Christmas 2019
David FRAME

The Globalist

The Globalist

PETER SUTHERLAND – HIS LIFE
AND LEGACY

**WILLIAM
COLLINS**

William Collins
An imprint of HarperCollins*Publishers*
1 London Bridge Street
London SE1 9GF

WilliamCollinsBooks.com

First published in Great Britain in 2019 by William Collins

1

A catalogue record for this book is available from the British Library

ISBN 978-0-00-832761-3

Typeset in Fairfield LH by Palimpsest Book Production Ltd, Falkirk, Stirlingshire

Printed and bound in Great Britain by CPI Group (UK) Ltd, Croydon CR0 4YY

For my wife Mary, my sons Hugh and Dominic,
and my parents, Tom and Maura.

CONTENTS

PROLOGUE

O N THE MORNING OF 11 SEPTEMBER 2016, A seventy-year-old Irishman suffered a heart attack and collapsed on a footpath in London. He had been walking to mass, as he had done every Sunday throughout his life.

A number of people rushed to his aid. He was carrying no identification. During the nine minutes it took the ambulance to arrive, those who attended to the stricken man could scarcely have realised who lay before them.

It was Peter Sutherland. 'The father of globalisation' and 'God's Banker' are among the soubriquets he had collected during his career. He was possibly the most influential Irish person ever and a key figure in world history over the past few decades.

In many ways, he was the personification of the changing relationship between Ireland and Britain. As a European commissioner for competition he had taken on the British government and prevailed. He would later become chairman of BP, one of the UK's largest companies.

He operated at the heart of the British establishment, yet he remained an outsider. He was a fiercely proud Irishman. And even though his influence spanned continents, he never strayed too far from his roots.

Early Years

1

GONZAGA AND
CHILDHOOD IN MONKSTOWN

PETER DENIS SUTHERLAND WAS BORN INTO A prosperous family in Dublin on 25 April 1946. His parents, Billy and Barbara, lived on The Hill in Monkstown, a middle-class village in south Dublin. Ireland had remained neutral during the Second World War, but memories of two painful conflicts that marked the birth of the Irish state over twenty years before were still an open sore; the country was economically underdeveloped and would remain so for another five decades. But Dublin retained characteristics of its former imperial past. There was the city's grandeur, its private schools and private clubs. This was the Dublin into which Sutherland was born, and which would mould his formative years.

Peter had two sisters, Karen and Gill, and a younger brother, David, who predeceased him in 2006. But it was his father who was a strong and enduring influence on his life. Billy Sutherland – along with the father of Peter Mathews, the late Fine Gael TD (Teachta Dála, a member of the Dáil) – was a partner in the insurance firm Mathews, Mulcahy and Sutherland.

William Sutherland and his two sons, William Jr (Peter's great-grandfather) and George, arrived in Ireland from Wick in Scotland around 1850. They were coopers by trade. William Jr, a Scottish Presbyterian, married Sarah Cooke, a Roman Catholic in Dublin in 1857. Five years later the couple moved to Cork, and George followed his brother to the city, where the two of them opened their own businesses. Records from 1870 show that George was a fish merchant at The Coal Quay, while William is listed as a publican at 27 Cook Street. By 1880 – when William and Sarah had eleven children – William and George are both listed as fish merchants with substantial commercial and residential property in Lavitts Quay.

Between 1880 and 1887, William moved to Newcastle in England on his own. He returned to Sarah shortly before his death, whereupon he converted to Catholicism. Sutherland's grandfather, also called Peter, was born in 1862. He moved to Dublin and became the Treasurer of Dublin City Council, marrying Mary Fitzpatrick in 1906. Sutherland's father, William George Anthony, was born in 1914.

Sutherland was educated at Gonzaga College, a Jesuit school in the affluent Dublin neighbourhood of Ranelagh. Even though Gonzaga had only opened its doors in 1950 – four years before Sutherland started – it had already established itself as the school of choice for Ireland's upper middle classes. It would soon eclipse the handful of other private schools in Dublin.

A former colleague of Sutherland's at the Law Library who attended Blackrock College described Gonzaga as 'Dublin 4 elitist . . . It had a "We will educate the next leaders of the state" mentality. Blackrock might have had pretensions but the Holy Ghost fathers were basically fellas building churches in Nigeria. There would have been a lot of boarders, farmers and merchants' sons in Blackrock – the sort of boy you wouldn't get at Gonzaga.'

Gonzaga profoundly shaped Sutherland. Colm Barrington – the son of Tom Barrington, the first director of the Institute of Public Affairs, and nephew of Donal Barrington, the former Supreme Court judge – was a contemporary of Sutherland's at Gonzaga. They subsequently became good friends. According to Barrington the Gonzaga boys had no idea how cloistered their existence was, 'because we didn't know any different. The Jesuits would make you feel that you were special rather than privileged and that Gonzaga was special and that you would go on to do special things.' Barrington said his father was at a parent-teacher meeting at which Garret FitzGerald, the former Taoiseach, asked Fr Hughes, the rector, if the school should put more emphasis on the sciences. Fr Hughes wryly responded that at Gonzaga 'we teach our boys to be the leaders of scientists'. Gonzaga instilled in Sutherland a lifelong passion for learning, although according to his friends and former teachers, the acquisition of knowledge was not one of his main priorities for most of his time at the school.

Tony Spollen met Sutherland on his first day at Gonzaga in 1954, and the pair remained lifelong friends, although their paths would cross in much more controversial circumstances in the 1990s. 'We became really good pals. I used to spend six weeks in the summer in his house in Monkstown. The Sutherlands would have been very wealthy – so from an early age, he would have been used to privilege. The family had a housekeeper called Polly. His mother was an extremely nice woman, Barbara. He was always used to having the best.'

Sutherland's typical summer would have revolved around Monkstown tennis club. He was a good, competitive tennis player. Another early childhood friend was John Arrigo, a neighbour in Monkstown. They too would remain lifelong friends. Sutherland had many passions in life, but in his early years nothing could compete with rugby. 'Myself and Peter became very good friends as we were both very keen on rugby. We were second row together initially and we then moved to front row with John Sisk in the middle,' says Colm Barrington. Underlining the rarefied social strata of Gonzaga, John Sisk was a member of the Sisk family, the founders of one of Ireland's largest construction groups.

Tony Spollen says that one of his earliest jobs was to get Sutherland elected captain of the Gonzaga rugby team, which involved extensive lobbying of the other players. Sutherland once secured a trial for the Leinster schools rugby team. Impatience got the better of him and he ordered Spollen to ring the sports desk of the *Irish Times* newspaper to check if he had made the team. He hadn't. 'He was never heavily into the academics. He did his homework, but just about. His two main interests were debating, he was a terrific speaker, and rugby,' says Spollen.

However, Gonzaga was not a good rugby school and it often had trouble putting fifteen players on the pitch. Adds Barrington: 'From a rugby point of view we got beaten a lot. We weren't allowed to play against any Protestant schools, who in rugby terms would have been more our size and smaller. Fr O'Connor wouldn't allow us to play against Protestant schools because of the Archbishop McQuaid philosophy at the time.' Fr O'Connor was the rector, while John Charles McQuaid, the Catholic archbishop of Dublin between 1940 and 1972, ensured that the church kept a vice-like grip on the state – in other words, Gonzaga were banned from playing against teams from Protestant schools. It was something of a miracle that on 5 March 2019, Gonzaga won the Leinster senior cup semi-final for the first time in the school's history by beating Clongowes Wood College 22–19. What's more, loose head prop Henry Godson, who scored three tries, is the son of Rory Godson, a close friend of Sutherland's.

Sutherland developed a lifelong relationship with Gonzaga. Indeed, the school's library is named in his honour, in recognition of one of the many generous donations he made over the years. Sutherland's ability to maintain lifelong relationships was one of his more striking characteristics. At his funeral mass on 11 January 2018, the church was filled with former friends from school, university and all the different strands of his storied career. Garrett Sheehan, a member of Sutherland's class who would also pursue a career in law, eventually becoming a High Court judge, gave the eulogy at Sutherland's funeral. 'Peter was great fun at school. He had a mischievous side but he was a natural leader. He was one of the only people to play [rugby] for the seniors and juniors in the same year. He was very good at keeping in touch with people. For example, no matter where he was or how busy he was he would always come back for UCD rugby dinner.'

Fr Noel Barber, the principal celebrant at Sutherland's funeral mass, took up a position at Gonzaga in 1961. Although he never taught Sutherland, the two of them subsequently struck up a friendship that again would endure over the subsequent decades, and Barber was one of the last people to see Sutherland before he passed away. 'I went to Gongaza when Peter was in fourth year. I trained a rugby team in sixth year when Peter was captain. As a young boy, he was chubby. Academically he wasn't stellar, he was a late developer. There were some brilliant fellows in his class but he wouldn't have been in that category in school. The most brilliant fellow in his class was Leslie Webb, who died in a drowning accident in India during VSO [Voluntary Service Overseas] straight after school. Peter was not in his category yet, but he always had a spark that showed up in debating society with Fr Veale.'

Fr Barber recounted a story from Sutherland's time at Gonzaga. 'A teacher overheard Peter and a pal discussing the strength and weaknesses of the priests whose masses they served. Peter with certainty said, "I like to serve Fr White."'(Fr White was the prefect of studies.) 'His companion retorted – it was in the days of corporal punishment – "But he biffs us." Peter countered pragmatically, "What are you talking about? He has to do it. That is his job and he does a good job."'

According to Barber, the same Fr White spotted something in Peter which eluded others at that stage. When a teacher remarked to him that young Sutherland was not doing so well, Fr White responded with uncharacteristic sharpness that when young Sutherland saw something he wanted he would go for it and get it. 'I overheard that conversation and I watched with pleasure how over the years the prophecy of the shrewd Fr White was fulfilled.'

All who knew him at Gonzaga say that it was Fr Joe Veale who left an indelible mark on Sutherland. 'Joe was absolutely inspirational. He taught us how to write. He established the debating society at Gonzaga. Peter was an outstanding debater from a young age. He made an immediate impact when he joined in fourth class,' says Sheehan. The debating society would become another passion in Sutherland's life and lead him to his career in law. Barrington remembers that Fr Veale was always ahead of his time in terms of openness. 'He encouraged us to read *The Catcher in the Rye* when everybody else was saying it should be banned.' Sheehan agrees that Fr Veale made a huge impression on Peter. 'Fr Joe was absolutely passionate about the Vatican council. I wasn't surprised to hear Peter did what he did with the Vatican because of Joe.' In 2011 Sutherland would become an adviser to the Vatican on its financial affairs. Sutherland is estimated to have made £120 million from Goldman Sachs' flotation in 1999. According to Sheehan, one of the first things he did with the proceeds was to buy Fr Veale an around-the-world travel ticket.

According to his former classmates, even when young Sutherland did not lack confidence and could add a self-serving gloss to events that were not necessarily merited by the facts. Sheehan recalls one particular week in sixth year when Fr Veale was handing back the boys' weekly essays after they had been marked. Sutherland had written his essay on Ernest Hemingway, the US novelist, who had died three years previously. 'Joe's comment was that there was too much hairy-chested sentimentality, which was meant as a criticism. But Peter took it as a compliment and proudly sent it around the class to show what a great writer he was.'

Fr Veale died in 2002. Described by friends and former students as a highly intelligent and complex man, he shaped Sutherland during his formative years probably more than anyone else apart from his parents. An appreciation which appeared in the *Irish Times* shortly after Fr Veale's death referenced an article he had written two years before, in which he addressed in very raw terms the life of a cleric. He described the 'private pain . . . loneliness . . . isolation . . . the desert in the heart . . . self-hatred . . . rage

. . . having no say in the disposition of one's own life . . . the longing for human contact . . . the ache for tenderness and gentleness.'[1] According to the newspaper, it was an 'outpouring of anger at the authoritarian, narrow-minded and philistine culture of the Church's leadership, both in Ireland and worldwide, and a cry too against the smug smile from the layman's armchair'.[2] He wanted people to ask why the scandals of clerical child-abuse had happened. What was the desolation that might explain, but not excuse, the depravity? This extraordinary article (in *Doctrine and Life*) appeared and disappeared with hardly a comment. His act of courage, the last act of his career, his 'J'Accuse', had been countered in an Irish way – by silence.

Bobby McDonagh was a former student at Gonzaga, although he entered the school eight years after Sutherland. He would become one of Ireland's most distinguished diplomats, and as Irish ambassador to the UK had close contact with Sutherland. They often discussed Fr Veale. McDonagh wrote an appreciation following Veale's death which appeared in the *Sunday Independent* newspaper on 4 November 2002:

> I remember Joe once saying that he believed in Christ rather than in Christianity. In making this distinction ('don't make a dichotomy out of a distinction' I still hear him saying), he was, of course, distinguishing the essence of faith from what is secondary. He promoted, with his formidable intellect and indeed the commitment of his life, the essentials of his faith. But beyond that his commitment to seeking the truth in all its paradox and complexity obliged him to have an open mind. He long recognised, for example, the central importance of women, especially mothers, in the church, as necessary leaders of opinion rather than as flower arrangers. He saw that the church urgently needs the involvement of the laity, as players rather than as cheer leaders. Tolerance of difference was at the heart of his belief.[3]

Fr Barber recalled that Sutherland hadn't stood out as having a deeper faith than any other boy in Gonzaga at the time. 'That became evident in later life. His last act was going to mass. His faith became evident in other ways, for example with migrants, and being involved with the Vatican.' According to Barrington, many of the nostrums that shaped Sutherland's life and career came from Gonzaga and the Jesuits. 'He was a liberal. He thought that by being liberal you helped people be better off and have a better life. That would have been a Gonzaga principle. Here were the Jesuits in a very rigid church and they were much more liberal than the rest of the church and that came through in Gonzaga people.' Friends say even though religion was very important to Sutherland throughout his life, he practised his faith privately and did not force his views on anybody else. His views were much more nuanced and progressive than he was sometimes given credit for.

In those days, boys attending Gonzaga did not have to gain the Leaving Certificate. Instead they took a matriculation exam and a sixth year, a pre-university year, on which great value was placed.* Matriculation was a separate set of exams used as a means to gain entrance to university, and was scrapped only in 1992, after eighty-two years. The idea of not taking the Leaving Certificate was to assert that what mattered was learning, not passing exams. Such an ethos was very strong when Sutherland was at the school, and it played a large part in shaping him in later life. According to Fr Barber it wasn't just about attainment, it was about ideals and values. Although Sutherland's matriculation was mediocre, 'I think he realised that even though he mightn't have worked very hard, an intellectual light was sparked. I think that really impressed

---

* The class of 1964 was as follows: John Barnewell, Ian Candy, Brian Carroll, Peter Costello, Dermot Eustace, Oliver Farley, David Fassbender, Con Feighery, Richard George, John Howard, Martin Kelly, Brian Kirby, Richard Lenehan, Philip MacMahon, Peter MacMenamin, Hubert Mahony, Sean McCutcheon, Brian McLoughlin, Hugo McVey, Nahor Meenan, Redmond Morris, Tom Morris, Chris Murphy, Brendan Murphy, Bill Nowlan, David O'Connor, Denis Quilligan, Garrett Sheehan, Anthony Spollen, Peter Sutherland, Brian Walsh.

him and he was always very generous to the school. He attributed what he got here to the Jesuits. They were very formative years for him, much more so than we thought at the time.'

In Barrington's view, the most important quality Sutherland took from Gonzaga was self-confidence: 'Gonzaga taught you to be self-confident. In my class everybody went to college. It was expected. You weren't going to join an insurance firm or anything like that. At Gonzaga you did feel special and when you went to college you did feel prepared for this.'

2

STUDENT DAYS AT UCD

SUTHERLAND WENT TO UNIVERSITY COLLEGE Dublin in 1964 to study law. But then again, he was hardly faced with an array of choices. Trinity College Dublin, academically superior at the time and with more of an international reputation, was out of bounds for young ambitious Catholics. Archbishop John Charles McQuaid, who had prevented Sutherland from playing rugby against Protestants, had also made an order that young Catholics were barred from entering Trinity, which had a Protestant ethos.

By that stage, Sutherland knew he wanted to become a lawyer, and that left him with one choice. In the 1960s, UCD was located in Earlsfort Terrace, now the site of the National Concert Hall, just off Stephen's Green in the centre of Dublin. At Gonzaga, Sutherland had been able to seamlessly mix his two passions, debating and rugby; but at university, some tough choices had to be made.

The Literary & Historical Society (L&H) had been founded in 1854 by Cardinal John Henry Newman. To become auditor of the L&H was seen as a rite of passage for any young person who had intentions of shaping Irish society, or at the very least becoming rich and famous. Patrick (Paddy) Cosgrave was auditor of the L&H when Sutherland arrived on the campus in 1964. Cosgrave was something of an anomaly. UCD, along with wider Irish society, was becoming more comfortable with its nationalist past. Like their counterparts throughout Europe, Irish students were on the march leftwards.

Cosgrave was very much to the right and revelled in the label 'west Brit', a pejorative term used to describe anybody still well disposed to Ireland's former colonial masters. He used to boast that his grandfather, a warden in Kilmainham Jail, had beaten up a young Kevin Barry, a Republican martyr. Following UCD, Cosgrave moved to London, where he plied his trade as a journalist before catching the eye of Margaret Thatcher. He went on to become a special adviser to the former British prime minister, although she cut ties with him when his drinking got out of control. He died in 2001 aged sixty.

Sutherland had shown no overt political leanings at that stage. Friends say he had no appearance of struggling for too long, if at all, with the choice of spending Saturday nights in the company of Cosgrave et al. in the L&H or the 'hop' at the Lansdowne rugby club. Neither was he active in politics at UCD, where many prominent members of Fine Gael – such as John Bruton, who was a few years behind Sutherland at college – were taking their first tentative steps towards elected office.

In those days, students took their degrees and Bar exams at the same time. Sutherland was awarded a law degree in 1967 and passed his Bar exams a year later.

In Sutherland's last year at UCD, Vincent Browne became the chairman of Young Fine Gael. Browne would later become a prominent journalist and harsh critic of the party. Rugby remained an all-consuming passion for Sutherland at UCD, yet he still found time to increase his circle of friends. Garrett Sheehan, Colm Barrington and other Gonzaga boys had made the same journey from Ranelagh to Earlsfort Terrace, although Barrington, being a year older and in the economics department, spent little time with Sutherland at UCD. Barrington was not a fan of his university experience. 'UCD felt very old fashioned. Having come from Gonzaga it felt in some ways silly. Girls were not allowed to wear trousers into the library. The pomposity of some of the lecturers was unbearable.'

Sutherland appeared to develop no strong feelings about his time at Earlsfort Terrace. Nicholas Kearns, who also studied law with Sutherland – they both started at the Bar on the same day – would go on to become a Supreme Court judge and president of the High Court. He and Sutherland met the summer before they started at UCD. 'I first met him when thirty-five lads went to Huntingdon in the UK for a summer to work for Batchelors Peas. Peter quickly emerged as the natural leader of the Irish group that was there. It was eight weeks of night shifts, eight at night to eight in the morning. We were all Irish guys from different backgrounds. If there were any workplace difficulties, Suds [Sutherland] sorted them out. He was big and strong in those days. He had a natural strength and energy. If he wanted something he got it.' 'Suds' was a nickname that would remain with Sutherland for the rest of his life.

Sutherland also studied economics and philosophy in his first year. Garret FitzGerald lectured him in economics, while Desmond Connell, the future archbishop of Dublin, taught him philosophy; according to Sutherland's eldest son Shane, the experience put his father off philosophy for twenty years. John Blayney, then a barrister and a future High Court judge, taught Sutherland constitutional law.

Declan McCourt, who met Sutherland at UCD, studied law and politics before taking his Bar exams. He enjoyed the experience. 'I found it very fulfilling. It was the Lemass era. Everything was opening up. It was great. We were in the centre of town. We made friends for life. There were plenty of colourful characters.' Sean Lemass had taken over as Fianna Fáil leader and Taoiseach from Eamon de Valera and immediately set about liberalising the economy.

The friendship between Garrett Sheehan and Sutherland developed further at UCD. 'He certainly didn't develop a passion for law in UCD. We were lucky if the lecturers turned up and we didn't mind if sometimes they didn't. He actually did really well in his final year of law. When he went to the Bar and started practising that is when he absolutely loved it. UCD was great fun. Our social life revolved around the rugby club. The L&H would have been an obvious path, but I think we were so determined to play for UCD.'

Sheehan explains that, contrary to the image of rugby players 'just being interested in drinking and talking about women, we actually had a lot of good discussions about politics and so on'. Sutherland's social life revolved around Hartigans and O'Dwyers on Leeson Street and The Pembroke on Pembroke Street Lower. There were also dances, or what were known as 'hops'. The Belvedere hop was very popular at the time. It was there that, in 1969, Sutherland met a young Spanish au pair, Maruja Cabria Valcarcel. They would marry two years later.

But Sutherland's time in UCD was mostly taken up with rugby. He played in the Freshman team which won the thirds league and then for the second team, which won the league and cup double in the Leinster league in 1967. Their ultimate aim, says Sheehan, was to be selected for the Leinster team, for which they both had trials. 'Peter was never far off making it.' John O'Hagan, who is now Professor of Economics at Trinity College Dublin, was captain that year, while Sutherland took over the captaincy of the senior team for the 1967–8 academic year. O'Hagan says that the first time the team got together, Sutherland gave an 'amazing speech. That team had been very successful the previous year. He managed expectations very well. He is the finest speaker of his generation.'

The first game of the year was the annual 'Colours' match against Trinity. Press clippings from the time described it as a classic. According to Sean Diffley in the *Irish Press* on 30 November 1967:

Beyond any doubt the 16th Annual Colours match finds an honourable place among the classic games of rugby. It had everything – drama, excitement, fantastic pace, a high degree of skill and artistry, heroic personal endeavour and, at the end, an element of pathos. On a dull, chilly afternoon, the two student teams revived the glory of rugby. There were no losers really. [For the first UCD try] Grace ran from inside his own half and then launched a huge kick that appeared to be far too much ahead. But the long-striding UCD player managed, remarkably, to field the kick and, despite the presence of several defenders, his momentum and sheer strength carried him to within sighting of the line, and a spectacular dive did the rest.

Meanwhile, according to Paul MacWeeney at the *Irish Times*:

Had there been All Blacks among the spectators they would have acclaimed UCD's second try as one of their own most precious vintage – no better combined movement is likely to be seen at Lansdowne Road, or elsewhere in Ireland for that matter, this season . . . From a scrum well inside the UCD half, Cooke served Murphy who sent inside to Bresnihan coming up on the burst. The forwards supported on each side of the man in possession, and at top speed, Deering, Gill, Sutherland and J. O'Hagan flicked passes in and out before Deering burst over near the posts.

Despite the best efforts of UCD, however, Trinity won the game.

In January the focus shifted to the Leinster Senior Cup. Unable to compete in height or weight with the other teams, the UCD students devised a two-man lineout.* This is how the legendary Con Houlihan described it in a piece for the *Irish Press* newspaper titled 'Ingenuity the key':

---

* The team that year lined out as: Peter Sutherland, Tony Hickie, Tom Grace, Frank O'Driscoll, Tadhg O'Glasain, Joe Cummiskey, Henry Murphy, Jimmy Kinahan, Tom Feighery, John O'Hagan, Con Feighery, Jim Doyle, Fergus Slattery, Gerry Halley, Shay Deering.

The students devised a scheme among themselves to beat Wanderers, then the top scoring side in the country and coached by Ireland's coach. But coaches, or at least most of them, follow the textbook . . . But they seem to forget ingenuity. And it was ingenuity which on Saturday made Wanderers wonder what had happened to them. Now as far as I know there's no rule asking that the two opposing forwards should stand shoulder to shoulder in the line. True, we have had four on each side peeling off, but UCD on their throw-in pulled out six forwards, leaving a couple in the line-out from each side . . . It was ingenuity, not organised by a coach, but by young-minded chaps.

It had the desired effect. UCD upset the odds to beat a number of more established teams on the way to the Leinster Cup final. The following piece appeared in the *Irish Press* on 17 April 1968, just a few days before the final, which was against Old Belvedere:

UCD will probably start favourites, and deservedly so, because they were most impressive when ousting Terenure 16–8, Wanderers 11–3 and Old Wesley 11–6, en route to the final. Against Old Wesley, in particular, they gave a magnificent exhibition of fast, intelligent, open rugby. The UCD team is one of the youngest to represent the College in memory – the average age being just under 21. What they may lack in experience they make up with exceptional fitness and attacking ability. A measure of this ability is indicated by the fact that they have scored 82 tries this season, an average of more than 3.5 per match. Another interesting feature of the line-up is that six of the team are studying law whereas the medical faculty has only two representatives this year.

Alas, it was not to be. Old Belvedere beat the students with a last-minute try in what was described as a thrilling final. O'Hagan says that Tom Grace, a member of the UCD team, is still resolute in his belief that the try should have been disallowed. Sutherland blamed the referee, who had given a different interpretation of the rules from that applied in previous games on the way to the final and clamped down on the students' 'ingenuity' (the two man lineout). (A full list of the team sheet for the game can be seen in Appendix 1.)

According to O'Hagan, one of the Old Belvedere trainers who went to the UCD dressing room to perform the customary commiserations suffered a heart attack, and despite the best efforts of Tom Feighery, then a medical student, to save him, he died. The post-match dinner was postponed by a week. Tony O'Reilly, who was coming to the end of his playing career, was the guest of honour. O'Reilly was capped 29 times for Ireland and played for the British and Irish Lions on two tours. He also became the chief executive of Heinz and one of Ireland's most successful businessmen.

Tony Hickie's son Denis played for Ireland, as did Tom Grace, Con Feighery and Shay Deering. Frank O'Driscoll got a few B caps for Ireland; although he decided to concentrate on his career in medicine, his son Brian became a rugby player of some note. Joe Cummiskey became a prominent medical consultant and a leading campaigner against doping in sports until his death in April 2018. Fergus Slattery, meanwhile, became one of the legends of the game, touring with the British Lions as well as winning numerous caps for his country.

Sutherland himself went on to captain Lansdowne in 1970, but retired from playing at the age of twenty-eight. According to O'Hagan he was never a star player as he needed to be bigger, but he has never played with anyone so driven. 'I have never seen anybody so upset at losing a match. He just saw black. He would descend into a slough of despond, but neither have I ever seen anybody to be so elated when we won.'

3

THE ARMS TRIAL

S UTHERLAND WAS CALLED TO THE BAR IN 1968, and devilled – 'devilling' being the period of training that every new Irish barrister has to undertake – under senior barrister Harry Hill along with another ambitious young barrister called Michael Moriarty. Aged thirty-seven at the time, the dapper Hill had a reputation as being one of the finest barristers in the Four Courts. A keen cricketer, who never married, he had a predilection for good food and fine wine.

Sutherland picked up more than the law from his master. About a year after Sutherland had begun practising at the Bar, Fr Noel Barber asked Hill how his former pupil was doing. 'Too well. I worry about him,' he replied. A couple of years later, Fr Barber reminded Hill of his concern and he replied that he was wasting his time worrying. 'Sutherland was going to the top.'

Hill would serve as Master of the High Court between 1984 and 2006, while Sutherland and his former master would remain close friends until the latter's death in 2006. 'Harry Hill never compromised his principles, or his opinions. He disliked above all posturing, cant and hypocrisy,' Sutherland wrote in an appreciation that appeared in the *Irish Times*. 'He sought to hide his light under a bushel, but what drove him fundamentally was personal relationships, sport and the Bar, probably in that order. Those who knew him know what a man of true quality he was.'[1]

Sutherland quickly established himself in the Law Library, the regulatory and representative body for barristers. David Byrne, who was called to the Bar in 1970, two years after Sutherland, and would also become attorney general (between 1997 and 1999) and a European commissioner (between 1999 and 2004), says that from the beginning Sutherland was ambitious, hard-working and very determined to be successful. 'He was excellent. He was a charming, clever man and he had a capacity to make and keep friendships. He minded his friends. He just had that way with people that was very attractive, and as a consequence he was able to build a practice in the Law Library fairly quickly. He'd a very good style in court.' Nicholas Kearns observed: 'He [Sutherland] was born with ambition. He was like a heat-seeking missile. No matter what he did he was always going to do well. He was a formidable rival and competitor in court and outside it. If he couldn't go around a problem he would go through it.'

Sutherland soon built up a lucrative civil law practice, helped in no small part by his father's insurance business. Insurance defence work would have been the holy grail among barristers. There was much less work around for barristers in the 1970s than there is today, but equally there were many fewer barristers. 'If you had connections with the law your start would be a lot speedier, and Peter's father had been involved in the insurance industry. So that gave him a running start, because he would have gotten work in the personal injury area and work from insurance companies. That would have been a good help to him. And then of course he had a wonderful network of friends and people that he knew from school, from rugby and all of that. He was an excellent networker. He identified and made friends easily,' another colleague from that era said.

According to former colleagues, Sutherland had a good court presence. In the Law Library there is a distinction between advocates and lawyers. Lawyers tend to be more academic, with an interest in how laws are formulated and how they relate to each other. Advocates are more drawn to the theatre of the courtroom and the gladiatorial nature of cases. Sutherland was very much an advocate. 'Peter would have been much more interested in fighting the case, looking after the client and so far as you can, making sure that you win,' says Byrne. 'Therefore, if you were to divide barristers into advocates and lawyers, he would have been in the advocates camp. That isn't to say he wasn't a good lawyer. He was of course, but advocacy was his strong point and that isn't surprising given his later career. He had great ability on his feet.'

John A. Costello, a former Taoiseach, gave a speech at the Law Library annual dinner in the early 1970s. Byrne recalls that, in making reference to the growing number of young barristers in attendance, Costello said, 'You might be wondering what are the successful characteristics that are necessary to have a successful career at the Bar.'

'I remember him saying you should fight every case as if it was your own and never write to the newspapers. They were the two bits of advice he gave.' Sutherland would have followed those precepts without a second thought, says Byrne. 'I'm not saying Peter was the only one who did that. That's what barristers did for a living – it was their job. But Peter was quite relentless and had a lot of skill in how he would go about that.' He was a formidable advocate. 'You knew, doing a case against Peter, that everything and anything would be used against you for him to win that case.'

Nial Fennelly, a Supreme Court judge between 2000 and 2014, was a colleague of Sutherland at the Bar and acted with him on a number of cases. 'I can't remember him being on cases that made huge advances in law. He wasn't on the human rights side of things like the late Donal Barrington [the former Supreme Court judge].' But, says Fennelly, 'He had a reputation of being very forceful as a barrister. He was always popular and well liked, but he was forceful and even aggressive as a young barrister making his way. He made a name from an early age at the Bar.'

The Law Library often appears a highly competitive environment, one that is riven with egos. A number of colleagues from that era say that Sutherland was one of the most competitive of all. Indeed, some of his tactics were legendary. One case pitted him against John Quirke, who would later become a High Court judge. They were good friends, but when Sutherland entered a courtroom friendships were left at the door. He and Quirke were appearing on opposite sides in a dispute between a landlord and a tenant, in a case heard in the Circuit Court by Noel Ryan. At one point, while the expert witness was giving valuations and evidence in the witness box, Quirke was on his feet, holding in his hand a report which he claimed vindicated his client, the landlord, and waving the report about with ever-increasing vigour.

The theatrics were getting too much for Sutherland. He leaned across, grabbed the report out of Quirke's hand and sent it in the direction of the nearest bin. 'The judge's response was amusement and he didn't admonish him. There was no row about it. Peter wouldn't have done it out of aggression; it was more of a playful act. He got away with a lot of things by reason of his own charm, yet at the same time he would use his charm to get away with a lot of things,' says David Byrne.

Alan Dukes, a former Fine Gael finance minister, recalls that even though Sutherland wore his ambition on his sleeve, his self-deprecating sense of humour had a disarming effect. Dukes recalls one story Sutherland told him about when he appeared before Judge Frank Roe defending a woman accused of shoplifting, not long after Sutherland's less than successful attempt to win a seat in the 1973 general election. The defendant claimed that she was unable to feed her children because she had no home. 'Frank Roe asked the woman would it help if she had a house. She said yes. He pointed his finger at Peter and said, "That man might be able to help you because he is a failed politician."'

One of the first cases that gave Sutherland a national profile was the so-called Arms Trial. The backdrop to the case was the flare-up in troubles in August 1969. Since the establishment of

Northern Ireland, Catholics in the province had been treated as second-class citizens, while state-orchestrated gerrymandering – until 1968 the system of property ownership had conferred greater voting rights on the Protestant population – had ensured that Catholic communities were politically under-represented. The nascent civil rights movement across Northern Ireland in the late 1960s demanded equal voting rights, among other basic conditions. The 'Battle of the Bogside' in Derry in August 1969, when residents of one of the most deprived areas in western Europe engaged the security forces in a week-long stand-off, is regarded as one of the seminal moments in the onset of the Troubles.

The ensuing violence was the worst that had erupted even by the turbulent standards of Northern Ireland. Simmering tensions mutated into a widespread and open conflict between the Catholic community and the forces of the state. As skirmishes escalated, the Loyalists' response was one of implacable resistance, and they turned on their Catholic neighbours. Nationalist communities were displaced and many were forced to seek refuge south of the border. For the first time, the Troubles had become a hugely emotive and political issue in the Republic. Although the exact details remain controversial and unresolved, the Irish government's response was to trigger a chain of events that would change the political landscape in the south.

Jack Lynch was then Taoiseach of a Fianna Fáil government. He set up a cabinet sub-committee to monitor events in Northern Ireland and co-ordinate a contingency plan in the form of emergency relief and assistance. The sub-committee had a budget of IR£100,000. Charlie Haughey, then Minister for Finance, and a future leader of Fianna Fáil and Taoiseach, took charge of the sub-committee alongside Neil Blaney, Minister for Agriculture. Deciding that there had to be a military component to the Irish government's response, the pair enlisted the help of military intelligence to formulate a plan. Captain James Kelly, originally from Bailieboro in County Cavan, was instructed to liaise with a number of defence committees established by nationalists in Northern

Ireland, and meetings took place from October 1969 onwards. It has been established that senior members of the Irish Republican Army (IRA) – an illegal paramilitary organisation – were in attendance.

Who knew about the meetings, and the decisions that were subsequently taken, became a constitutionally loaded question. In early 1970, Captain Kelly made contact with groups in Hamburg, Germany, with a view to importing arms. He was sent to Hamburg that April to organise a shipment of guns, earmarked for nationalist resistance groups in Northern Ireland, to the Republic via Dublin airport. Coincidentally, Jack Desmond – the father of Dermot Desmond, a businessman who would strike up a friendship with Sutherland in later life – was the customs officer in charge at the airport.

Peter Berry, then Secretary General of the Department of Justice, and *éminence grise* of the Irish state, had become aware of the scheme, which he described as a subversive plot. He ordered that the arms be impounded upon arrival at Dublin airport. When Liam Cosgrave, the leader of Fine Gael, the main opposition party, learned about the smuggling operation, he demanded a response from the government.

Lynch publicly sacked Haughey and Blaney. Both men, along with Captain James Kelly, Belfast Republican John Kelly, and Albert Luykx, a Belgian national who had acted as an intermediary in the deal, stood trial in May 1970 on charges of illegal arms smuggling. Sutherland, who had just turned twenty-four, was retained as a junior counsel on Captain Kelly's defence team, under senior counsel Tom Findlay. There was initial surprise in the Law Library at the choice of Sutherland: his speciality was civil law and he did not have a reputation as a criminal lawyer. He did however have a relationship with Fitzpatrick's, the firm of solicitors who represented Kelly.

To the outside world Sutherland would also have seemed politically an odd choice for Kelly's defence team. He had a deep antipathy to paramilitaries of any hue, and one of the early factors attracting him to politics was his opposition to Haughey and all

24

he stood for. However, there is a long-standing tradition in the Law Library to retain barristers from 'the other side'.

Patrick Connolly, the future attorney general, acted for Haughey, with a young Dermot Gleeson, who would also go on to become attorney general, as his junior counsel. Captain Kelly's defence was that he was not a rogue operator and had not acted outside legal channels. His case was that Jim Gibbons, Minister for Defence at the time, had been apprised at all stages of the work of the cabinet sub-committee, including the intention to import arms. Captain Kelly had been following orders at all times, it was argued. Gibbons denied that he had been aware of the plot. Crucial to Kelly's defence was the evidence of Colonel Michael Hefferon, the head of Army Intelligence at the time.

When, a few years before his death, Sutherland put together his private papers, they included extensive writings about the Arms Trial. According to Sutherland's account, Hefferon was regarded by the prosecution team as a significant witness in support of their case. However, the opening statement by Seamus McKenna, senior counsel for the prosecution, outlining the nature of the state's case, had a profound effect upon him. Hefferon met Frank Fitzpatrick, solicitor for Captain Kelly, and told him that Kelly was innocent of the charges and that he could not with a clear conscience give evidence to support a case to the contrary. Fitzpatrick conveyed this conversation to McKenna in the belief that it would halt proceedings. Instead, according to Sutherland, it changed the prosecution's stance towards Hefferon and the deployment of what had been intended as their strongest witness. Hefferon had headed the original witness list. But as the first trial progressed he was held back and was only called as the twenty-first witness, long after Gibbons had given evidence. Nevertheless, as Sutherland recalled in his account of the trial, 'his contribution was crucial to the tenor of the case'. Sutherland continues:

Hefferon's evidence to the first trial (28 and 29 September 1970) confirmed that: The State was engaged in training

[Northern Ireland] civilians from Derry in the use of arms at Dunree (something Gibbons had emphatically denied in the Dáil on 9 May 1970). There was an active military policy for the defence of minority population in the North (as articulated by Jack Lynch's broadcast on 13 August 1969 and elaborated in the Army directive of 6 Feb 1970). There was a specific and explicit Government directive relating to the preparation and training of the Army for incursions into Northern Ireland. When the prosecution attempted to indicate that no such directive could be located, Hefferon was very precise as to where copies were available within military files and was able to affirm that he had had the contents of that directive confirmed to him by serving staff officers (at this point Hefferon was retired from service).

Hefferon also said that: Captain Kelly was acting at all times as a serving army officer and in an official capacity. Captain Kelly was acting on orders from the Minister for Defence who was aware of his activities. Both Minister Gibbons and possibly Minister Blaney had promised arms to representatives of the Northern Defence committees. Any arms would remain at all times in a designated place and under the control of Captain Kelly and the army until a decision was made and orders given as to their disposal.

There were two trials. The first trial collapsed because of allegations of bias. The second trial would eventually collapse because of a number of flaws in the prosecution's case, including contradictions in testimony given by Haughey and Gibbons. But that was not the end of it for Captain Kelly, nor for Sutherland. The government tasked the Public Accounts Committee of the Irish parliament to investigate the IR£100,000 spent by the cabinet sub-committee. According to Suzanne Kelly, a prominent tax lawyer and daughter of Captain Kelly, Justin Keating, then a Labour Party TD, privately told Kelly that the Public Accounts Committee had been told that its remit of looking into the money was a political fig leaf. Its real purpose was to rerun the trial, except this time it was to deliver a guilty verdict.

This time Sutherland represented Captain Kelly pro-bono. According to one former colleague, anything that Sutherland did, 'he did with all the might of a front row forward'. The first real example of this was that Public Accounts Committee. The junior barrister cross-examined Gibbons, who was by then Minister for Agriculture, with an intensity and robustness that effectively derailed the case against Kelly.

When the second trial commenced Hefferon had been dropped from the prosecution case as a witness. His original statement remained in the book of evidence and the State justified not calling him on grounds of unreliability. He was eventually called as a 'bench witness' by Mr Justice Henchy during the second trial.

McKenna's examination of Hefferon on 13 and 14 October 1970 was an attempt to salvage the State's case during the second trial. However, it only served to highlight a number of critical issues:

The change of official policy evidenced by the directive of 6 February 1970 and as confirmation of this policy, the movement of rifles and ammunition to Dundalk on 2 April 1970 on Gibbons' orders for possible distribution. The central role of Minister Gibbons in the whole affair, of his close advance knowledge of Captain Kelly's activities, of the plan to store the weapons and of his knowledge of the precise location for storage (in a monastery), knowledge which gave him effective 'control' over the weapons. The unreliability of Gibbons' own testimony during the trial.

At the conclusion of his evidence during the second trial, as he left the witness box, Hefferon was applauded by members of the public in the gallery.[2]

The night of Sutherland's appearance before the Public Accounts Committee, Sutherland had dinner with his father in the United Services Club on Stephen's Green. Billy Sutherland told his son that it was a fatal mistake to take on the establishment in that manner and it would surely undermine his career prospects in Ireland. In the event, it evidently didn't.

*

The arms crisis has remained an open sore in Irish political life. Allegations of a state cover-up have persisted. Under the terms of the National Archives Act, papers relating to the 1970 trial were released into the public domain at the end of 2000. On 18 February 2001 newspaper reports alleged that an attempt had been made, by altering Hefferon's witness statement, to suppress evidence that would have supported the defence case, and in particular what Jim Gibbons knew about the plan to import arms and ammunition. On 10 April 2001 a *Prime Time* programme broadcast by RTÉ examined the issue of Hefferon's statement in much greater detail.

The issues raised in the press and on television were the subject of a debate in the Dáil on 11 April. In the course of the debate John O'Donoghue, the Minister for Justice, accepted that the programme's contents gave cause for concern. Pledging to make enquiries and to report back on his findings as soon as he was in a position to do so, O'Donoghue asked attorney general Michael McDowell and the Garda commissioner to respond to specific aspects of the issues raised by the programme; their contributions were to form part of the final report.

The report, prepared by McDowell, considered the allegations of conspiracy and in doing so examined the preparation and editing of Hefferon's statement and the preparation of the Book of Evidence (the case for the prosecution), by reference to practice and procedure at the time. It considered the procedure by reference to the law of hearsay, the relevance of the state and nature of Gibbons' knowledge as to the guilt or innocence of the accused in the trial. The scope of the investigation also included a number of documents that were not released into the public domain, including Garda reports and intelligence files felt to contain material that, if made public, could possibly lead to an action for defamation or otherwise cause distress or danger to individuals. At the time the report was compiled several items were found to be missing, including the prosecution case file, the original Garda investigation file, and the transcripts and sound recordings of both trials.

The overall report concluded that, notwithstanding the limitations of the passage of time, the absence of key evidence and the fact that some of the key witnesses and actors were now deceased, it was reasonable to infer that while the possibility of an attempt to suppress evidence could never be definitively ruled out, the likelihood was remote.

Sutherland retained Dr Brian Jackson, the head of postgraduate studies at Carlow Institute of Technology, to look at the report. The following is an extract from Sutherland's papers based on material provided by Jackson:

While there is no doubt that the statement made by Michael Hefferon to the Gardai was extensively edited before it was included in the Book of Evidence as served on the accused, this was usual practice and was done to eliminate hearsay and other irrelevant material and was consistent with the duty imposed by S 6 (1) (d) of the Criminal Procedure Act 1967, to provide the accused with 'a statement of the evidence that is to be given by each of them (i.e. the witnesses)'. The Book of Evidence was prepared by three lawyers on the prosecution team. They were Aidan Browne BL, Edward Durnin of the CSSO and Declan Quigley of the AGO who appears to have undertaken the bulk of the work. He received clerical assistance from Garda John Gallagher – now John Gallagher SC (identified by Michael McDowell during the course of our discussion of 24 September). The Attorney

General concluded in his report that there was no evidence of any Ministerial or any Department of Justice involvement in the process around the preparation of the Book of Evidence.

Furthermore, Michael McDowell concluded that:

There was no conspiracy or strategy on the part of the Department of Justice to deceive or otherwise influence those engaged in drafting the Book of Evidence as to the true nature of Michael Hefferon's statement to the Gardai. Notwithstanding the edited form in which the statement appeared in the Book of Evidence, the Attorney General concluded that the original statement would have been available in the court if required under S 3 and S 4 Criminal Procedure Act 1865. Evidence from heavily annotated papers belonging to Michael Hefferon and now in military archives suggests that Capt. James Kelly had sight of and was aware of the contents of the original witness statement. Given the number of actors involved within Justice, the Gardai and the legal profession, any 'conspiracy' would have required wide and conscious participation and in view of the inherent risk this can be discounted (a) on the basis of the absence of compelling evidence and (b) the likelihood of a more coherent and probable explanation.

Although there were no formal guidelines for the preparation of books of evidence extant in 1970, the process can be re-imagined with the help of documents from the early 1980s. By this process the AG concluded that: There was an accepted 'editorial' approach employed in the preparation of books of evidence in order to eliminate hearsay and other irrelevant material. It was never practice to include witness statements in their entirety. The complete statement would have been available in the court as a matter of standard procedure. Rules and practice around disclosure of documentation at the time of the trial differed from current practice and there was no general duty to disclose, as a matter of course all witness statements to the defendants.

However, there was a duty to call all material witnesses and to disclose all relevant evidence.

At this point the AG refers back to the charge before the court, a conspiracy to import arms into the State in contravention of S 17 of the Firearms Act 1925. Principally, he focused upon the terms of the specific exclusion under S 17 (8) of the Act which provides for the legitimate importation of arms and ammunition 'under the authority of the Minister for Defence for the **use of the Defence Forces**'. This is a crucial distinction and Michael McDowell concluded that those preparing the Book of Evidence may have taken the view that the case turned on the intended **use** of the arms (not on the knowledge or authority of the Minister for Defence) and that any evidence as to the Minister's state of mind (which accounts for a significant amount of the excised material from Hefferon's original Garda statement) may have been justifiably excised as prima facie hearsay. While this may indicate a very narrow and specific view of the case it does not support the charge that evidence was tampered with in bad faith or that it was improperly suppressed.

The Attorney General concluded in his report that: Prosecution was already in train before a statement was taken from Col. Hefferon. While the original statement made to the Gardai may have contained material that was politically embarrassing for James Gibbons and for the Government, it did not (as was suggested by the programme and by a number of commentators) remove the basis for a return to trial of the defendants. Col. Hefferon's evidence as given in court was consistent with his original statement and it did not provide grounds for a direction to acquit.[3]

In other words, there was no conspiracy.

*

31

After the trial, Sutherland went back to burnishing his credentials at the Four Courts as one of a clutch of young barristers who were destined for greater things. The Four Courts refers to the Supreme Court, High Court, Court of Appeals and the Dublin Circuit Court. Sutherland was involved in some of the highest-profile cases of that decade. In June 1970 Daniel Brolly, from Lifford, Co. Donegal, a 51-year-old foreman employed by the Board of Works, claimed damages against Patrick McGowan, forty-three, a Fianna Fáil senator, chairman of the county council, hotelier and potato merchant of Ballybofey, Co. Donegal, for alleged 'criminal conversation' with his wife, 34-year-old Anne Mary Maxwell, and for 'enticing her away from his house and society'. (The offence of criminal conversation has now been abolished, but at the time it enabled a husband to claim damages from his wife's adulterous partner.) Sutherland acted on behalf of Senator McGowan. The case generated acres of coverage across the national press as salacious details of the affair were disclosed during the trial.

An application was made by McGowan's legal team to have the case heard 'in camera', but this was rejected by the judge. In his statement of claim Brolly asserted that he and his wife had been married since April 1953 and that she had lived with him and their five children until May 1969. Since that time at various dates she had been 'debauched', 'enticed' and 'procured against her will' to 'depart and remain absent from his house and society'. For prolonged periods she had been 'harboured and detained' by McGowan at various places around Ireland, in Donegal, in Sligo and in Dublin. As a result, Brolly was deprived of the services of his wife, his inalienable family right had been violated, the constitution and authority of his family destroyed, and he had suffered great mental distress. McGowan's defence was that Maxwell had left the marriage of her own free will.

The case was eventually settled and McGowan agreed to pay a sum of IR£3,900, although there was no admission of liability. Marie Fleming, one of Brolly and Maxwell's five children, who suffered from multiple sclerosis, unsuccessfully brought a case against the state for the right to end her own life. She died peacefully in 2013, having written extensively about her father's case against McGowan in her memoir.

Sutherland was also involved in one of the highest-profile cases of the early 1980s. The Stardust was a nightclub situated in the north Dublin suburb of Artane. Forty-eight young people lost their lives when fire destroyed the club on 14 February 1981, dozens more being left with life-changing injuries. A Tribunal of Inquiry into the tragedy was held under Mr Justice Ronan Keane, Sutherland representing the manager and leaseholder of the Stardust, Eamon Butterly. It was not a popular cause, and Butterly was the target of widespread public disapproval. The tribunal found that it was 'probable arson'. It was one of the last cases Sutherland would defend. He was soon to become attorney general.

4

FINE GAEL

SUTHERLAND HAD DISPLAYED VERY FEW POLITICAL inclinations while at UCD. In a choice between rubbing shoulders with the country's future leaders at the L&H Society and playing rugby, the latter won out every time. But a successful career at the Bar hinges on vaulting ambition as well as cultivating the right sort of political ties. Ireland was a two-and-a-half-party state in the 1960s. For thrusting young barristers looking to make an impression, it was generally a choice between Fianna Fáil and Fine Gael. The two parties dominated the Irish political landscape from the foundation of the state onwards. Fianna Fáil, for most of its existence, was a cultural movement more than an orthodox political party. It was nominally left of centre but, in reality, it attracted people from across the ideological spectrum. What united all of them was the party's commitment to a united Ireland. Being sound on the 'national question' was a pre-condition for membership of the 'Republican Party.' Fine Gael was almost the mirror opposite. It was firmly centre right and had a natural antipathy to the sort of nationalism displayed by Fianna Fáil. Its membership tended to be big farmers and the middle classes.

Some young barristers opted for Labour, but their choice was motivated by ideology rather than ambition. Many people, including new entrants to the Bar, cleaved to one party or the other based on civil war considerations. Not so Sutherland. He came from a Fine Gael background, but not because it was the side his grandparents had taken during the foundation of the state.

Sutherland's grandfather had been the treasurer for Dublin Corporation. When he died in 1921, the family were bereft. Sutherland's grandmother went to W. T. Cosgrave, the Minister for Finance, and explained her family's straitened circumstances. She was a qualified public health nurse and Cosgrave ensured that she was put on the public payroll. According to Sutherland, Cosgrave's benevolence was one of the reasons why he was affiliated to Fine Gael. But then again, Fine Gael would probably have been a natural home for the Sutherlands. They were after all a prosperous south Dublin family.

Sutherland was also drawn to the party thanks to Declan Costello's 1965 policy pamphlet, 'Towards a Just Society'. Costello cited the grinding poverty and poor housing conditions in his Dublin North West constituency as one of the main reasons for writing the document. 'Share the resources of economic recovery fairly and, when an ill wind blows, prioritise the protection of the weak and the vulnerable,' was one of its main themes. In calling for much greater economic planning and more government intervention in the economy, it was an attempt to address the shortcomings of an increasingly sclerotic Irish state.

Garret FitzGerald also joined Fine Gael because of the pamphlet. FitzGerald, who had struck up a good rapport with Sutherland at UCD, was another Jesuit-educated middle-class boy from Dublin. His parents came from a mixed marriage: his mother, Mabel McConnell, was from Northern Ireland and had converted to Catholicism upon her marriage to Desmond FitzGerald, the Minister for External Affairs in the first Irish government.

A schism developed within Fine Gael around the late 1960s. A Dublin-centred liberal wing had formed around Costello, whereas a more rural, law and order wing remained loyal to party leader Liam Cosgrave. Sutherland and FitzGerald were firmly on the liberal wing, while future Taoiseach John Bruton was in the

Cosgrave camp. According to party sources, Sutherland and Bruton, while very respectful of each other, never developed a close relationship. On the other hand, Sutherland's relationship with FitzGerald, probably more than any other in his life, would have profound consequences. But then again, while he remained loyal, he was not unaware of FitzGerald's otherworldliness.

'All of us had an ambivalent relationship with Garret – he could drive you bananas,' says Gemma Hussey, a former Fine Gael minister. 'I mean I was a great friend and an admirer of Garret's. He was a good, honest, clever internationalist, but he was very scattered. And he'd have his mind changed very easily.' If she was going to meet FitzGerald about something, her husband Derry would tell her that it might be a good idea to find out who the last person FitzGerald had spoken to was, because that person would have changed his mind. 'I think it probably drove Peter a bit mad.'

Sutherland decided to dip his toe into the bearpit of elected politics. Friends are divided as to whether by doing so he was merely laying down a marker to be used as leverage when Fine Gael got into government, or whether he was intent on pursuing a career in the Dáil. He ran for Fine Gael in Dublin North West in the 1973 general election. Comprising as it did the working-class areas of Ballymun and Cabra, this would have been far from his natural constituency. 'I have often wondered why he did it,' Gemma Hussey says. 'But then you have to throw your mind back to the times.' Sutherland, she believes, would have felt strongly that a Fianna Fáil government with Charles Haughey in its ranks would not be good for the country. 'He did it out of a sense of duty. A lot of things that Peter did were out of a sense of duty, I think.'

Michael Sweetman had originally been selected to run for Fine Gael in Dublin North West. One of Ireland's first committed Europhiles, Sweetman had spearheaded the 1972 referendum on Ireland's entry into the European Economic Community, having helped Declan Costello put together 'Towards a Just Society'. Tragically Sweetman was one of twelve Irish businessmen killed in an air crash on 18 June 1972. The group, who were among the most prominent industrialists in the country, were on their way to Brussels to set up a bureau to lobby on behalf of Irish businesses following accession to the EEC. The plane went down near Staines, west of London, shortly after taking off from Heathrow. All 118 people on board were killed.

Mary Robinson, then a Senator, and Garret FitzGerald were among those who paid tribute to Sweetman. In many ways he had foreshadowed Sutherland – he had advised Fine Gael on Europe and Northern Ireland – so it was perhaps fitting that Sutherland should take his place in the election.

Costello had been the TD in Dublin North West from 1951 until 1969 when he stood down, although he contested the 1973 election in the Dublin South West. He would serve as attorney general in the Fine Gael–Labour coalition between 1973 and 1977, and as a judge in the High Court between 1977 and his retirement in 1998. According to Peter Prendergast, head of elections for Fine Gael in the 1973 election, the rationale for running Sutherland in Dublin North West was that the seat had been held for eighteen years by Costello, who was also a barrister and came from a similar social background to Sutherland. However, friends say Sutherland was well aware that his personal circumstances jarred with his putative constituency and that is why he put Carraig an tSionnaigh, the Irish version of his address, in his campaign leaflets to disguise the fact that he lived in Foxrock.

Hugh Byrne was Sutherland's running mate. A somewhat eccentric character with colourful and controversial views, when François Mitterrand, the former French president, was on a visit to Ireland, the Department of Foreign Affairs was staggered and dismayed in equal measure that he wanted to meet Byrne, who he had met at a EU council meeting years earlier and found to be a very agreeable companion. 'He was normally kept well away from civilised company,' says one Fine Gael source.

In 1973 Byrne was a Fine Gael councillor in the area, with well-established links in the community: he was a GP and a member of the local boxing club. Although the odds were heavily stacked against him, Sutherland took the election very seriously. 'Anybody who runs thinks they are in with a chance,' says Prendergast. The constituency may not have been Sutherland's natural territory, yet he took to the campaign trail with the same vigour he displayed on the rugby pitch. The dashing young barrister with an abundance of charm soon began to make an impact on the doorstep. One of the peculiarities of Irish politics is that there can often be more rivalry between party colleagues running in the same constituency than between candidates from opposing parties. The electoral system is based on multi-seat constituencies with TDs elected through a system of proportional representation by a single transferable vote. The logic is that there is a much better chance of unseating an opposing candidate in a subsequent election, than unseating a party colleague.

This particular dynamic has given the normal cut and thrust of electioneering an added edge. But even by the standards of campaign subterfuge that have prevailed in Ireland, what happened in Dublin North West in 1973 has attained a unique place in the pantheon of strokes and cute *hoorism*. Social media has raised (or lowered) the dark arts of campaign interference to a highly sophisticated level. Before the era of mass communications, however, political parties intent on undermining a rival candidate had to resort to much cruder tactics. Byrne's camp, who as they entered the election had estimated Sutherland's chances at somewhere between nil and zero, became alarmed at the feedback they were getting from the doorsteps.

Locals were taken with the handsome young barrister with the silver tongue. When moreover, rumours began to circulate that Sutherland had a beautiful and exotic wife, the Byrne camp collectively decided that a more interventionist approach to their party rival would have to be taken.

Sutherland spent one evening knocking on doors around Cabra, to a generally positive response. Meanwhile a team of volunteers in the Byrne camp had reputedly found a Nigerian student from the Trinity medicine faculty. Asked to accompany them to the same houses that Sutherland had visited the previous evening, she was introduced as Mrs Sutherland. The consensus formed among Byrne's volunteers was that in early 1970s Ireland, proof of an interracial marriage was enough to break any fledgling political career.

Prendergast insists that Byrne had no direct role in the underhand tactic. But whether he played an indirect role remains one of the great unanswered questions in Irish political life. According to Nicholas Kearns, Byrne and Sutherland 'were made for each other. He [Sutherland] wouldn't have minded that. He would have expected it.'

In the event, Sutherland lost the election. He secured 1,969 votes, or 6.24 per cent of the votes cast and promptly lost his deposit. Overall, though, it was a respectable performance. He had come sixth out of ten candidates: Jim Tunney of Fianna Fáil came first, Byrne took the second seat, David Thornley of Labour took the third and Fianna Fáil's Richard Gogan took the fourth. It was one of the few setbacks in Sutherland's career. According to Garrett Sheehan, however, losing the election did not greatly distress him: 'If it was a disappointment, it was a very brief one.'

Mark FitzGerald, Garret's son and the owner of auctioneering firm Sherry FitzGerald, the biggest in the country (FitzGerald sold Sutherland's Foxrock home when he moved to Sydney Avenue in Blackrock in 1976), had politics in his blood; indeed it was one of his main passions in life. In an illustration of the tight-knit social circles in Dublin, Mark FitzGerald first met Sutherland at a party thrown by the latter's sister Karen in 1974. Mark, who was there with one of his good friends Gerry Sheehan, a younger brother of Garrett Sheehan, says that Sutherland harboured a desire to have another go at seeking election and that he probably regretted that the opportunity never arose, but his career took a different path. 'But I think when he got involved later in life and the whole migration thing, the commitment to public service was definitely about that. His business career was about giving him the financial independence ultimately to go back into public service. That's what I felt about him. That's what my father felt about him,' adds Mark.

Happenstance played a prominent role in Sutherland's career trajectory. Exploring alternative scenarios in the lives of public figures can throw up some interesting counter-narratives, and in Sutherland's case more than most. For example, what would have happened if Sutherland had been elected in 1973? One former colleague said he wouldn't have had the patience to sit on the backbenches. It is also doubtful he would have relished the endless constituency clinics and funeral attendances required to ensure re-election. Nor, if elected, would he probably have become attorney general in the next Fine Gael government. And it was because of Fine Gael's wafer-thin majority at the time that Sutherland got the nod to go to Brussels as Ireland's European commissioner. That was the launch pad for international stardom. On the other hand, the one role Sutherland prized more than any other in his life was to become president of the European Commission. It is normally a pre-condition that candidates for this position have been elected to office.

When Fine Gael and Labour formed a coalition following the 1973 election, Sutherland went back to the Bar and worked on what was now a thriving practice. The next general election in 1977 was not a good one for Fine Gael; it went from fifty-five seats down to forty-three, while Fianna Fáil surged from sixty-five to eighty-four seats and was able to form a government. Liam Cosgrave stood down as leader of Fine Gael and was replaced by Garret FitzGerald.

Sutherland may have stood back from the political fray in the mid-1970s, but his relationship with the FitzGerald family blossomed over that period, Mark FitzGerald recalls. 'They had a very close relationship and Peter and Maruja would have come to dinner a lot. They got on with my mother. Peter got on particularly well with my father, but my mother also. He was very close to my mother.' Sutherland's relationship with Joan FitzGerald would play a crucial role in one of his most important career moves.

The 1973–7 government contained some heavyweight figures. Garret FitzGerald was Minister for Foreign Affairs, Justin Keating Minister for Industry and Commerce. Michael O'Leary was appointed Minister for Labour, Conor Cruise O'Brien Minister for Posts and Telegraphs and Peter Barry Minister for Transport. Historians of that era generally agree that there has rarely been more intellectual heft sitting around a cabinet table. But that was too little to put the country on the right path. The government was a victim of unfortunate timing: Ireland had experienced a rare spurt of economic growth in the early 1970s, but by 1977, the oil crisis had tipped the economy back into recession. The government reconfigured every constituency boundary in the country in ways that allegedly benefited Fine Gael and Labour. Despite the best efforts of the coalition to rig the election in its favour, Fianna Fáil swept to a crushing victory.

After the 1977 election, Peter Prendergast took over as Fine Gael's national secretary and initiated a party-wide restructuring. A steering committee was set up to formulate party policy, its members including Sutherland alongside Derry Hussey, Jim Mitchell, Peter Barry and some senior unelected party members. 'Peter was a very valuable member, to put it mildly,' says Gemma Hussey, who first got to know Sutherland around this time.

According to Prendergast, Fine Gael's grassroots organisation was in a parlous state. A two-pronged strategy was proposed to put the party back in power. First was the establishment of structures that would put Fine Gael on a much more competitive footing before the next election. Running parallel to this process was the creation of a coherent policy platform. Sutherland was a key player in putting the party's manifesto together. The preparation paid off: Fine Gael reversed many of its losses in the 1981 general election.

Brendan Halligan first met Sutherland in the late 1960s. An economist by education, Halligan had a lifelong association with the Labour Party. He was a TD, an MEP and the party's secretary general over a period of three decades. Another committed Europhile, he set up the Institute for International and European Affairs (IIEA), a think tank, in Dublin and developed a close personal and professional relationship with Sutherland. Halligan attributes Fine Gael's success at this period to a particular skill: 'There was a culture in Fine Gael of being extremely good at drafting, a combination of politics and law and sometimes economics. It was part of the organisational culture of Fine Gael that goes back to the foundation of the state. They did after all draft the first constitution.'

He continues: 'The best drafter in the English language I have ever come across was Jim Dooge.' Widely considered a polymath, Dooge served as Minister for Foreign Affairs in 1981; he was also an engineer, a climatologist and an academic. Halligan and Dooge had written Fine Gael and Labour's joint 1973 manifesto together. 'Then there was Alexis FitzGerald, whom I wrote the 1977 election manifesto with, and also Declan Costello. On top of that Garret FitzGerald was also very talented. Peter [Sutherland] was part of that culture,' Halligan says.

It was a training that would serve Sutherland well in later years. His ability to draft a contract in a very short period of time saved the Uruguay Round of trade talks from collapsing at the eleventh hour.

Any time a new government is formed there is always intense speculation about the identity of the new cabinet, and 1981 was no exception. According to one senior legal source who was in the Law Library at the time, the expectation in legal circles was that Nial Fennelly would be appointed attorney general. A former Law Library colleague of Sutherland's has said that 'Fennelly's reputation as a lawyer was superb and he went on to be advocate general in the Courts of Justice in Luxembourg and a Supreme Court judge, and an excellent Supreme Court judge at that. He was a top-class lawyer, one of Ireland's best lawyers in the last forty years. So there probably was a little bit of surprise that – well, certainly the feeling was that Peter came on the outside and overtook Nial on the line.'

On 26 June 1981, Garret FitzGerald appointed Sutherland attorney general. Still only thirty-five, Sutherland was by far the youngest man to occupy the role in the history of the state, a record that still stands. At the time he was also the highest-earning barrister in the Law Library. 'I suppose his name would have been in the ring but Peter wouldn't have had a reputation for being a lawyer. His reputation was as an advocate. I suppose at that time the feeling was that somebody who had a very strong legal reputation would be the one who might go in as AG. Of course Peter was charming. He was excellent at tactics, he was a good advocate, he knew how to win, he knew how to campaign for something and therefore he obviously conducted a campaign for himself to become the attorney general, and he was successful,' the same former Law Library colleague stated. But Sutherland mounted a very effective campaign. 'He would have gone to every Fine Gael Árd Fheis [party conference]. He was deeply involved with the party in terms of putting policy together. He did the hard yards. Fennelly did not, and ultimately that was the difference between them.'

Fennelly declines to comment on whether he was linked to the post. But he says: 'Don't forget there is an unavoidable political element to the role. Peter was a good lawyer with good instincts. He wasn't noted for his academic approach to the law. He wasn't noted as a writer of learned articles. But the AG is the legal adviser to the government, and is equipped with an office staffed with experts. It wasn't a surprise at the Bar. He was noted for being active in Fine Gael. Peter had huge political clout and had a huge self-confidence about him.'

According to Mark FitzGerald, his father was conscious of the fact that he had been elected Taoiseach for the first time at the age of fifty-five. And that is why he made a conscious decision to appoint as many young TDs to the cabinet as possible. Alan Dukes, Michael Noonan and John Bruton, who were all in their thirties, were given cabinet positions. It was in that spirit that he picked Sutherland, says FitzGerald, adding that his father was also conscious about promoting women into senior positions, but that in 1981 there was a dearth of suitable candidates. Eleven female TDs were elected to the 166-person chamber that year, and there was just one female TD in the cabinet: Eileen Desmond, the Labour Party Minister for Health.

'Was Peter then natural choice as attorney general? Well, I think he was young to be attorney general and I don't think it was necessarily an absolute given, but I think that the work Peter did with my father was very important. They quickly got themselves on a wavelength. My father was full of policy ideas and Peter was a pragmatist who could see how they could be executed, and the fact that they did that work on the manifesto showed the depth of his brain,' says Mark.

It was certainly a bold move on his father's part. According to Alan Dukes, the role would have been agreed between FitzGerald and Dick Spring, the Tánaiste (deputy prime minister) and leader of the Labour Party. 'There was never any tension in government about Peter's political background. The protocol with the AG is that he or she attends all cabinet meetings but speaks only when spoken to. It was obvious Peter had things to say outside the strict remit of the AG. He always managed a way of being requested to speak.'

Towards the end of the summer of 1981, when Sutherland was invited to speak to the Irish American Lawyers Association at a meeting in Dublin, he used the opportunity to address the issue of the need for constitutional change. He set out a clear manifesto calling for a thorough review of the constitution and for a programme of social and institutional change that would reflect and implement what was becoming, for some, the uncomfortable reality of plurality. A constitution 'is made for people of fundamentally differing views', according to Sutherland.

Pluralism, he said, was the essence of the Republican ideal; the state had an obligation to protect the rights of individuals in the context of diversity of belief and take cognisance of the rights and the sensibilities of non-nationalists in the North. The following is an edited extract of that speech:

Promote pluralism, reconciliation and peace; our constitution had provided stability and coherence to civic society and it had allowed it to flourish and to function.

But a constitution should not give cause for alienation; rather it should assist in the process of reconciliation. For fifty years, the Irish constitution had served us well, it had provided stability and coherence, based on the rule of law, but in the process it had, understandably, acquired an aura of immutability.

But it is vital that we did not permit our reverence for that authority to blind us to some of the inadequacies or shortcomings that were now becoming apparent as society developed and changed. Debate and an openness to change are positive for a democratic republic. The mystique and excessive reverence accorded an iconic text, such as a constitution, can only serve to damage its long-term sustainability and its integrity.

Informed and healthy debate ensures that the constitution remains a living, vital expression of the rights and liberties of each individual in the specific context of the complexity of their relationship with society. Debate protects the citizen just as it preserves the authority of the constitution.[1]

The speech generated significant publicity. In response, the Fine Gael–Labour coalition set up a constitutional review commission and a working group comprised of leading academic experts, together with a number of legal practitioners. The group met on a number of occasions. Having established its terms of reference and a work plan, it produced a series of detailed working papers in which consideration was given to areas of particular complexity such as citizen rights, the right of referral and review and the jurisdictional extent of the courts.

This presaged a decade of social, political and constitutional upheaval.

Public Office

5

THE EIGHTH AMENDMENT TIME BOMB

S UTHERLAND'S CAREER CONSISTED OF TWO PARTS: the public servant and the businessman. His first public sector role, as attorney general in the 1981 Fine Gael–Labour Party coalition, was hardly the most auspicious beginning. The government lasted only 279 days. Against a highly unfavourable economic backdrop, it was a particularly turbulent time in Irish politics. The national debt was climbing to unsustainable levels. The unemployment rate was 15 per cent and rising. The lack of a coherent industrial strategy and short-sighted protectionist policies ensured that levels of economic activity remained anaemic at best. Hunger strikes among Republican prisoners in the Maze prison in Northern Ireland brought worldwide attention to the Troubles, and made the prospect of peace even more remote. IRA murders and loyalist reprisals became a depressing staple of the daily news cycle.

The minority coalition collapsed on 27 January 1982 when it failed to get its budget through the Oireachtas. John Bruton, then Minister for Finance, had attempted to put VAT on children's shoes; it was a move that alienated the independent TDs propping up the administration. Another election in March returned Fianna Fáil to power.

Then, in the summer of 1982, a series of shocking and

random murders convulsed the country when Malcolm MacArthur killed a nurse, Bridie Gargan, in Phoenix Park and a few days later took the life of Thomas Dunne, a farmer from County Offaly. MacArthur went on the run. In an effort to evade capture, he went to the house of an old acquaintance, Patrick Connolly, then attorney general. The two men attended a match in Croke Park, the headquarters of the Gaelic Athletic Association (GAA), and discussed the murder with Garda commissioner Paddy McLoughlin.

MacArthur was arrested at Connolly's Dalkey home in August 1982. The attorney general immediately resigned and a very colourful description of events was given by the then Taoiseach Charlie Haughey. The episode seeped into popular culture through the acronym GUBU – grotesque, unbelievable, bizarre, unprecedented. (It was Sutherland's former master, Harry Hill, who successfully prosecuted MacArthur for Gargan's murder.) Later that year, the Fianna Fáil government itself fell over proposed budget cuts needed to stabilise the country's fiscal position. An election was held in November 1982, and as a result Fine Gael and Labour formed another government.

Sutherland now began his second and much more eventful stint as attorney general alongside Michael Noonan, the newly installed justice minister. The two men would develop a close working relationship and a lifelong friendship; their earliest encounter, however, was the phone-tapping scandal. According to newspaper reports in December 1982, earlier that year the Fianna Fáil administration had ordered that the phones of two prominent political journalists – Geraldine Kennedy from the *Irish Press* and Bruce Arnold from the *Irish Independent* – should be tapped in an effort to detect the source of cabinet leaks. The phone tapping had been instigated by Sean Doherty, a Fianna Fáil TD for Roscommon and justice minister in 1982. At the time, the state could only sanction the phone tapping of persons suspected of subversive activity. Even though the work of Kennedy and Arnold had greatly upset the government of the day, under no circumstances could it be deemed a threat to the security of the state.

When the story broke it caused a political crisis that quickly embroiled the two most senior members of An Garda Síochána, the Irish police. As Michael Noonan explains: 'I had to have conversations with Garda commissioner Paddy McLoughlin and deputy commissioner Joe Ainsworth. I was relying on Peter [Sutherland] for legal advice on what was appropriate and not appropriate to say. It was very good advice.'

In 1978, Gerry Collins, Fianna Fáil justice minister at the time, had dismissed Garda commissioner Ned Garvey when it emerged that Garvey had placed Eamonn Barnes, the director of public prosecutions, under surveillance. When Garvey initiated proceedings against the state on the basis that it had abrogated his constitutional rights, the case went all the way to the Supreme Court, with Garvey emerging victorious. 'The essence of the advice he gave me,' continued Noonan, 'was that when Gerry Collins was justice minister and the government dismissed Ned Garvey, Garvey won his case in the Supreme Court on the grounds of inappropriate procedure. He went through Supreme Court judgment so that I didn't make any legal errors in conversations with McLoughlin and Ainsworth.' Sutherland's advice to Noonan on how to deal with McLoughlin and Ainsworth was sound because he had represented Garvey. He knew what, and more importantly, what not to do in such circumstances. As a result, both McLoughlin and Ainsworth retired from the force.

*

The phone-tapping scandal was only a minor skirmish, however, compared with what was to come next. In the early 1980s, the Catholic right was uniting under a banner of implacable opposition to abortion. The broad aim of the two main groups, the Society for the Protection of Unborn Children (SPUC) and the Pro-Life Amendment Campaign (PLAC), was to insert an amendment into the constitution that would prohibit abortion in Ireland in all circumstances. Moreover, they wanted to ensure that no Irish woman could travel abroad for an abortion – and that meant removing access to information about abortion services in other jurisdictions. In many ways Ireland was starting to resemble a theocracy more than a fully functioning democracy. There were very few developed countries at that time where the forces of the church and religious groupings could shape society to such an extent through state legislation.

The Catholic right had such heft that politicians ran scared rather than confront them. Dr Julia Vaughan was the leading figure in the Pro-Life Amendment Campaign, while some PLAC members were very senior lawyers in the Four Courts. The religious right took the view that it was necessary to place in the constitution an amendment that would do two things.

First, they wanted to rule out any possibility that the constitution would be used in the future as a vehicle to identify an unremunerated right to abortion by an interpretation of the rights to privacy – in other words, the kind of thing that had happened in the Roe v. Wade case in the United States. Second, there was also an even more radical group who believed that there should be a positive expression of the right to life in the constitution. In that period there were three elections, so any powerful advocacy or lobby group would obviously get a keen hearing from the political leadership of both parties. As a result, both Fianna Fáil and Fine Gael gave commitments to include wording in the constitution that would have the desired effect for the pro-life groups.

The religious right occupied key positions across the state and in Irish society. The number two civil servant in the attorney general's office when Sutherland took over, a colourful figure called Matt Russell, was closely associated with PLAC. Even by the conservative standards of the time, he occupied the outer fringes of the right wing. A prominent member of Opus Dei, Russell was also instrumental in the collapse of the Fianna Fáil– Labour coalition in 1994 when it emerged in November of that year that he had not processed nine warrants for arrest of paedo-phile priest Fr Brendan Smyth.

PLAC had lobbied all parties before the 1981 general election to insert an amendment in the constitution that would make Ireland's abortion laws ironclad. Garret FitzGerald, as leader of Fine Gael, made such a commitment but failed to follow through in the short-lived government. When Charlie Haughey was in government in 1982, PLAC had again come up with the wording it wanted inserted into the constitution. Haughey promised that he would hold a referendum to honour his commitment to PLAC. The pledge followed Haughey on the campaign trail when the government collapsed in November of that year, but put Garret FitzGerald in an invidious position. If Fine Gael failed to match Haughey's commitment then it risked incurring the wrath of – and electoral rejection by – social conservatives. They had mobilised in such large numbers that they could potentially sway the outcome of the election.

FitzGerald opted to take a conservative approach and matched Haughey's pledge. According to Mark FitzGerald, his father made the judgement that if he hadn't given such a commitment he wouldn't have won the election. 'If he hadn't won the election, I don't think personally it would have bothered him if he hadn't become Taoiseach. But he was very interested in solving the problems in Northern Ireland. He made the gamble on the Eighth Amendment even though his heart wasn't in it, because he knew that if he didn't then between the Church and Haughey they would wipe the floor. Well, they nearly did, it was a very close election.'

Alan Dukes, finance minister in the Fine Gael–Labour govern-ment formed in December 1982, recalls a meeting held while the party was still in opposition. He and a few like-minded party members, he says, had taken to referring to the Society for the Protection of Unborn Children, after the abbreviation of their name, as 'Spuccers'. 'The Spuccers were invited to make a pres-entation to the Fine Gael parliamentary party in October 1982.

I remember it well. It was a bright sunny morning. The Spuccers came in and made the presentation, which I found very unusual. They then said they would like the views of every Fine Gael member present, which they would faithfully report back to their constituents. I remember having to make a conscientious effort not to tell them that it was okay, I would tell my constituents myself. But anyway, I didn't. Then we had the election in November '82. Then we were in government and Peter [Sutherland] was faced with the task of steering this through.'

Somewhat unusually, Michael Noonan became the sponsoring minister to steer through the Eighth Amendment in 1983. It should have been the responsibility of the health minister; in 2018, Simon Harris, Minister for Health, would be given responsibility for managing the referendum that removed the Eighth Amendment, and it was assumed that in 1983, Barry Desmond, the Labour Party health minister, would take charge of the proposed legislation. But Desmond vehemently opposed the proposal and refused to have anything to do with it. That is why Noonan was asked to take charge. 'So it was transferred to me, the file was transferred from health to justice. There was nothing in the file except the words,' Noonan recalls.

Normally a file containing a proposed piece of legislation, particularly one as contentious as the Eighth Amendment, would contain reams of analysis and legal opinion. There was nothing in the file bequeathed by the previous administration. 'Except the little green words printed by Fianna Fáil, which said "to be included in the constitution". It looked initially, my officials thought, that the words had been produced without analysis, but we found out subsequently that the words had been considered but there was no written analysis. It was produced outside the system,' explains Noonan. It emerged that the wording of the amendment had not been prepared in consultation with any government department. It is the understanding of this book that the original proposal for the amendment was put together by Sutherland's UCD lecturer in constitutional law, Justice John

Blayney, a Supreme Court judge between 1992 and 1997. Blayney died in June 2018, aged ninety-three, one month after the Eighth Amendment was repealed through a referendum.

The wording of the amendment was as follows:

The State acknowledges the right to life of the unborn and, with due regard to the equal right to life of the mother, guarantees in its laws to respect, and, as far as practicable, by its laws to defend and vindicate that right.

Noonan says that when the proposed legislation was published, it looked as if it would have a seamless passage through the Oireachtas. Then there was speculation that there could be trouble over the wording. Peter [Sutherland] gave informal advice first that there were problems with the wording. Then it became very difficult to proceed. There were a number of problems with the wording but he focused on possible risks to the life of the mother.'

According to Noonan, his officials in the justice department also identified problems with the wording of the amendment. In particular they believed that it was ambiguous and that it would be challenged in the Supreme Court, which could poten-tially pave the way for the introduction of abortion in certain cases. 'Both Peter and myself were telling the government there was a difficulty, there was a different emphasis. He said there was a risk to women and the risk I was bringing to cabinet was that the amendment was not fit for purpose and instead of closing out abortion, which was the intent, it would open the door to it.'

The following passage is taken from Sutherland's private papers:

I had considered the proposed amendment carefully, over a number of months and had sought and consulted with a range of expert opinion (medical and legal) both in Ireland and further afield (principally from the US). The text of the proposed amendment presented a number of problems and these stemmed from a lack of precision in drafting. In my opinion, it was not a suitable implement with which to copper fasten the status quo. The language used, specifically around the notion of 'unborn' and of 'equal right to life', appeared to leave the matter open to interpretation in the (inevitable) event of a future appeal to the courts. This was precisely the outcome that those behind the proposal had intended to frustrate. The proposed amendment offered neither clarity nor closure on the issue. It was not fit for purpose. I presented my opinion on the wording by way of a memorandum to cabinet. The text of that opinion was subsequently released for publication.[1]

When it emerged that Sutherland had raised concerns about the amendment and its potential consequences, there was a furious backlash in the Dáil, and indeed on the part of the pro-life lobby groups. They interpreted it as an attempt by the government to renege on the pledge it had made during the election campaign. Fianna Fáil in particular had a sizeable contingent of ardent pro-lifers within its ranks, but Fine Gael also had a considerable number. FitzGerald was on the horns of a dilemma. Knowing that the wording was deeply flawed, but that politically the matter had become toxic, he took the unprecedented step of publishing Sutherland's advice on the wording:

In summary: the wording is ambiguous and unsatisfactory. It will lead inevitably to confusion and uncertainty, not merely amongst the medical profession, to whom it has of course particular relevance, but also amongst lawyers and more specifically the judges who will have to interpret it.

Far from providing the protection and certainty which is sought by many of those who have advocated its adoption, it will have a contrary effect. In particular it is not clear as to what life is being protected; as to whether 'the unborn' is protected from the moment of fertilisation or alternatively is left unprotected until an independently viable human being exists at 25 to 28 weeks.

Further, having regard to the equal rights of the unborn and the mother, a doctor faced with the dilemma of saving the life of the mother, knowing that to do so will terminate the life of 'the unborn' will be compelled by the wording to conclude that he can do nothing. Whatever his intention he will have to show equal regard for both lives, and his predominant intent will not be a factor.

In these circumstances I cannot approve of the wording proposed. [See Appendix 2 for Sutherland's full advice.]

The most politically expedient thing for Sutherland to do would have been to put his conscience to one side and proceed with the proposed legislation as best he could. After all, opposing the pro-life lobby on this issue was a strategy freighted with risks – not least the very public backlash from SPUC and PLAC. Nicholas Kearns says it was a very traumatic time for Sutherland and his wife Maruja. 'Things were arriving at home in the post, nasty letters and so on. I know he was more concerned about Maruja than himself. His warning on the Eighth was brushed aside at the time, but it subsequently came to pass.' Sutherland was a practising Catholic, but events relating to the Eighth Amendment would suggest that he had great courage and his convictions were much more nuanced.

Dukes says that Sutherland was a man of deep faith 'but he was a powerful thinker as well. I think what he proposed for that amendment in no way compromised his faith. I think Peter, as a lawyer and AG, would have been quite categoric about the need for separation of church and state, although I never discussed that with him.'

According to Gemma Hussey it was one of Sutherland's 'finest moments . . . He was very clear and despite his own inner convictions about abortion and everything, he was absolutely clear about it. Yes he was an extraordinary Christian in the best sense of the word.'

But then again, Hussey says, she didn't know exactly what Sutherland's views on abortion were. Neither did his close friends. He was a man of deep faith, but he certainly didn't broadcast his beliefs. In this case, he was first and foremost the attorney general to the government and he saw it as a moral obligation to flag any potential legal problems with a piece of legislation.

Mary Robinson, who would become president of Ireland in 1990, was at the time a member of the Senate and one of the leading campaigners in the country against the Eighth Amendment. 'Peter was trying to get Fine Gael to come out on the right side of the issue. I was actively warning in the Senate about the implications of equating the right to life of the mother with the unborn and that this proposal would be a terrible future for women. Peter was aware of these dangers. He was a very serious Catholic but in my view he wasn't a conservative Catholic,' she says.

Garret FitzGerald eventually announced that he was unhappy with the wording and that an alternative form of words would have to be found. The attorney general's office said it would find words that would work. Sutherland consulted widely on the next course of action. It is understood he took soundings from Niall McCarthy, one of the leading members of the Law Library and another future Supreme Court judge. According to Garrett Sheehan, Sutherland had been very close to the Maynooth theologian Enda McDonagh, and had discussed the issue extensively with him.

Sutherland produced an alternative wording: 'Nothing in this constitution shall be invoked to invalidate, or to deprive of force or effect, any provision of a law on the ground that it prohibits abortion.'

The new wording was put in a memorandum, copies of which were made in the Irish Life building on Abbey Street where the Department of Justice had a sub-office. During the process, a copy was leaked to Oliver Flanagan, a Fine Gael TD who had a reputation as a fire-and-brimstone arch-conservative. When

Flanagan brought up the memorandum at a Fine Gael parliamentary meeting, consternation ensued.

David Byrne says Sutherland's performance as attorney general at the time was 'masterful . . . His wording for the Eighth Amendment I thought was excellent. I agreed with him then and I still agree with him to this day.' Byrne had campaigned against the original wording. At the time he was a member of Fianna Fáil, and among a very small minority of the party who opposed the Eighth Amendment. He initiated, together with Frank Clark (who is now the Chief Justice), a petition signed by one hundred barristers in the Four Courts which expressed dissatisfaction with the wording that was being advanced.

'The reason why I got involved in that was because I was at home one day having my lunch, and I heard a leading member of the Bar express a view that all lawyers were in favour of this wording – that was the conservative wording – and I knew that wasn't the case. I was so upset about it that I went back into the Law Library that afternoon and spoke to a number of friends and colleagues and said I believed this was wrong. I believed it should not be allowed to be expressed out there that we were in favour of it in this way. The petition did not expressly favour Peter's wording, we just said that the wording that was chosen was inappropriate and we wanted to make it clear that it ought not to be sent, that lawyers take the view that this is the right way forward. If somebody had asked me at the time – I'm sure they did, also Adrian Hardiman was heavily involved in that as well – I would have said Peter's wording. He was absolutely right about that.'

Byrne says he believed that Sutherland's wording was better suited if there had to be a wording. 'I believed that the wording that included a positive right to life or equal right to life would cause an enormous amount of trouble.' He added that 'it couldn't possibly be properly adjudicated on by the courts; it put a very, very unfair burden on the judiciary if ever there was a dispute, which would be inevitable . . . I also felt that something like that would be better dealt with by statute rather than by constitution.

I'm a great respecter of constitutions but you have to be very careful what you put into a constitution because you must remember that it is intended – and was in this instance intended – to fix the law into the future irrespective of the shifts or changes in public opinion. If you do things by statute rather than by constitution it allows for changes in the law to take place more easily, where the elected representatives of the people who make laws in parliament are the ones that can respond to the new changes or ideas that were there.

'I believe that, as a matter of law and politics, is a better way to respond to things. That's the very thing that the pro-life lobby did not want to happen. They wanted to lock this into the future and that's what I felt was wrong. I felt at the time that Peter's answer to that was a good one because it responded to the request of the pro-life lobby that the constitution should not be used to interpret in an unexpected way a right to abortion. Peter's amendment would have dealt with that, but that wasn't enough for the pro-life lobby, they wanted an expression of a positive right to life. As we know, that created so much trouble and Peter was absolutely right about that.' David Byrne discussed the dilemma with Sutherland at the time. 'He felt passionately about it.'

The task of going through with the proposal again fell to Michael Noonan. Many members of Fianna Fáil, unhappy that the original wording of the Eighth had been replaced by what they considered a watered-down version, decided to act. They enlisted the help of eight diehard pro-life members of Fine Gael, and between them they were able to get a parliamentary majority to reinstate the original wording of the amendment. Noonan and Fine Gael then had to steer through an amendment to which they were opposed.

On 7 September 1983, Ireland voted by a majority of 66.7 per cent to 33.3 per cent to adopt the Eighth Amendment. Over the next thirty-five years Ireland's abortion laws were rarely out of the headlines, and usually for the wrong reasons. In particular, what became known as the X-case in 1992 (referred to as such as the girl involved could not be legally named) received widespread international condemnation. That year a fourteen-year-old girl reported to the Gardai that she had been raped and as a consequence was pregnant. When her parents informed the Gardai that the girl was travelling to the UK for an abortion, attorney general Harry Whelehan sought an injunction to prevent the girl, whose identity could not be revealed for legal reasons because she was a minor, from leaving the country (stridently pro-life civil servant Matt Russell played an active role in proceedings). Justice Costello, sitting in the High Court, granted the injunction, but the Supreme Court set aside the ruling and the girl was allowed to travel. Michael Noonan comments: 'My senior officials thought the problem with the wording was subsequently what turned out to be the X-case. They actually thought it would go wider than the terms of the X-case. They were right in the sense that the wording gave rise to abortion in circumstances in line with the X-case. But they thought it would be a wider consequence arising from Supreme Court cases.'

Sutherland's concerns about the Eighth Amendment, however, were most clearly illustrated in the tragic case of Dr Savita Halappanavar. The Indian-born dentist died in University Hospital Galway in October 2012, having developed a sepsis infection during a miscarriage. It subsequently emerged that she had requested an abortion when she began to miscarry, but she was denied the procedure on the grounds that it was illegal. If the abortion had been performed it would probably have saved her life.

When the story broke it hardened public opinion. The government pledged to hold a referendum on reforming Irish abortion laws; when it took place on 21 May 2018, 69 per cent of the Irish people voted in favour of repealing the amendment.

6

THE TROUBLES: NEGOTIATING
THE ANGLO-IRISH AGREEMENT

ALONGSIDE DIVISIVE SOCIAL ISSUES SUCH AS THE Eighth Amendment, events in Northern Ireland formed a prominent backdrop to Sutherland's time as attorney general. Ever since the foundation of the Irish state, relations between Dublin and London had been shaped by distrust and enmity. But the level of hostility escalated when the Troubles flared up in the late 1960s. There was a view in Dublin that the British government neither understood nor cared about the plight of the nationalist community in Northern Ireland. Allegations of collusion between security forces and loyalist paramilitaries, as well as evidence of a shoot-to-kill policy on the part of British armed forces based in Northern Ireland, deepened the level of antagonism in Irish government circles.

By the early 1980s, the IRA had extended its campaign of terror to mainland Britain. The assassination of Lord Mountbatten in Sligo in 1978 increased the level of distrust. Airey Neave, a Conservative MP who was close to British Prime Minister Margaret Thatcher, was killed by a car bomb planted by the Irish National Liberation Army (INLA), another Republican paramilitary organisation, outside the House of Commons. If anything, these events stiffened the resolve of the British government to take a yet more hard-line approach to Northern Ireland. Dáithí Ó Ceallaigh, one of Ireland's most distinguished diplomats, served as ambassador to the UK between 2001 and 2007. In the late 1970s he was the press attaché at the Irish embassy in London. 'I felt like I was in an enemy country,' he says.

When Garret FitzGerald was elected Taoiseach in 1981, he set about changing the Irish government's approach to Northern Ireland; by extension, he hoped that this would form the basis of some sort of rapprochement between Dublin and London. Among those FitzGerald selected to play a crucial role in the formulation of the Anglo-Irish Agreement was Michael Lillis.

FitzGerald had come across Lillis when he was based at the Irish embassy in Washington. Lillis had been very influential in getting senior Irish-American politicians such as Tip O'Neill to focus on Northern Ireland. He had helped prepare a speech for Jimmy Carter which for the first time didn't by default side with the UK government in relation to Northern Ireland. In the short-lived 1981 government, Lillis was appointed diplomatic adviser to the Taoiseach, a post that had never existed before and has never existed since. He struck up an immediate relationship with Sutherland, who he says referred to the Fine Gael–Labour coalition as Camelot: 'You didn't know from one moment to the next if the government was going to fall.'

The attorney general's office at the time was in the basement of the Department of An Taoiseach, with the Taoiseach's office on the first floor. Lillis had an office next door to FitzGerald. Alexis FitzGerald, the Taoiseach's special adviser (the two were unrelated), also had an office on the first floor. Liam Hourican, who would become Sutherland's deputy chef de cabinet in Brussels, was at that stage the government press secretary. Declan Kelly, the Taoiseach's private secretary, completed Garret FitzGerald's inner circle.

Lillis and Sutherland would go for a coffee every day in a café across the road from Government Buildings. 'There was a confectionery shop and a café. We would go there every morning about eleven. Peter was very fond of the cakes, but he was clearly under instructions not to be eating so many of the things. He used to hold them behind his back in case I would see them. And then he would gobble it. He had a weakness in that regard,' Lillis recalls.

'He had a very powerful personality, even at that stage. He was extremely good company. He was brilliant but somewhat downright in his views. When he was getting a bit tense about what Garret was up to, he would kick my door open and come in and utter a few very rude words and accuse me of screwing up. It was just a way of letting off steam. I always enjoyed it though.'

Lillis, Sutherland, the Taoiseach and Alexis FitzGerald would meet regularly to discuss the ongoing hunger strikes in Northern Ireland. IRA inmates in the Maze prison had stopped taking food in protest at the conditions in which Republican prisoners were held, their demands including the right to political prisoner status and to wear civilian clothing. The British government was implacable in its resistance, and when one prisoner, Bobby Sands, died on 5 May 1981, the already volatile situation in Northern Ireland deteriorated still further. The FitzGerald government developed a close relationship with John Hume, the leader of Northern Ireland's Social Democratic and Labour Party (SDLP), the moderate nationalist party. Hume was a regular visitor to Government Buildings and to the Taoiseach's private residence.

But FitzGerald wanted to give people in the South a perspective on Northern Ireland Unionism. Even though Ireland was a small country and it was only seventy-five miles between Dublin and Belfast, the border was to all intents and purposes hermetically sealed. Apart from the Troubles being broadcast on RTÉ, very little was known about daily life in the North, particularly among the Unionist community. Equally, people in the North knew very little about what was happening in the South, although where Unionists did have a view it was overwhelmingly negative. The South was seen as insular, economically underdeveloped and controlled by the Catholic Church. In other words, there was no compelling reason why Unionists should extend the hand of friendship south of the border.

Lillis was given the job of finding Unionists to come to Dublin to articulate issues from their viewpoint. 'I found a group of them. They were barristers. There was a guy called Robert McCartney. He was a very brilliant man but very prejudiced. There was a man called Smith. Both of them were QCs.' Sutherland, says Lillis, played an important role in persuading both men to come to meetings in Dublin. 'Peter's personality and reputation was such that they treated Peter with respect. He was one of the better-known barristers in Dublin.' The meetings were private, although the government announced that they were taking place and explained what they were intended to achieve.

With the fall of the government in March 1982, Charlie Haughey, the leader of Fianna Fáil, formed the twenty-third Dáil, which lasted until December 1982. During this unstable period, the development was not lost on Margaret Thatcher, and it helped confirm her outlook on Anglo-Irish relations. Throughout 1982, relations between Dublin and London deteriorated further. Thatcher accused Haughey of treachery when in May 1982, he withdrew Irish support for the UK's United Nations sponsored sanctions of Argentina over the Falklands war. The prospects of a breakthrough in relations with London looked remote when FitzGerald formed the twenty-fourth Dáil at the end of 1982. Sutherland was again appointed attorney general. By the time the new government was formed, Dáithí Ó Ceallaigh had been posted to the Anglo-Irish division of the Department of Foreign Affairs in Dublin. He got to know Sutherland well over this period.

Sutherland's background and personality, Ó Ceallaigh explains, were very important factors in finding common ground with London: 'Personalities play a huge role in complex and sensitive negotiations.' Sutherland developed a close relationship with Sir Michael Havers, the UK attorney general (perhaps better known as the father of the actor, Nigel Havers), and their relationship provided an important axis in negotiations.

'In the 1980s there was an instinctive dislike among the English of the Irish,' Ó Ceallaigh says. 'But equally there was a very simple nationalism in Ireland that was anti-English. Sutherland's background, particularly his Jesuit education, was not like that. He didn't have that innate dislike or mistrust of the English. He didn't feel as if he had to bang on the table as many Fianna Fáil politicians did. It made it very difficult for them to engage with the British. There was a retreat into a green jacket by Irish politicians and the same on the other side. Sutherland was above that. He had an incredible intellectual capacity, a huge moral backbone.' Sutherland's attitude, says Ó Ceallaigh, enabled him to engage with the British and convince them not only that they could deal with the Irish, but that the Irish were not in favour of violence.

Lillis agrees with Ó Ceallaigh's assessment: 'The role of Sutherland was very important. Sutherland was the right sort of guy to deal with the Brits on these issues. He was never dismissive or hostile.'

FitzGerald instructed Lillis to take the first step in making a series of proposals to the British government. At the time, the main forum of discussion between the two governments was the co-ordinating committee of the Anglo-Irish intergovernmental council. Although it enabled senior officials to meet, in reality it was nothing more than a talking shop, focusing mainly on what the two governments could do together in uncontroversial areas such as agriculture and education.

'I took an initiative with my opposite number, Sir David Goodall, who was number two in the Cabinet Office to Lord Armstrong. We got the ball rolling,' Lillis says. 'I made a bid which was considered to be outrageous by the British. I was setting the bar high. Things were in an appalling condition in Northern Ireland. The Provos' – the Provisional IRA – 'were recruiting. The Unionists would not give ground. The SDLP was under pressure. Loyalists were engaged in sectarian shootings. The UK had no idea what to do. I made a proposal that things were so bad there was nothing that the UK could do which would address the issues, or at least put the brakes on in terms of the alienation of the minority nationalist community. I proposed they needed our help. They needed the involvement of the Irish government through security and the court system, including the guards and the army. The idea was that the involvement of the Irish government would help the minority population accept the system of authority in the North. Behind that was our project, which was to have a system of the two governments involved in ruling or governing Northern Ireland.'

FitzGerald, Hume and Sutherland were aware of what Lillis was doing, but very few others at that stage had any idea. To the surprise of the Irish government, Thatcher reacted with interest to Lillis's proposals. 'She knew that they were in a mess,' he says. As a result, exploratory talks began in 1983. The inner circle that were kept privy at all times were the Taoiseach; Dick Spring, the Tánaiste; Peter Barry, the Minister for Foreign Affairs; Michael Noonan, the Minister for Justice; and Sutherland. A marathon negotiation began, which lasted two years. Thirty-six meetings were held over that period, often going on for two or sometimes three days.

Sutherland and Havers held numerous important meetings, organised by Richard Ryan at the Irish embassy in London, which covered a range of complex issues. One such was the idea, proposed by Lillis, of a mixed court system in Northern Ireland, whereby an Irish judge would sit with two Northern judges. The Irish government believed that it was the most effective way of ensuring that the nationalist community accepted the judicial system in Northern Ireland, which was seen as biased and unfair. 'Unfortunately,' says Lillis, 'our side screwed up on the mixed courts issue.'

The Taoiseach, by his own admission, was the main culprit. Before the issue of how a mixed court system had been properly explored in the main channel of negotiation, which was headed on the Irish side by Dermot Nally, secretary general of the

Department of An Taoiseach, and by his UK counterpart Robert (later Lord) Armstrong, FitzGerald attended a rugby match at Lansdowne Road with his son Mark and Sutherland. The Lord Chief Justice of Northern Ireland, Lord Lowry, was also present. FitzGerald started discussing with Lowry the benefits of a mixed court system and the next stage in the development of the initiative. Lowry was completely unaware of the proposal and subsequently sent a hostile message to Lord Hailsham, the UK Lord Chancellor.

The Lord Chancellor was then semi-independent of the UK government and responsible for the court system. Both Hailsham and Lowry threatened to resign if the mixed court proposal went ahead. 'We messed up on that one. Hailsham didn't just dislike the Irish but to an unusual extent he was deeply anti-Catholic. Thatcher was deeply upset. She wanted mixed courts. But she couldn't overrule Hailsham. Sutherland tried to get us back on that one through his channel with Havers, but to no avail,' says Lillis.

Another very important development over this period was the New Ireland Forum, an attempt by the Irish government to reach a consensus among nationalist communities on both sides of the border on an agreed constitutional settlement for Ireland. There was no input from Unionist communities. Sutherland was in regular attendance at the forum, and an official called Richard O'Toole from the Department of Foreign Affairs caught his eye. O'Toole would play an important role in Sutherland's next career move.

When the New Ireland Forum reported in May 1984, it suggested three possible solutions for the crisis in Northern Ireland. These were a federal united Ireland; a confederated united Ireland; and joint sovereignty over Northern Ireland between Dublin and London. One of the most memorable episodes of the long and tense negotiations that culminated in the Anglo-Irish Agreement was Thatcher's very public rebuke of the proposals in her infamous 'out, out, out' press conference in November 1984, which was damaging to FitzGerald and the government at the time. 'But it wasn't actually her intention. She was like an elephant in a china shop in many ways. She had no subtlety. She couldn't deal with any ambiguities,' Lillis says. 'They had told us the three proposals were already not acceptable. We already knew that, but it was the way she said it. There was a lot going on in the background.' Thatcher made the comments after a scheduled summit meeting at Chequers. The summit had been convened so that both sides could assess what progress had been made in the talks. Lillis says that until then, negotiations had been going along relatively smoothly. There were disagreements between the two sides – and interestingly, numerous disagreements within the British side – but the Irish government had kept a tight rein on the talks. Information was shared only between FitzGerald, Spring, Barry, Noonan and Sutherland. 'They were informed on everything. There was a lot of back and forth with London. Thatcher would blow hot and cold. She could get very vituperative. One day she would tell the Irish where to go, then a few days later it would be back on again. It was very hard for the British side because their boss couldn't make up her mind. On the Irish side there was much more uniformity and coherency. Sutherland kept a very sharp eye on all of that. He was regarded by the rest as an expert on how to read the British.'

On 12 November 1984, before that Chequers summit, a meeting was held of the entire cabinet. One of Lillis's jobs was to write a memorandum about the state of negotiations. 'We tend to think of Fine Gael as being less nationalist than Fianna Fáil. If you rub them up the wrong way they can be worse than anyone,' he says. Before that meeting in Chequers, a couple of issues had arisen. Lillis shared with the cabinet certain documents from Britain proposing that the Irish government's role in the future governance of Northern Ireland would be conducted at a very low level. But in return for this consultative role, the Irish government would have to change Articles 2 and 3 of the constitution, which because they made a claim on Northern Ireland were a source of deep antagonism among Unionists. (The articles were eventually ditched by plebiscite following the Good Friday Agreement in 1998.) Furthermore, the documents said, the SDLP would have to accept that it would have no role in a Northern Ireland government and would have to accept a subordinate role as a member of the Northern Ireland Assembly.

'It was unfortunate it was expressed in those terms because it wasn't really the British position. We knew that. It was a document that was given to us at that time that didn't reflect the British position positively and it was a reflection of a meeting the British side had with Thatcher. She had become highly irate about what the Irish side was looking for,' Lillis says.

But the cabinet reacted with outrage. It felt that London had been bullying the Irish negotiating team. The cabinet demanded that before FitzGerald went to Chequers, the officials would deliver a strongly worded response. 'Sutherland was dragged into it. It ended up in diplomatic terms with what is known as a speaking note. It is basically a letter except you read it out. It's a way of delivering a message from one government to another, especially if there is tension between the two. I got the job of delivering it to the British government. I could see it would end up doing a lot of damage to our relationship with London. Sutherland didn't want anything to do with it, but was given the job of drafting it. It came out in belligerent, hostile terms. In the end I was sent over to my opposite number David Goodall. He was very well disposed to doing a deal. He knew that Thatcher would blow a gasket if she saw the demands coming from Dublin. It was the only time Sutherland took an extremely hard nationalist line. It wasn't the real Sutherland.'

When Lillis phoned FitzGerald from London and told him it would be a very unwise move to deliver the note, the Taoiseach gave him permission to draft an alternative, less strongly worded letter. Lillis had a meeting with Goodall and the two drafted a second letter of protest. Delivered just before the Chequers summit, it ended up being a mild rebuke rather than the dark green fusillade originally intended.

Sutherland was not at Chequers, but the meeting was quite positive and had made a lot of progress. It was afterwards, when the two governments each went off to their respective press conferences, that things went awry. It was mistimed. The British government did not hold its press conference at the scheduled time, so the Irish government did not know about the 'out, out, out' comments when FitzGerald addressed the assembled media.

Running parallel to the Anglo-Irish talks, Sutherland had been dealing with another sensitive area that was a source of deep tension with London: the refusal by the Irish courts to extradite Republicans suspected of paramilitary activities. From 1965 onwards, Irish courts had refused extradition warrants based on terrorist offences because they were deemed to be political crimes.

The case of Dominic 'Mad Dog' McGlinchey happened under Sutherland's watch. Formerly a member of the IRA, McGlinchey had transferred to the INLA in the early 1980s. Even by the standards of the time, he was a particularly violent individual – he claimed in a 1983 interview that he had been responsible for at least thirty murders, and was believed to have been responsible for the 1982 Ballykelly disco bombing which claimed the lives of six British soldiers and eleven civilians. In 1981, extradition proceedings had commenced when a warrant was issued by Ballymena District Court on 24 June. Laurence Wren, the deputy commissioner of An Garda Síochána, endorsed the warrant for execution in the state. McGlinchey, at that point still in Portlaoise prison, challenged the process, claiming that the offence specified in the warrant was 'political' and that once extradited, he would also be charged with other offences of a political nature.

McGlinchey's case was heard in the High Court on 17 May 1982. By the time of the appeal he had been released from prison and was living at an address in Dublin, at Colliers Avenue, Ranelagh. After Mr Justice Gannon dismissed the appeal on the grounds that no evidence had been presented to substantiate the 'political' nature of the offence, the case was taken to the Supreme Court. Here, McGlinchey's counsel abandoned the 'political'

71

defence to the original offence, relying instead on the argument that there were substantial grounds for believing that if extradited he would be prosecuted for political offences. The appeal was again dismissed. Although 'political offence' had not been claimed, the Chief Justice went out of his way to assert that terrorism had rendered obsolete many judicial authorities on political offence, and that the burden of proof in establishing whether an offence was political or not should rest, not with the offence, but in the particular circumstances of specific cases and 'what reasonable, civilised people would regard as political activity'. The judge ruled that the plaintiff had failed to prove his case.

Sutherland wrote in his private papers that in the context of extradition law, and in the wider contexts of the Irish political landscape, cross-border and Anglo-Irish relations, this was a landmark judgment:

> Chief Justice O'Higgins' ruling effectively removed the motivation of individual perpetrators from consideration and tilted the balance toward the specific nature of the case. The case did not produce a flood of extraditions. Edgar Graham's exaggerated claims of 'safe haven' were unfounded. But the case was a significant step in shaping public perception and political opinion at a very delicate moment in our history.[1]

McGlinchey skipped bail during the hearing, but he was subsequently apprehended in March 1984 following a gun battle with Gardaí. In a last-ditch attempt to avoid his removal to the North, his legal team sought an injunction from the High Court to place a stay on his extradition pending a further appeal on grounds that the Extradition Act 1965 was unconstitutional and the original warrant issued by the District Court in Ballymena had expired. When Judge Barrington granted the injunction, on the afternoon of Saturday 17 March, Sutherland convened a sitting of the Supreme Court on the same night.

It was a controversial move. In his judgment, the Chief

Justice had recognised McGlinchey's right to lodge an appeal; however he noted that, as the original case had been based on an appeal for protection under the Extradition Act, it was a cynical abuse of process to now seek to challenge the constitutionality of that legislation. He dismissed the appeal and noted that as the Extradition Act was a complete piece of legislation it could not be limited by the rules of a district court in another jurisdiction. McGlinchey was immediately extradited to Northern Ireland.

Sutherland's decision to order the Supreme Court to sit on a Saturday night divided opinion in the Law Library. When Tom O'Higgins contacted Brian Walsh on Saturday afternoon to check whether he was available for a sitting of the Supreme Court that evening,[2] Walsh said that he was available but he opposed the extradition. He was not contacted again. O'Higgins subsequently said that he had already enlisted Justice Henchy and Justice Griffin and therefore did not need Walsh's services.

There was a considerable backlash against the move. A colleague of Sutherland's at the Law Library at the time comments: 'I had reservations about Sutherland's McGlinchey decision where he got the Supreme Court to sit at night on St Patrick's Day in the cold and the dark.' Tom O'Higgins, he says, was a deeply conservative figure who was sitting as the Chief Justice at that time, and who, regarding an application to have McGlinchey sent to the North immediately, would have been 'the right judge to make that application to'.

'A lot of people were concerned that this was done at night, on St Patrick's Day, without any opportunity for the issue to be adjudicated upon in a calm way in the full light of day,' said one of Sutherland's former Law Library colleagues. The view from this colleague was that Sutherland wanted it done quickly and promptly.

'It's not an illegitimate view. I didn't agree with it. I'm not saying he was wrong, I'm just saying we would have had a divergence of view. But it's again an indication of Peter's approach to things.

There certainly would have been – and still to this day there would be – a body of opinion that wouldn't have agreed with his stance on that, but it's another example of Peter acknowledging that there was already a decision of the court in relation to the issue and all that he was doing now was copper-fastening it: get this thing done, we need it done quickly, let's move on before a head of steam builds up for the opposition,' added Sutherland's former Law Library colleague.

The Anglo-Irish Agreement was designed and negotiated by another cabinet sub-committee, comprising Taoiseach Garret FitzGerald, Minister for Foreign Affairs Peter Barry, justice minister Michael Noonan, Tánaiste Dick Spring and attorney general Sutherland. 'Within that group Peter was influential,' Noonan says. 'We met regularly for a long time. Peter had very good insights and contacts. His relationship with Havers was particularly important.'

Noonan attended a meeting in London with Tom King, the former Secretary of State for Northern Ireland, whom he told about the change of position on extradition. 'He was absolutely delighted. He left the room to make a phone call, I presume to Thatcher. As a government, the two Peters, myself and Garret and Dick were *ad idem* on this. We all wanted legal cover to make terrorist offences extraditable on the grounds that they were not consistent with democratic societies. Terrorist offences, which would not be considered political in any democratic humane country, would no longer be political. So that opened the way for extradition. The British were pressing us very hard,' says Noonan.

Dukes says that there was agreement at cabinet level about McGlinchey's extradition. 'Peter would lay out the legal case and then there would be a political discussion. He would say that these are the limits in which you have to make a decision. It was always very clear. Peter's reasoning on McGlinchey was particularly clear. What he was being accused of was a crime in the Republic just as it was in the North, so we had no reason not to extradite him. He made the point that if somebody was in the North and had committed a crime down here, we would expect the authorities in the North to be amenable to an extradition. He was very clear that politics cannot abrogate the rule of law.'

The case against McGlinchey, however, fell through in Northern Ireland, prompting criticism of Sutherland's decision to extradite him. Adrian Hardiman, at the time a prominent barrister and later a Supreme Court judge, went on RTÉ's *Morning Ireland* radio programme in October 1985 and launched a blistering attack on Sutherland, who by then had taken up the role of European commissioner.

During the course of the interview, Hardiman rejected the view that the collapse of the McGlinchey case reflected badly on the legal profession in Dublin. 'I think that the person who would be very considerably embarrassed if he were still around to be embarrassed is the former attorney general Mr Peter Sutherland,' Hardiman said. 'He was the attorney general at the time this charge was brought against McGlinchey. It looks very much as if Mr Sutherland, who presumably could have had access to the evidence, allowed the case to go forward through the Irish courts knowing that there was practically no evidence.'

After the interview, Peter Prendergast rang RTÉ with a statement. It read:

It was said by Mr Adrian Hardiman, a Fianna Fáil candidate in a recent election, supposedly speaking as a barrister, that the previous attorney general Peter Sutherland could or should have checked the case against McGlinchey which the Northern Ireland authorities had. Under the 1965 Extradition Act . . . Irish courts extradite against a sworn warrant that a case exists rather than having the capacity or the right to explain the case. That is the law; the attorney general has nothing to do with it. The courts decide. Mr Hardiman, as a lawyer, knows that. One can only assume that his words this morning were quite malicious and dangerous.[3]

When RTÉ broadcast the statement it was in edited form, leaving out the reference to Fianna Fáil and the 'malicious and dangerous' allegation. The following day, however, the *Irish Daily Mirror* published the claims in full. Hardiman threatened to sue Prendergast but the contretemps was resolved before proceedings were launched.

The Anglo-Irish Agreement was eventually signed in November 1985, giving the Irish government an advisory role in the affairs of Northern Ireland. Dáithí Ó Ceallaigh says that Sutherland played a vital role in the agreement. 'We were pushing the boat out in constitutional terms. Peter was excellent at giving advice.' Lillis agrees with this assessment. 'He wouldn't have been as important as the two prime ministers, but he was hugely important.'

The agreement stipulated that there could be no change in the constitutional position of Northern Ireland unless expressly decreed by a majority of the population at the ballot box. It also set out the template of a devolved government. Needless to say, Unionists were furious. Ian Paisley, the leader of the then fringe Democratic Unionist Party, led the charge, organising rallies that brought Northern Ireland to a standstill. By that stage, however, Sutherland was in Brussels.

Getting the Anglo-Irish Agreement over the line had been stressful for everybody, probably none more so than Michael Havers. When the Irish government's papers were released under the thirty-year rule in December 2018, they contained a note written by Richard Ryan, of the Irish embassy in London, recounting a meeting he had with Havers at which the former British attorney general revealed that, when he regained conscious-ness following heart surgery in 1987, he had blurted out the words, 'Paisley must die.'

*

In the summer of 1984, Garret FitzGerald faced a dilemma. He had to pick Ireland's next European commissioner, but because of Dáil arithmetic he couldn't afford to lose any sitting TD as the government had the slimmest of majorities. The question of how Sutherland came to be in the frame to replace Dick Burke, the outgoing commissioner, has many possible answers. A political source says that FitzGerald initially offered the position to Jim Dooge, who was then in the Senate, but he turned it down. According to Michael Noonan, he was having coffee one day with Sutherland in the Dáil bar. Sutherland mentioned the dilemma facing FitzGerald over filling the role. 'I said to him, would you be interested. He came back a few days later and said he would. I told him there was no point telling me and he should tell Garret.'

Mark FitzGerald claims that it was his mother Joan who put Sutherland in the frame, during the course of a Sunday lunch. 'My memory is that she was instrumental. I think she came up with the idea. But the thing about my father was, he didn't run a commanded, controlled household like a lot of men of their time, who were chief executives or heads of organisations. I mean anyone who was in the family or anybody who was at the table, he'd regard them as equal. He'd listen to opinion, so it wasn't all about him talking about his great ideas. So my mother made the suggestion of Peter and my father immediately saw the benefit of it.' Peter Prendergast meanwhile says that it was he who, in conversation with Joan FitzGerald, floated the idea of Sutherland.

Whoever may have seeded the idea in his mind, FitzGerald confided in Alan Dukes that he was indeed thinking about nominating Sutherland. 'I said he'll be very good, but I hope that doesn't mean I will be excluded, at which his face dropped. He didn't want to have to make that difficult decision. I said it to indicate I didn't want it to be an automatic decision. We had got back from Brussels in 1981 and we were just getting bedded in. The girls were at school. Although I would have loved the job, I told Garret a few days later I wouldn't be pursuing it, to his immense relief. I don't think there was anybody else in for it. Very few would have understood its importance and been comfortable doing it.'

Gemma Hussey claims that Justin Keating was interested.

'I think he was disappointed, and he might have well been a very good commissioner because he was a person just like Peter who was a broader thinker than most. But I think Garret definitely had his mind made up. And it turned out to have been one of the best appointments that any Irish government ever made.'

There was only one wrinkle in Sutherland's accession from attorney general to European commissioner. Up to that point, it was the senior partner in government who had nominated the attorney general. But now that Sutherland was leaving the post halfway through his term, Dick Spring proposed that John Rogers, at the time a junior counsel, replace him. There was a backlash against the move in the Law Library. Colm Condon, a previous Fianna Fáil-appointed attorney general, had convened a special meeting of the Bar Council, intending that it would issue a statement raising its concern about Rogers' appointment. Sutherland, who shared his colleague's concerns, made a number of representations to the Taoiseach about the appointment. It is understood that he canvassed Dermot Gleeson, who had recently been appointed the youngest senior counsel in the history of the state, to see if he would be interested.

Having made his own enquiries about Rogers, and after a period of deliberation, FitzGerald agreed to the appointment. But it strained relations between Spring and Sutherland.

Dukes saw little of Sutherland following their time as cabinet colleagues. 'I was never very close to him afterwards. I met him in London after he had cancer. Before that he had the appearance of a seventeenth-century squire – the philosopher king; the smooth talker with a cigar. That day I met him he looked pale and diminished in stature. I got a shock. He didn't make much of [his] Fine Gael connections after that. He moved off the national stage after [going to the] commission. He was never really a convinced partisan politician. He certainly approved of Garret's direction. If Garret had been in Fianna Fáil he would have been in Fianna Fáil. And Declan Costello before that.'

*

Reflecting on Sutherland's period as attorney general, Garrett Sheehan cites his significant role in drafting the 1984 Criminal Justice Act, an 'extremely important piece of legislation' in which for the first time the state recognised the rights of persons after they had been arrested. Brendan Halligan says that when Sutherland was attorney general 'he had a reputation of having a brilliant brain and out-of-the-ordinary intellect. He was seen as Garret's man and everybody knew that Garret had absolute faith in him. But he was also known for being his own man and a very independent thinker, so when he came out with this analysis on the Eighth Amendment, most people sat up and took notice. Peter was always very self-confident and assertive. He was one of the best AGs ever. Constitutional law was a mixture of politics and philosophy. It suited him. He had a real aptitude for it. If you asked him to draft an amendment to the constitution, he would do it and very quickly. He was one of the very few people who could do it.'

Overall, says Nial Fennelly, Sutherland was a very good attorney general. 'Nobody would have any doubt that he was an exceptionally able man. He was terrific. He managed to combine great ambition with very human qualities. I don't think anybody disliked him even though they all had stories about what he got up to in cases. He was always well liked.'

7

GETTING COMPETITION:
BECOMING A EUROPEAN COMMISSIONER

I RELAND JOINED THE EUROPEAN ECONOMIC Community in 1973 following a referendum the previous year. It is not clear exactly when Sutherland developed his passion for Europe, but friends say that even from their earliest days at Gonzaga he always had an international outlook. According to Garrett Sheehan, when boys were asked to write their addresses on their school books, Sutherland always went that bit further: 'Hilmont, The Hill, Monkstown, Dublin, Ireland, Europe, The World' was imprinted on each one of his books. But then again, his political awakenings were shaped by people who were committed Europhiles.

The first step towards Ireland's official membership of the EU had been taken at a meeting in the Shelbourne Hotel in Dublin in 1954, with roughly one hundred people in attendance. That night there were seven signatories to a document formally launching the European Movement in Ireland. Garret FitzGerald, Declan Costello and another barrister named Denis Corboy were among the signatories. Sutherland was close to all three. 'I don't think it was any great mystery. The core figures in Fine Gael were all passionately pro-European,' says Brendan Halligan.

When the European Economic Community was created by the

Treaty of Rome in 1957, each country had its own reason for joining. Most saw it as means of ensuring that war between member states would never break out again. According to Mark FitzGerald, however, his father's commitment to Europe stemmed from the shortcomings of the Irish state. 'He had looked at Ireland as a young man and seen that in 1959, when he was thirty-three, 50 per cent of the people born in Ireland were no longer in Ireland. They either died – we had lost sixty thousand kids between 1932 and 1948 through TB – or the rest had emigrated. Two of his three brothers had emigrated. So what drove people like my father was the fact that the new state had failed dismally. So he bought into the European idea, and went to Brussels himself in 1957 because Lemass and Whitaker had encouraged him.'

Mark goes on to explain that Seán Lemass brought his father, Denis Corboy and a few others into the Department of Industry, where he was the minister in the Fianna Fáil government, that year, encouraging them to strengthen ties between Ireland and Brussels. T. K. Whitaker, the influential secretary general of the Department of Finance, was at the meeting. Lemass's discussions with FitzGerald had to be kept under the radar at the time because Éamon de Valera, the Taoiseach, had a natural antipathy to the fledgling EEC and blocked any official contact with Brussels. But after Lemass became leader of Fianna Fáil in 1959, a political consensus formed that Ireland's strategic interests were tied to EEC membership. That resolve grew from the early 1960s onwards and hardened as the decade progressed.

When Britain voted to leave the EU on 23 June 2016, a view quickly formed among prominent Brexiteers that Ireland would be forced to follow the UK out of the exit door because the two economies were so closely aligned. It was a dated worldview, belonging to an era before Ireland joined the EU. In the 1960s, it would not have been feasible for Ireland to join the EEC unless the UK joined at the same time. Ireland may have been a sovereign country, but economically it was in effect a region of the UK. Over 80 per cent of Irish exports went to Britain and the punt was pegged to sterling. Britain was willing to join but its path was blocked by French President Charles de Gaulle, who spent most of the 1960s saying 'non' to Britain's applications. French resistance thus thwarted any chances Ireland had of becoming a member state.

There is a story that the Department of Finance had put together an application for Ireland's membership of the EEC in 1961. It presented a comprehensive and rousing argument as to why Ireland should be allowed to join the community. There was just one snag – the submission was sent to the wrong address in Brussels. 'I think it is an apocryphal story. I have heard it many times, but I don't believe it,' says Brendan Halligan, who by that stage had joined the Labour Party. 'In 1961 we applied along with Britain. The following January, Lemass went to Brussels and gave a presentation to the Council of Ministers. He said "We are not looking for money, and we will join in the defence of Europe if we become a member." Everything was put on ice because of de Gaulle. I don't think our application was ever taken seriously at that point. It was put in the desk of a drawer and the drawer was never opened. I wouldn't make a thing about the wrong address. I'm sure it isn't true.'

Towards the end of the 1960s, attitudes towards the UK changed and it was agreed that it could join the bloc. Ireland's application was accepted on the UK's coattails. By the time the Irish government held a referendum to ratify Ireland's accession to the EEC on 10 May 1972, Sutherland was becoming active in Fine Gael. He helped in the campaign in support of membership. Although Official and Provisional Sinn Féin campaigned against entry, the mainstream parties, as well as most civic groups, were in favour of Ireland's membership. The result was never in doubt; 83 per cent of Irish people ticked yes on the ballot paper.

There had been three Irish European commissioners before Sutherland's nomination. Former president Patrick Hillery was the first, holding the social affairs brief. He was replaced by Fine Gael nominee Richard Burke, who held the taxation and consumer affairs portfolio. Burke was succeeded by Fianna Fáil's Michael O'Kennedy, whose stint as commissioner for personnel and administration was short-lived; after nine months he was himself replaced by Burke in what was something of a political stroke on the part of Charles Haughey. Because of the tight Dáil arithmetic he could not risk a Fianna Fáil nominee, which would have triggered a by-election; instead he called on Burke to return to Brussels. According to Francis Jacobs, who joined the European Parliament in 1979 as an official, both Burke and O'Kennedy were underwhelming commissioners: 'I have to choose my words carefully, but I saw the O'Kennedy and Burke eras as being extraordinarily lacklustre.'

The European Commission is the executive arm of the European Union, in effect the bloc's civil service. It can formulate policy, and it has the job of implementing policies when they have been ratified by member states. In the first few decades of its existence, the commission was by far the most powerful of the institutions that made up the European Union. There was a double edge to this strength, however. A powerful commission coincided with the relatively smooth functioning of the European Union. But because it is a body of unelected officials, the view arose, especially among Eurosceptics, that the EU suffered from a democratic deficit. Over time, the European Council and the European Parliament have clipped the wings of the commission, but this has led to stalled decision making and the inability to push through necessary reforms.

From the time Sutherland was given the nod by FitzGerald in the summer of 1984, he embarked on military-style preparations. When he joined the commission in 1985, it was at the peak of its power. His first task was to put together a cabinet.

As attorney general he had a number of connections with the New Ireland Forum. Richard O'Toole from the Department of Foreign Affairs, deputy head of Ireland's diplomatic mission in Switzerland, had been seconded to the forum's secretariat, returning to Geneva at the forum's conclusion. Sutherland knew him by reputation, as O'Toole had been head of the Union of Students in Ireland back in the 1960s. Sean Donlon, then a senior official in the Department of Foreign Affairs in Dublin, rang O'Toole to tell him that he was being mentioned as a possible chef de cabinet for Sutherland. O'Toole was asked to fly to Dublin, where he met Sutherland in his office in July 1984.

Sutherland told O'Toole that he had been putting a lot of thought into the portfolio he should pursue and added that he was initially attracted to the development aid brief. 'I said to him very clearly that Ireland had never fully understood the power of the commission,' says O'Toole, 'and that to my mind the real power lay in the competition area. And I would definitely advise him to go for competition. So I had the impression at the time that he reacted to that.' Sutherland told O'Toole that a number of other people had also mentioned competition, and the two men had a long discussion about the EU. 'He had a very good knowledge of the treaties. He was less well versed on the intergovernmental processes. And we had a conversation . . . I'd say it was due to last for about half an hour, but it lasted for about an hour.'

Sutherland asked O'Toole whether he was free that evening for dinner. 'He told me at dinner that he wanted me to join the cabinet. And I said okay, but in what position? He said that he hadn't decided yet, but he was thinking of me as either chef de cabinet or deputy chef.' Sutherland had also been looking at Liam Hourican as a possible chef de cabinet. Hourican, a former journalist with the *Irish Independent,* had served in Burke's cabinet and was highly rated in Brussels. The pair had developed a good relationship when Hourican was government press secretary in the 1981 Fine Gael–Labour coalition.

O'Toole says he would have been happy to take either position. He also told Sutherland that his success as commissioner hinged on putting the right cabinet together. The most effective commissioners in the past had been well briefed not only in their own areas, but across most other portfolios as well.

Following the meeting, O'Toole took a leave of absence from

his post in Geneva, while Sutherland made the necessary arrange-ments to set him up with a desk in Brussels. The plan was that O'Toole would spend the next six months preparing the ground for Sutherland's arrival. After a month in Brussels, Sutherland rang O'Toole and asked him to be chef de cabinet, informing him that he was going to make Hourican deputy chef.

With his chef de cabinet in place, Sutherland pursued the compe-tition portfolio with his trademark intensity, enlisting all the help he could get. Ireland held the rotating presidency of the European Council for the first six months of 1984. Even though Garret FitzGerald and Margaret Thatcher had sparred openly over Northern Ireland, they had good personal relations, and FitzGerald was able to persuade Thatcher to accept Jacques Delors, a French socialist, as the next president of the commission. When his nomination had been formally ratified, Delors visited FitzGerald at his home in Palmerstown Road in Dublin, where the Taoiseach asked Delors for Sutherland to be given the strongest possible portfolio.

Competition was mentioned but nothing was agreed. So Sutherland went on his own charm offensive, making direct contact with Delors and visiting him twice in Paris. At the outset the two men seemed like uneasy bedfellows: Delors was a socialist with a trade union background. Then they discovered they had both attended Jesuit schools and were practising Catholics, and that helped cement the relationship.

While Sutherland lobbied Delors for the competition portfolio, he also went about striking up relationships with the newly minted commissioners. 'As he said himself, if there were going to be any cliques, he was going to be in the most important ones,' says Garrett Sheehan. Sutherland invited the commissioners to Dublin at his own expense for a series of bilateral meetings. 'He developed a genuine friendship with a lot of the other commissioners and they with him. And I think that stood the test of time during his term of office. Even when they had differences on views, a very good personal relationship was maintained with the commissioners at all times,' says O'Toole.

Delors held a meeting in the Château de Rambouillet in the north of France in November 1984 to finalise his team of commissioners. Sutherland went to bed on the Saturday night knowing that he was a strong contender for the competition portfolio. On Sunday morning he went to mass at the Church of St Lubin of Rambouillet. Delors was there, and he gave Sutherland a gentle nod to say that he had prevailed.

The focus now turned to putting the rest of the cabinet together. David O'Sullivan, who was then working in the EU embassy in Tokyo, was the first name on the list. O'Toole rang O'Sullivan in early December to say that he was going to be Sutherland's head of cabinet and ask whether O'Sullivan would be interested in joining. 'He said I think you could be a good fit, and I said that I would be very interested. And then a few days later, he rang me and said no, it's not going to work out, we only have a limited number of places.' O'Sullivan headed off with his wife on a long trip to New Zealand and Australia. 'Then just before Christmas [1984] we were staying in a rather grotty hostel-type place with no telephone or anything near Ayers Rock. And there was a sort of hand-scrolled message literally nailed to the door saying, "call Richard O'Toole".

'We didn't know where to find a phone, so we went off and found a Sheraton Hotel a few miles away and I asked could I make a foreign phone call, which you can imagine in those days was quite complicated.' O'Sullivan eventually called O'Toole, who told him there was now a very live possibility that he would be given the position, but he needed an answer more or less immediately. 'It was typical Richard. So I said, will you give me a half an hour with my wife. We went into the bar and had a quick chat.' O'Sullivan was due to leave Tokyo in the summer of 1985, so his departure would be coming six months early. 'But on the other hand I had nothing in particular lined up, so this was an exciting opportunity, so I decided to take it.'

When O'Sullivan told the head of the EU delegation to Japan he was leaving early to take up a role in Brussels, he was accused by his boss of being duplicitous. 'He did all he could to try and delay my departure and I know that Richard had some epic discussions with Emile Noel, the secretary general of the European Commission, insisting that I be brought back very quickly.' O'Sullivan returned to Brussels in the middle of January, leaving his wife to sort out the move from Tokyo. 'I remember it was snowing very heavily when I arrived in Brussels, and I remember treading the streets trying to find somewhere temporary to live and then somewhere more permanent to set up house.' O'Sullivan says his first meeting with Sutherland did not go as he had hoped. 'He was slightly intimidating when you first met him, when he was in his "I'm the man in charge" mode he could be quite assertive.' Sutherland told O'Sullivan that he had taken him into his cabinet 'on the word of Richard'.

'He said to me, "I hear good things from Richard, but I want to be very clear above all else, I need loyalty." It was a very gruff encounter and I came away thinking okay, this is going to be interesting.' But the next day, when O'Sullivan met Sutherland again, quite by chance, he apologised for being so abrupt, saying, 'I think I was a bit aggressive with you yesterday, don't take me wrong. I'm pleased you are here and I'm sure you'll do a great job.'

'And that was Peter. I always found him to be the warmest and most considerate human being. But it was always mixed with this ability to be tough and sometimes quite abrasive. But usually with a reason behind it – it wasn't just that he was being bad tempered. He wanted to assert himself and I understand when I arrived, he wanted to be clear that he was the commissioner, I was the member of cabinet. We had never met before, this was going to be on his terms, and I accepted that.'

As soon as they started talking about substantive issues, says O'Sullivan, he knew instinctively that Sutherland was intent on making his mark as a commissioner. 'It was clear that he was extremely intelligent, he had an amazing grasp of detail.' O'Sullivan attributes this to Sutherland's training as a barrister, whereby he had gained the ability to grasp detail and digest it, to simplify it and identify the essence of an issue. 'I was very impressed and I quickly formed the view that this was someone who was going to do something with his life. I think the remarkable thing about Peter is that he established himself in the commission very quickly as a force to be reckoned with.' Sutherland, says O'Sullivan, worked very hard to establish himself; competition was a hugely impressive portfolio for an Irish commissioner to have obtained, particularly one so young and with no real political background.

O'Sullivan worked on social policy in his first year at the commission, before taking on relations between the commission and the European Parliament. 'Richard was an outstanding head of cabinet. They were a remarkable team because Peter was the front office and the one who put it all together, but Richard did a fantastic job in understanding what he needed and in getting the rest of us to deliver it for him.'

Catherine Day was next on the list. The Trinity-educated economist, who prior to meeting Sutherland had been in Dick Burke's cabinet, joined the European Commission in 1979 following an open competition. When she had breakfast with Sutherland at the hotel where he was staying before his move to Brussels, Day says her initial impression was that he was extremely focused. He asked her what she knew about his fellow commissioners. Day had already been offered a post in the cabinet of Grigoris Varfis, the incoming commissioner from Greece. 'So I strongly suspect that Richard had advised Peter not to make any opening offer to me. He wanted Peter to meet me and see. I still am not very tactical, and I certainly wasn't then, but I was trying to brief Peter as much as possible because I felt comfortable I had another option.

'So I was interested in working with him but it wasn't my only option. But I was also trying to fill him in on different people who were his colleagues, and so I said to him that I had an offer from Varfis that I was thinking of accepting.' By the end of breakfast Sutherland had told Day he would like her to be on his team. 'And Richard then came and joined us, and I interpreted from

Richard's face that this was not Richard's plan but Peter had jumped the gun.' It was typical of Sutherland, says Day, to decide on his own gut instinct. 'But what was very obvious from the start was that Peter was determined to make his impact.'

Sutherland had a very powerful portfolio, observes Day, and he was determined to make his presence felt. But he also had to learn about the continental way of doing things and about diplomatic procedures: 'I'd say the first half dozen meetings that he had with different people who came to discuss state aid or competition cases were in and out in ten minutes.' Sutherland would make up his mind, listen to them and say yes or no. He had to learn to make meetings last half or three-quarters of an hour; he grew into such ways, because he realised he had to. But, says Day, 'He could still be very punchy when he needed to.'

Eugene Regan had worked in the Brussels office of the Irish Farmers' Association in the late 1970s. With a background in agriculture, he wrote to Sutherland when he was made commissioner to put himself forward for the agriculture role in his cabinet. 'He had done the rounds before he came to me. He was very well briefed. I met him at his home in Blackrock. I found the interview very intimidating and tough. He wanted to know what school I went to. I think he wanted to know did I go to Gonzaga or Blackrock, that sort of thing. I told him I went to the Christian Brothers in Glasnevin. Anyway, I got the job. He didn't know agriculture very well, but he made it his business to understand it.' Regan went on to develop a very good working relationship with Sutherland, while Michel Richonnier, a Frenchman, completed the team. Richonnier was an economist who had spent years working in the French civil service. He joined the cabinet of Manuel Marín when the Spanish commissioner took over the education portfolio at the start of 1986.

Pascal Lamy was Jacques Delors' chef de cabinet. 'For a commissioner in Brussels Peter was incredibly young,' observes Lamy. 'This sort of position is usually given to people who have a more senior career or at least track record. Delors had very quickly developed a very good impression of Peter. He thought he was a very straight guy who was quite to the point and rather ambitious. He thought this was a big move in Peter's career. Hence this idea of giving him competition.'

According to Lamy, Sutherland was the 'real junior' compared with the other commissioners, who had all held senior political posts in their home countries. 'But Delors' intuition was that this guy had real talent.' Sutherland's legal training was useful, according to Lamy, because at the time the competition portfolio was more legal than political. He was able to convince Delors of his value – although, says Lamy, 'that is not enough in my view. So it was a big bet and it worked.' Competition is one of the few portfolios that is almost exclusively a competence of the European Commission. That means that other commissioners had to be on good terms with Sutherland. 'Peter could be quite bold. He could be pretty authoritarian and sometimes a bit arrogant. But he had, you know, the Irish temper,' says Lamy.

Sutherland described those early meetings with Delors at a speech he gave in London in 2011:

Jacques Delors became a crucial part of my life when I was nominated. Probably, like Sir Thomas More, I was a turbulent priest who was to be moved out of Ireland after a turbulent time as attorney general, but I was asked by my Prime Minister to become the Irish commissioner in Brussels. The four years that I spent there, with Jacques Delors, were a vitally important part of my life.

Sometimes people wonder here why it is that those who are sent to Brussels go native, as so many have done. Every commissioner that has gone from this country that I can recall, on his return, after four years, is a transformed personality in terms of their attitude to Europe. The reason for me why it was important was that I saw a nobility of purpose, however ineffective it may be in practice, in taking on and challenging nationalism, which is the core rationale for the existence of European integration. It was founded following the Second World War on a philosophical base.

I was struck, when I went first to Paris to meet Jacques Delors, before he became president or before I became a commissioner, but in the immediate aftermath of our selection. I had lunch with him in a restaurant called Chez Edgar, off Avenue Montaigne in Paris, and he asked me whether I was a European and I replied that I was. I remember him telling me that he had been inspired by a Christian philosopher, Emmanuel Mounier, and Jacques Maritain, another philosopher, who wrote immediately following the Second World War, who, in turn, had inspired, at that time, the founders of the European movement – Jean Monnet, De Gasperi, from Italy, Adenauer, from Germany, and Schuman, above all, from France.[1]

Francis Jacobs says Sutherland's cabinet is regarded in Brussels as one of the best ever put together by any commissioner. David O'Sullivan went on to be secretary general of the European Commission between 2000 and 2005, and was more recently EU ambassador to the US from November 2014 until his retirement in September 2018. Catherine Day succeeded O'Sullivan to become the first ever woman secretary general of the European Commission, serving two terms between 2005 and 2015. There is a school of thought that Ireland sent its brightest talents to Brussels in the early days as a tactical strategy to get the most out of its membership. Certainly, O'Sullivan and Day are regarded as among the top operators in Brussels over the past few decades.

Colm Larkin, who had been working as an official at the European Commission, replaced Liam Hourican halfway through the term. Hourican was on holiday in Kerry with his family in the summer of 1993 when he suffered a fatal heart attack at the age of forty-nine. Sutherland was about to board a flight for Geneva when he heard the news, and it affected him deeply. He had developed a very close bond with Hourican and his family when they were in Brussels. Hourican left behind a wife and six children; his daughters Emily and Bridget are both journalists.

Regan trained as a barrister when he returned to Dublin and is now a judge at the European Court of Justice. O'Toole and Sutherland would maintain a lifelong working relationship; after Sutherland joined him on the GPA board O'Toole went to Geneva, with Sutherland as his number two, when he took up the role of head of the General Agreement on Tariffs and Trade (GATT) in 1993.

8

SHAPING EU COMPETITION POLICY

O
N THE LAST DAY OF AUGUST 2016, MARGRETHE
Vestager, the European Commissioner for Competition,
caused a minor political earthquake in Dublin. Two
years previously the commission had publicly launched an investigation into Apple's tax affairs in Ireland, suspecting that the
country had struck a sweetheart deal with the US technology
giant in return for jobs and investment. When the investigation
concluded that in 1991 and 2007 Apple had negotiated two
separate accords with the Irish Revenue enabling it to avoid paying
billions in corporate taxes, the commission ordered the Irish
government to recoup €13.1 billion plus interest from Apple.
Although the Irish government and Apple both deny wrongdoing
and have launched separate appeals, the tech giant eventually
paid the Irish state €14.3 billion into an escrow account in 2018.

Vestager had used all the tools at her disposal to take on one
of the biggest companies in the world. And by ordering the Irish
government to recover the money allegedly bestowed on Apple
through state aid, she was employing a template developed by
Peter Sutherland when he was competition commissioner.

Sutherland made no public pronouncement on Vestager's move,
but he must have had conflicting thoughts on events. The government felt humiliated, while the decision prompted a furious

backlash in Dublin. There had been an expectation that the commission would find against Ireland, but senior government sources had been briefing in the days before the decision was made public that the amount would be in the order of a few hundred million euros, or possibly a maximum of €1 billion.

Nobody, in even the most senior political circles, suspected what the actual amount would be. Enda Kenny, the Fine Gael Taoiseach, made the unprecedented move of attacking Martin Selmayr, the secretary general of the European Commission, at the first EU summit following the Apple decision. The feeling in Dublin was that the Apple decision was the opening salvo in a broader and potentially much more dangerous offensive by the commission, and that the target was Ireland's corporate tax regime.

Ever since corporate tax in Ireland had been lowered to 12.5 per cent in the early 1990s, it had been a lightning rod for disaffection on the part of other member states. The view was that Ireland's corporate tax regime fostered unfair competition and had facilitated very aggressive tax planning among US multinationals. It was an argument that Sutherland had repeatedly dismissed. Ireland's low corporate tax and business-friendly regulatory regime chimed with his broader vision for Europe. Two months before the European Commission's decision on Apple, the UK had voted to leave the European Union. Both events reflected the evolution of the bloc over the previous three decades.

*

When Sutherland officially took up his position as European commissioner for competition in January 1985, the UK government was trying to create, rather than exit the single market. The Treaty of Rome had been signed in 1957, yet twenty-eight years later it had failed to deliver in its efforts to create a common market. The EU at that stage was a single economic zone in theory only. Individual member states still retained their own internal barriers to trade. The UK had become impatient with the potential economic benefits that were being squandered because of national and sectoral self-interest.

It underlined the differences in approach to European integration. The UK saw the EU purely in transactional terms, as a convenient market on its doorstep. Mainland European member states, particularly France and Germany, had a much deeper emotional attachment. Their watchword was the forging of closer ties between countries that had twice in that century plunged the continent into war. Ireland's enthusiasm for EU membership lay somewhere between the two. It was an underdeveloped country desperately looking for economic patronage. But it was also looking to overcome its dependence on the UK.

Margaret Thatcher, the British Prime Minister, sent Lord Arthur Cockfield to Brussels in 1985 to drive the establishment of the internal market. She trusted Cockfield, who was dour and dependable, but most importantly had a reputation for being mildly Eurosceptic. Her rationale was that he would not stray outside the strict remit she had given him of creating a single market for British goods. The following passage is taken from a British government paper prepared at the time of Cockfield's departure for Brussels:

The Treaty of Rome, which established the European Economic Community (EEC) on 1 January 1958, had as its objective the creation of a common market through the elimination of internal trade barriers between Member States. The free movement of goods was to be accompanied by the free movement of persons, services and capital as the 'four freedoms'. Despite the subsequent removal of tariff barriers, the free movement of goods and services continued to be hampered by non-tariff barriers such as national technical rules governing products and the requirement for service providers to comply with a wide range of national regulations in each Member State. Anti-competitive practices such as the use of state aid also continued. These barriers meant that the common market continued to exist in name only.

In March 1985, the European Council approved the aim of creating a fully fledged internal market and asked the commission to prepare a programme and timetable for implementation. A white paper, *Completing the Internal Market*, proposed by Cockfield was published in June 1985. It detailed 300 legislative proposals, including measures to eliminate a series of physical, technical and fiscal non-tariff barriers. The approach was given added impetus with the signing of the Single European Act in February 1986. As well as setting a deadline for the completion of the single market by 31 December 1992, the Act made Council decision making more effective by introducing qualified majority voting (QMV), removing the requirement for unanimity in some areas which had previously hindered the adoption of legislation. Alongside the greater use of the principle of mutual recognition, which enabled member states to recognise the rules of another member state, rather than a strict reliance upon the harmonisation of national rules, this allowed the EEC to overcome bottlenecks and make progress in completing the single market. For the first time the European Parliament also became involved in the legislative process through the co-operation procedure.

Unfettered competition was the sine qua non of the internal market, and that is why so much hinged on Sutherland. Competition had always been a powerful portfolio, but previous commissioners, mostly for political reasons, had rarely exercised its powers. Albert Borschette had been Commissioner for Competition from 1970 to 1976. Even by the drab standards that prevailed at the time, Borschette was seen as particularly grey and uninspiring. The competition commissioner briefs the European Parliament once a year on developments in the portfolio. Elections to the European Parliament started in 1977, but before then member states nominated candidates to sit in the Parliament. John Prescott, the firebrand Labour MP for Hull who was to become deputy leader of the party under Tony Blair, and who infamously engaged in a physical altercation with a protester before the UK general election in 2001, sat on the Economic

Affairs Committee of the European Parliament at the time. Following Prescott's unsparing style, a number of members savaged Borschette during the commissioner's appearance before the committee on 8 December 1976. Borschette felt unwell during the bruising encounter and asked to leave the committee room to take a break; having done so, he promptly collapsed of a heart attack and died.

'If you read the Treaty of Rome, the chapters on competition are extremely developed,' says Pascal Lamy. And the reason for that was when the Treaty of Rome was being negotiated, Germany had been heavily brainwashed by the Americans and the Brits. So, at the time, the Germans wanted a very precise, legal structure in order to root the principle of a firm competition policy. And Peter Sutherland pushed on the accelerator with the consent of Delors.'

From 1957 onwards, competition had largely been a fiefdom controlled by the core member states. These countries recognised the potential impact of competition; as Lamy says, 'The reality is that from 1957 to 1985, the potential of the competition portfolio was not used.' The process of pivoting the EU towards a more fluid internal market involved many politically sensitive steps, the foremost of these being the removal of state aid. Some governments used state aid for economic purposes to prop up industries that were no longer viable but were seen as strategically important, while others used it for overtly political purposes to support sectors or regions that would deliver an electoral advantage in return. In some cases the removal of state aid would lead to the collapse of companies, and inevitably thereafter to job losses.

A social dimension to European integration was therefore required, as there had to be a safety net for the workers and regions affected. Structural funds were the commission's answer. Ireland, which in the 1980s was one of the poorest member states, benefited significantly from structural investment.

Member states had always been obliged to notify the commission when they intended to extend state aid, but it was seen as a formality that permission would be granted. In many cases governments went ahead with state aid programmes well before they had received formal approval. In some cases, no formal application was ever made. According to Claus-Dieter Ehlermann, director general of the legal service of the European Commission when Sutherland became commissioner, state aid was not a politically sensitive issue, or something that gave member states undue concern. 'Member states were not too fussed about getting formal authorisation because it was seen as a noble cause not to allow workers to lose their jobs. The percentage of state aid cases approved of which the commission were told was very small.' That, says Ehlermann, changed under Sutherland, who insisted that any such aid that had not been given approval was paid back to the state.

The scale of the challenge facing Sutherland was formidable. Dutchman Frans Andriessen had been in charge of competition in the previous regime, but according to Ehlermann 'he didn't get very far. He didn't have the stamina to fight for a decision which obliged the member state to claim the money back [from the recipient].'

How Sutherland would fare as a commissioner hinged on his relationship with Jacques Delors. The Frenchman was sixty-two when he took over as president of the commission. Having been an MEP between 1979 and 1981, he had spent the following three years as French Minister for Finance. A committed socialist, he had spent his entire career in the public sector. He had a formidable reputation – he was not known for suffering fools gladly, he placed a great deal of heft in his own opinions and he was immensely headstrong – but very few would argue that he wasn't the right person to take over the commission in 1985. At that stage, people were rightly questioning the role of the EU. Without a properly functioning single market, it would never be able to deliver the economic benefits which were the most compelling argument for European integration.

Bold decisions needed to be taken. Although he was perhaps

tin-eared to political sensitivities, Delors had never publicly shied away from a fight. It is one of the great ironies of European politics that in 1985, Margaret Thatcher was one of the most vocal champions of the single market and the ambitious reform programme of the Delors Commission. Yet the Frenchman's decision to speak at the British Trade Union Congress in 1988, where he pledged robust labour laws for member states, was probably the starting point in the Brexit debate. Delors' intervention prompted a furious backlash from Thatcher, whose speech in Bruges on 20 September 1988 became a bible for Eurosceptics.

At the outset, Sutherland and Delors seemed like uneasy bedfellows. According to Lamy there was a very interesting subtext to their relationship. 'Irish politics doesn't work right or left. There are many other components and both men had something in common, which is that they were Catholic. Delors never raised his Catholic belief anywhere, but it has had an influence on his particular way of thinking. That is true of Peter as well.' But, adds Lamy, in terms of politics, Sutherland leaned towards the right, while Delors was more a man of the left.

Catherine Day agrees, saying that the relationship between Sutherland and Delors was complex and at times very fraught. 'They both had enormous respect for each other, but they differed in their political philosophies; Delors was coming from the trade union left and Peter was very much a Christian democrat in the European sense. He very much oriented towards markets being allowed to do their thing.' When it came to issues like state aid, Sutherland's approach was quite strict; his view was that a lot of state aid was wasted money. 'He didn't agree that it was a sort of compensatory mechanism which didn't have consequences. Whereas Delors thought of state aid as necessary in cases where Peter did not. So they had clashes, but I think Peter saw the opportunity, sized it up pretty quickly and went for it.'

At the first meeting of the Delors Commission, it was obvious that the president had one eye on the history books. There was a woman seated at a table at the back of the room. When one of the commissioners asked what her role was, Delors said she was there to catalogue every detail of what took place.

During his first week in office, Sutherland forensically went through the Treaty of Rome, demonstrating the ability to master a brief that according to former colleagues in the Law Library was one of his most impressive attributes. He then considered all the European Court of Justice rulings that had been made on competition, which provided him with a roadmap of what he could and could not do. Until the mid-1980s, the commission had been interpreting the rules on competition in ways that were politically expedient. Coming from a small, poor country, Sutherland had a very strong view that Ireland could never compete with the kind of subsidies offered by the larger member states. When the college of commissioners convened for the first time, Sutherland therefore had a very clear idea of what he wanted to achieve. He also knew that it would pit him against Delors and many of his fellow commissioners. If he was to prevail then he would have to lay down a marker.

The first item on the agenda presented the perfect opportunity. Andriessen, the Commissioner for Agriculture, read out a few lines about the commission's policy on milk quotas. When Delors sought to wave it through, Sutherland objected. He felt there had been insufficient time to review such an important policy. Delors gave him two minutes to make his case. Sutherland took twenty minutes, concluding that in deference to the president he would stop there, before demanding that a vote should be taken. He lost narrowly, but the other commissioners sat up and took notice. 'He made his mark from the word go,' says Eugene Regan.

Agriculture was the setting of many of Sutherland's more interesting tussles as commissioner. The way the system worked was that Ireland would be offered a concession, say on milk quotas, and the UK would object. Ireland would eventually be granted the concession, which enabled Irish farmers to produce more milk than the official quota, and the UK would insist that

Northern Ireland farmers be allowed the same. However, on the first such occasion, the British government took the concession earmarked for Northern Ireland farmers and spread it throughout the UK. After the Northern Ireland Farmers Union went to Sutherland to protest, he made several representations to Andriessen, who turned the screw on the British government. Eventually London relented and the concession for Northern Irish farmers was restored. According to Regan, the head of the Northern Ireland Farmers Union, which would have been a heavily Unionist organisation, told Sutherland that they saw him as 'their commissioner'.

Sutherland soon developed a reputation among the commissioners, and before long he was being noticed more widely. It was a tussle with the French that brought him to the attention of the media. France had been operating a system whereby it would give interest-free loans to cereal producers who were exporting to the Egyptian market. The French government extended this to all agriculture products destined for Egypt; the country had always been a big market for Irish beef, and the French support strategy was seen as an interference with competition policy. Sutherland managed to secure a proposal to bring France to the European Court over the scheme. Having gone through a few committees, it finally went to the commission – at which Delors was not present – for a vote. There was a show of hands, and all hands shot up in favour of taking France to court.

Delors would meet the French media every Wednesday for a lunchtime briefing, but he failed to appear on the day of the vote, and his fellow French commissioner, Claude Cheysson, deputised. Cheysson was furious with Sutherland and called him '*Le petit shérif*'. On the back of the French broadside, the *Financial Times* ran a prominent story on Sutherland.

In the first year of the Delors Commission it was not unusual for meetings to go on all day. Neither was it uncommon for Delors to have too many drinks at lunchtime, which made afternoon sessions colourful and sometimes turbulent affairs. Catherine Day reports that at times, Delors would let his frustrations get the better of him, and would lash out at various commissioners he believed were underperforming. On more than one occasion Delors singled out Grigoris Varfis for the hairdryer treatment. Among the many less than affectionate terms he used included 'glorified Greek innkeeper'.

Sutherland tried to intervene on a number of occasions in an effort to defuse the situation. 'Delors would say "I'm not talking about you, Peter, you are a man of principle," recalls Day. 'He put him into a different category,' she adds, 'he clearly respected Peter.'

The personal relationship between Delors and Sutherland was not the only factor that would determine the success of the competition portfolio. Delors' cabinet and Sutherland's would also need to develop a good working relationship. According to Day, that relationship was harder to bed down. 'But we kept pushing. We thought if we could have a long meeting with Delors and his cabinet we could explain where we were coming from. They were very resistant to it but eventually they agreed and we were convinced they did this deliberately. They always felt superior, that they were harder-working than anybody else.' And so, she says, they deliberately picked the Friday morning or the Saturday of the typical Brussels bank holiday, which lasted from Thursday to Sunday, saying they would be available for such a meeting. 'It was a way of saying that we don't take holidays, we are working. We felt they were daring us to say oh well, it's a bank holiday weekend so we can't. So we gritted our teeth and said of course we will be there.'

Sutherland's first major skirmish with Delors was over the car industry. In 1985 the German government had introduced fiscal advantages for clean energy cars, whereupon Renault, Peugeot and Citroën complained because they felt they had ceded an unfair advantage to the Germans. Feeling that the environmental benefits outweighed the level of aid, Sutherland decided not to take a state aid procedure, on the basis that the French were free to introduce a similar system and there was no constraint on them doing so if they wished. There was a tussle with Delors, who was sensitive about anything to do with France. When a vote was held in the commission, Sutherland won.

He then took on the Germans. The case was an investment subsidy for an industrial facility which Sutherland deemed was an unnecessary waste of public money. But it was politically important because the prime minister of Baden-Württemberg, where the facility was located, was a key ally of Chancellor Helmut Kohl. The move did not go down well in Berlin, but Sutherland stuck to his guns.

Next came his first skirmish with London, when Sutherland took the view that support extended by the British government to the textile industry contravened state aid rules. At a meeting with Norman Lamont, the UK Minister of State for Trade and Industry, Sutherland argued that he was creating a level playing field; his intention was not only to remove such aid from the UK textile industry, but to target similar support in other member states. Lamont accepted his argument.

With a few early victories under his belt, and with Delors' backing, Sutherland set his sights on much bigger prizes. At the time, there was a paucity of competition in airlines, energy and telecoms; the three sectors that most affected the lives of Europe's citizens were mostly dominated by state-controlled monopolies. Sutherland went about breaking up these cartels. For example, the national airlines of member states had been allowed to set the price of plane tickets between countries. By 1987, he had not only removed restrictions that enabled governments to protect national carriers by blocking the introduction of low fares, but successfully encouraged new entrants to the market. He thereby put the necessary building blocks in place for the creation of the single aviation market, which was completed in 1992.

Opening national markets and creating an EU single aviation market spurred competition, providing more routes and more destinations to places in the EU and further afield. According to the

European Commission's factsheet on aviation, today there are almost eight times as many routes as there were in 1992, giving the consumer more choice and ensuring more places are connected regularly. A good example is Dublin airport, where the number of intra-EU routes grew from 36 in 1992 to 127 in 2016. Consumer demand has driven the continued expansion of new routes. In 2015 for example, almost 920 million passengers passed through 450 EU airports, nearly three times more than in 1992. In addition, smaller regional airports continue to expand, helping to contribute to more balanced economic growth in all parts of the EU.

Perhaps the most tangible evidence of the dismantling of state control of aviation is the emergence of Ryanair – in the late 1980s a one-pilot operation – as the largest airline in the EU and one of the biggest in the world. Michael O'Leary, Ryanair's colourful chief executive, is not known for holding politicians or public servants in high regard. In fact, most of the time his relationship with politicians would be similar to that between a dog and a lamppost. Sutherland was one of the very few exceptions. In a 2017 interview with the *Irish Times*, O'Leary credited Sutherland with reforms in the airline sector: 'Peter Sutherland drove all of this in the face of massive opposition from the German and French flag carriers, who did everything in their power to stop him. It's very much an Irish success story in Europe. It broke up the flag-carrying monopolies and ushered in competition.'[1]

O'Leary pointed out that Ryanair would be unlikely to exist without Sutherland's intervention. Europe's open skies regime allows an airline registered in one member state to operate freely throughout the bloc. 'In 1987 Ryanair had no passengers. This year we will have 130 million. We're an Irish airline but we are the world's biggest international airline by passenger numbers.'

*

When Sutherland also blocked the merger of British Airways and its smaller rival British Caledonian, as well as the Rover takeover of Leyland in the car sector, the two cases received full headline treatment across the UK media. In many ways they highlighted tensions between the UK and the EU that would fester for thirty years and would ultimately lead the country to leave.

Even though Margaret Thatcher was an unalloyed supporter of free markets, she was not averse to depicting Sutherland as a potentate impinging on UK sovereignty when he cited her government for anti-competitive practices. She was particularly incensed over his ruling on Rover, as he described in a speech he gave at Gresham College in 2011:

At the time I was Commissioner for Competition, and I remember one day shaving in my house in Brussels and listening to the news, and there was a G5 meeting taking place in Toronto. I had been a rather turbulent priest in Brussels as well as in Dublin, and I had blocked the British Rover takeover and I had also been rather difficult over the merger of the Scottish airline – Caledonian and BA. Mrs Thatcher had not enjoyed this, and she was asked something about interest rates on the radio, and as I was shaving, she said, 'Oh, I do not want to talk about interest rates,' she said, 'I want to talk about that man in Brussels!' and of course, I am afraid it was me!

I had the revenge of at least being able to laugh at the following situation. When she came to give her famous Bruges speech, which was the denunciation of all things European, she gave it in the European University Institute in Bruges. It was in a very ancient hall, and the Rector of the University was a German, who was very much a European integrationist, and when she finished her speech, out of four speakers in the hall came the blaring movement of 'Ode to Joy', the European national anthem. Mrs Thatcher, immediately, with her Ambassador, jumped to attention with everybody else, she thinking, as it transpired, that she was standing to the Belgian national anthem whereas, the rest of us, with tears rolling down our face, were standing to the European national anthem.[2]

One senior EU official who was in the commission the same time as Sutherland says that he was successful because he was able to articulate his policies very clearly to other commissioners. His rationale was not that he was taking an anti-French view or an anti-German view, or that he had any agenda other than ensuring there was fair competition across the region. After initial resistance the other commissioners, and by extension other member states, would grow to trust and respect him.

Eugene Regan describes Sutherland as a force of nature in the commission. So well briefed was he not just on his own area but on most issues that the commission was dealing with, says Regan, that he shaped the entire commission agenda.

'None of the commissioners since have tried to row back on what Peter achieved, so it was a clear victory for Peter and for neoliberal thinking,' says Ehlermann. 'I got on very well with him. I remember one disagreement between him and me, which was rare. We had a very delicate case where Directorate General (DG) for competition and legal services were not on the same wavelength initially on the extent to which competition law limits intellectual property copyright. I don't know why, but he was emotionally on the side of an Irish newspaper.'

The case Ehlermann is referring to related to *Magill* magazine and concerned the copyright on TV listings. Back then, if a newspaper wanted to publish TV listings, it had to get permission from each individual broadcaster, on the basis that broadcasters had exclusive rights to their listings. Vincent Browne, the editor of *Magill*, started publishing the listings without permission. The Irish courts held that the broadcasters did indeed own the copyright on their own listings and found against *Magill*. The magazine took its complaint to the European Commission, and was successful: the commission found that this was an abuse of their dominant position by the broadcasters and they must license their listings.

Ehlermann comments of Sutherland's approach to the case: 'He thought that in that case the use of copyright was abusive. It was the sort of copyright that should never have been granted, but largely that is a matter for a member state and not the commission. The only lever was competition law. I found that to be interfering with intellectual property rights, because it is property, and we were opening up a Pandora's box.'

Nial Fennelly says he remembers discussing the case with Sutherland when he returned from Brussels. Fennelly stated that Sutherland didn't pay much attention to the copyright law in the *Magill* case. Sutherland agreed. Fennelly remembers, 'I always thought that personified Peter. He knew what the outcome should be and he just went for it'

Dermot Desmond was the driving force behind the creation of the International Financial Services Centre (IFSC), a specially designated zone with tax incentives to attract financial services companies, in Dublin in the 1980s. He persuaded Charlie Haughey to back a proposal to establish the IFSC, and it became part of government strategy. But first it had to get clearance from Brussels. The decision was considered by the commission to see whether it involved state aid. The Irish corporate tax rate of 12.5 per cent was not considered to be state aid since it was the general tax regime and applied to all corporations. However, if applied on a selective basis, say to one region or sector, then it would be state aid. After examining the situation, the commission agreed that the inclusion of all financial companies in the 12.5 per cent rate was not sufficiently selective to be state aid, and so Ireland was free to go ahead. Sutherland effectively gave the IFSC the green light.

*

The first pillar of competition policy is the removal of illegal state aid. The second pillar of competition policy is anti-trust legislation. Sutherland had developed a comprehensive legislative framework on mergers and acquisitions. Margaret Thatcher had meanwhile grown increasingly disillusioned with Lord Cockfield, accusing him of going native. Even though it was expected that he would serve two terms, he was called back to London after four years and replaced by Leon Brittan – although Thatcher also quickly turned on Brittan. The final touches and formal approval of merger legislation occurred under Brittan, who was to succeed Sutherland as commissioner.

Leon Brittan had been elected as a Conservative MP in 1974 and while serving as British Home Secretary in the mid-1980s, he took a hard-line approach during the miners' strike. He had originally been close to Thatcher, though she lost confidence in him because of his underwhelming media performances. He was moved from the Home Office to Secretary of State for Trade, before being shunted off to Brussels in 1989.

Ehlermann says it was extremely interesting to compare the two men. 'I would say Sutherland was a total success. Leon was a peculiar product of neoliberal thinking in theory, but while Peter always remained pragmatic and knew when to stop, Leon did not. I don't think Peter ever had any problem with his colleagues. Leon had. He was too doctrinaire, too ideological. Peter was much more collegiate. Sutherland did not have any case to decide on mergers because legislation was not approved until he left. But he struck the essential compromise. He raised the threshold on whether the matter remained the concern of a member state or whether it should be decided by the commission. That was a very important breakthrough. His main legacy is really a credible and sustainable fight against state aid. In anti-trust, he had an important contribution, but not as important as his fight against state aid.'

This is how Sutherland concluded his 2011 speech on his time at the commission:

I remember that day in Chez Edgar when Jacques Delors said to me, with a wry smile, that, as a theme for this first

Commission, we would have a very specific one – we were going to try to create a functioning internal market of free movement of goods, persons, capital and services by 1992. He said that one of the strongest advocates of this, for once, if I may say so, on the positive side of the argument vis-à-vis Europe, was the United Kingdom, which is why it appealed to him as an idea. It appealed to the United Kingdom because it was the crystallisation of a pragmatic, rather than an airy-fairy ideal, as some of the European thinking is often described. This was something practical and something that fitted in with the British concern about free markets and the opening of markets.

I think that Jacques Delors had a somewhat different intention to that expressed at that time by Lady Thatcher, or Mrs Thatcher as she was, because he recognised, and I remember him saying it to me, almost in a conspiratorial way, that the only way that you could ever have an internal market was by having more European legislation, and the only way you could have more European legislation, binding member states, was by having more majority voting. If you had majority voting, which could outvote individual member states, you were attacking the very core of national sovereignty, which is exactly what Jacques Delors intended to do, and, ultimately, it became apparent that he was right.

That was driving him to a view, not merely that European integration was desirable, but that the more you could have sharing of sovereignty and the voting across the interests of individual member states by majority voting, the more you would get that integration.[3]

As Sutherland was quick to point out, it could be seen as ironic that the Single European Act, which provided for that majority voting, was adopted during the time of Margaret Thatcher.

Sutherland's success as a commissioner was a double-edged sword for Britain's membership of the bloc. On the one hand, his drive to create an efficient, competitive single market chimed with Thatcher's vision of European integration. On the other hand, he was responsible for increasing the importance of the commission – which was ultimately one of the driving forces behind Brexit.

9

PRESIDENT OF THE
EUROPEAN COMMISSION?

SUTHERLAND WAS THE FIRST COMMISSIONER FROM Ireland to embrace the Brussels lifestyle. He and his wife, Maruja, moved to Brussels with their daughter Natalia, although the two boys, Ian and Shane, were sent as boarders to Glenstal Abbey in County Limerick. Sutherland knew that if he followed the template set by previous Irish commissioners – fly home on Thursday night and back again on Monday morning – he would miss out on the weekend dinner party circuit. This was when the real business was done in Brussels. Most importantly, he did not intend to allow any cliques among other commissioners to develop behind his back.

There was a peculiarity in Sutherland's first year as a commissioner. With Spain and Portugal due to join on 1 January 1986, the portfolios that were to be allocated to the two new member states were temporarily shared out among existing commissioners. Sutherland was given education. The newly appointed commissioner already had his hands full with the competition brief, so it would have been understandable if he had paid scant attention to education during 1985. On the contrary, he gave it his full attention. As it turned out, education would give Sutherland one of the achievements he was most proud of during his time as commissioner.

In 1985 Hywel Jones was a director for education and training in DG Social Policy, Employment and Industrial Relations. Sutherland had been in the job about a week when he summoned Jones for a meeting. It was a Friday evening and Jones arrived with a sizeable dossier full of the main issues relating to the education portfolio. 'We met again on Monday morning and he knew the contents of the dossier backwards,' remembers Jones. 'He had an astonishing grasp. He was on top of it from the word go.' Tucked away in the dossier were two related projects that Jones had been working on. 'I gave him the embryonic outlines of two programmes. One was Comett, which was education training and technology. The other one was Erasmus.' Comett involved building alliances between education, technology and industry on a pan-European basis, while Erasmus was an exchange programme for tertiary-level students.

Sutherland was encouraged by Michel Richonnier, a member of his cabinet, to take forward the two flagship programmes. He saw the potential in both. If Europe was to move to a fully fledged single market, then the free movement of ideas would be a key building block. But the big member states were very nervous about having a legal basis in the treaty for anything to do with education because it was closely related to the idea of sovereignty.

'The internal market idea Sutherland was very supportive of. On the back of that we were able to get a lot of impetus behind the two programmes. The year before, the Adonnino report was published by the European Commission, which looked at the idea of European citizenship and how to develop a social Europe: feeling European and seeing the future in European terms. I grew to realise in later years how much of a passionate European he was,' says Jones.

Erasmus had a very difficult birth, particularly as it seemed to have no legal basis. Thanks to his background, Sutherland knew that without any such basis, it would be impossible to secure financing for Erasmus. Salvation came in the form of Article 128 of the Treaty of Rome, which established common principles in the field of vocational training. The question then arose as to what constituted training and what education. Sutherland, Jones and the rest of the team spent much of 1985 preparing a legal and political basis for Erasmus.

During that year, the Gravier judgment issued by the European Court of Justice profoundly influenced legal debates about the place of education and training in the treaty.[1] A case had been brought by a student, a French national who wished to pursue a course in cartoon design at a Belgian art school. She took the Belgian authority, the City of Liège, to court on the grounds that, as an EC national, she should have been given a place on the same terms as Belgian students and not charged the higher foreign student fee, called the minerval. The European Court had accepted that there should be no discrimination between EC nationals in terms of access to training and that the word 'training' should be deemed to cover university education. The result of the case was to have a profound effect on political discussions concerning the legal basis for the EU to promote and finance educational co-operation.

In December 1985, it became apparent that France, Germany and the UK were steadfast in their opposition to the proposal. Even a smaller member state can theoretically block a proposal if the relevant vote needs unanimity; if one or more of the big member states is against anything brewing on the legislative agenda, then it is normally dead on arrival.

'I witnessed an amazing incident between Peter and Delors,' says Jones. During a very difficult meeting at the Council of Ministers, ministers from the larger member states had told Sutherland that they would never accept Erasmus. 'We broke off from the meeting and went to see Delors. It was a very tough meeting. Peter told Delors he had to back it even if it meant going for a majority vote. I think that meeting was Peter at his finest.'

Once Delors got behind Erasmus, it tilted the chances in favour of success. Even there, though, the opposition did not stop. The method of voting the Erasmus programme through was contested by a minority of member states, although when the issue was brought before the European Court of Justice it ruled in favour of Sutherland, allowing the majority decision to be upheld. '1985 was the year of setting up the battle and 1986 was the year of winning the battle. I don't believe it would have been won without Peter and his mastery and drive,' Jones says. Comett was a parallel programme to Erasmus, he explains, designed to bridge technology and industry. 'I thought it was more important than Erasmus.' Then there was a process of rationalisation: Comett was folded into the Erasmus programme. 'The official title Erasmus, with its historic symbolism and immediate appeal, also worked perfectly as an acronym – European Community Action Scheme for the Mobility of University Students (or, as I preferred, Studies).'

Once Spain joined the EC at the start of 1986, Manuel Marín took responsibility for the education portfolio. The negotiations which led ultimately to the adoption of the Erasmus and Comett programmes, says Jones, owed a great deal to the determination and dynamic leadership of Sutherland and Marín, both of whom were passionately attached to winning what turned into a difficult confrontation in the negotiations within the Council. Since then the Erasmus programme has gone from strength to strength, with 200,000 students from more than 2,000 educational institutions taking part in exchanges every year.

Sutherland was clear, however, that Erasmus wasn't only about education; the programme was a tool to further the wider project of European integration. 'The ultimate objective was the process of integration between Europeans rather than the purely educational advantages that it would give. The reality is that we needed to create a new attitude to the EU, which we still need to do today,' he said in an interview with the UCD student publication, *Connections*, in 2010. 'This requires young people to recognise a common cultural and value-based system the European countries share; and not to feel alien and different from others.'

One of Sutherland's other main responsibilities during his time as commissioner was relations with the European Parliament. 'I would honestly say that he was responsible for a qualitative transformation in the commission relationship with the European Parliament,' says David O'Sullivan. The Single European Act had significantly increased the role of the Parliament in EU affairs. 'We had to codify those procedures and Peter was heavily instrumental in that, and in taking a very leading approach about how we should deal with the European Parliament.' Back then, says O'Sullivan, the Parliament was regarded with deep suspicion by most people in the commission and elsewhere. 'Peter took it very seriously and I think the new procedures that we adopted, although they were a bit boring and bureaucratic, gave the Parliament certain rights and roles.' These formed, says O'Sullivan, the platform on which the Parliament built its subsequent grab for power through a series of treaties, culminating in the Lisbon Treaty.

Sutherland received the Gold Medal – an award conferred on those who have made an important contribution to European integration – from the European Parliament in 1988.

*

Francis Jacobs first came across Sutherland as an official on the secretariat of the Committee for Economic and Monetary Affairs in the European Parliament. The committee dealt with the single market project and competition. The Parliament's formal role in competition matters was minimal, its main function being to review how the commission had dealt with competition policy in the previous year. The commission would put together an annual report; the Parliament then reviewed the report and published a comment. 'So we did a report on the report. We did our report in September after the commission report came out in July,' says Jacobs. 'Peter made an appearance before the committee once a year. It was always a classic. He would outline the main themes and then take questions on any aspect of policy, including areas that were not in the report.'

115

The floor was open to members of the committee to ask Sutherland any questions they wished – and they often did. Jacobs says it was not uncommon to hear questions about car dealerships, or even complaints from the Campaign for Real Ale in the UK about tied houses. 'He would deal with all of that,' Jacobs adds. 'One day I was in a lift with him and to my incredible surprise he said thank you very much, Francis, for your report. He had been briefed that I was the ghost-writer.

'I was thirty and a lowly official. He was thirty-eight and a commissioner. In a very hierarchical structure, where first names were unusual, to be called by my first name by the commissioner, whom I had never been formally introduced to, was a surprise. Some people say he was a stuck-up international tycoon figure. He wasn't. He had great warmth. The ghost-writer is very rarely acknowledged within the system. It was an incredibly nice touch for me.'

Sutherland had a reputation as being a market liberal. The most important elements of his portfolio were the dismantling of state aid and the removal of distortions in competition, and his approach was hated by the left. But at the time there were no attack dogs similar to John Prescott. 'Certainly in the UK context, it was the period when [Neil] Kinnock was wrestling Labour back from the hard left. The party was so riven by internal struggle I don't think they were bothered by what was happening in the committee,' says Jacobs. 'Sutherland was a very capable performer. Style can be as important as substance. He was very charming. He called people by their first names. He was respectful but forceful. He was generally liked by the committee.'

The committee's main focus was the single market, so they were broadly positive towards anybody who was pushing this agenda. And Sutherland would have been at the forefront. 'My main recollection is that in a hierarchical environment he seemed like a breath of fresh air,' observes Jacobs. 'Sutherland gave Ireland this dynamic image which was utterly lacking previously. Burke was pompous and not impressive. O'Kennedy just didn't want to be there. He was appointed late by Haughey, he was given the leftovers and he seemed ill at ease in the commission. Ireland at the time was seen as this strange little country with no left and two centre-right parties.' According to Jacobs, Ireland was seen at the time as friendly and pragmatic, leaning to the centre right but not particularly ideological. It supported the Common Agricultural Policy (CAP) but that was hardly a liberal measure. 'That is why Sutherland wouldn't have been targeted as much by the left.'

*

When Sutherland came to the end of his period of office in 1989, many people in the commission thought he should be given a second term. He was certainly interested in remaining in Brussels. After all, his friend and mentor, Jacques Delors, was staying on as president. But domestic politics would deal Sutherland's prospects a fatal blow. Charlie Haughey was now Taoiseach and Fianna Fáil was in power. Haughey may have crossed the floor once to appoint a Fine Gael nominee as commissioner, but he certainly wasn't going to do it a second time. In some ways, Sutherland had become the victim of his own success. He had lifted the currency of being a commissioner. Previously it had been seen in Ireland as having little relevance to political life, but Sutherland had shown that in the right hands, it was a powerful lever at the disposal of the government. When Haughey sent Ray MacSharry to Brussels, MacSharry turned out to be a very effective Commissioner for Agriculture, and introduced sweeping changes to the CAP.

Sutherland went about ensuring that his cabinet were taken care of before he left office. Catherine Day joined the cabinet of Leon Brittan, the incoming Commissioner for Competition, while Liam Hourican became chef de cabinet for MacSharry. Eugene Regan went back to Ireland and trained as a barrister. Richard O'Toole joined aircraft leasing company Guinness Peat Aviation, whose board Sutherland had also agreed to join.

117

On leaving the commission, Sutherland returned home and went back briefly to the Law Library before taking up the role of chairman of Allied Irish Bank (AIB). But the commission never left Sutherland. From 1990 onwards he plotted his return one day as president. Rated very highly as he was both within the commission and among member states, his ambition was not without foundation.

*

His chance appeared to arrive in 1994. The process of replacing Jacques Delors was initially a fiasco. At the Corfu summit at the end of June 1994, the expectation had been that Ruud Lubbers, the Dutch prime minister, would become the next president. He was seen as having the right credentials and background: he was a Christian Democrat from one of the core member states; more importantly, he had the backing of the big member states. But then, weeks before the summit which was supposed to be his coronation, the German government had a change of mind and backed the Belgian candidate, Jean-Luc Dehaene. The Germans persuaded the French to also throw their support behind Dehaene. It now looked as if the Belgian would succeed Delors. But then John Major, the British prime minister, came out very publicly against Dehaene, saying his objection was based on how the contest was being conducted. Or that, more importantly, it was a power grab by the Franco-German axis.

Major was also under pressure from the Eurosceptic wing of his party. Dehaene had a reputation as an arch-federalist, while the Conservative Party at that stage was already on the way to self-immolation over Europe. Any suggestion of a push towards federalism heightened the party's Euro-neurosis. Major was pushing for Leon Brittan to become the next president, but his candidacy secured very little support among other member states.

Going into the Corfu summit, Sutherland was seen as a cred-ible but outside choice to succeed Delors. But as political horse-trading got into full swing and his rivals were eliminated, Sutherland came into the frame. Having just successfully concluded the Uruguay Round of trade talks, his stock had risen at an international level. Major was known to be an enthusiastic supporter.

The facts of that summit are still not clear. There is a question mark over whether Sutherland had the support of the French government. John Major said in his autobiography that François Mitterrand was opposed to Sutherland because he viewed him as too Anglo-Saxon. If Paris was not on board, that would scupper his chances. But his prospects were dead in the water already if he didn't have the backing of the Irish government. At the time another Fianna Fáil–Labour coalition was in government and Albert Reynolds was Taoiseach. Two senior EU sources have confirmed that at the Corfu summit a consensus formed among member states that Sutherland could emerge as a compromise candidate. Both sources have said his candidacy was withdrawn because he did not get the backing of the Irish government.

Dick Spring, who as Minister for Foreign Affairs attended the summit, says that his only memory of the event is that the Irish and British governments were at loggerheads over Northern Ireland. He claims to have no recollection of being asked to support Sutherland's candidacy. 'I honestly do not recall. It is a very long time ago.' Spring is adamant, however, that Sutherland did not canvass the Irish government for support in the run-up to the summit. Reynolds, who died in 2014, also played down the possibility that Sutherland was in contention. 'He has not been ruled in. There is no substance in stories that there is support for Sutherland,' he said at the time.[2]

There are a number of possible reasons why the Irish government failed to row in behind Sutherland. The most basic is the tribal nature of Irish politics. Fianna Fáil simply would not support a Fine Gael candidate. There are other reasons, however. According to Brian Cowen, the Minister for Transport in 1994, Sutherland's candidacy was never raised at cabinet level.

Fianna Fáil minister Pádraig Flynn was a controversial figure. During the 1990 presidential election campaign he sparked an enormous controversy when he made offensive remarks about Mary Robinson, the Labour Party's favoured candidate, on a programme on RTÉ radio. Flynn lashed out at Robinson in comments that were laced with misogyny, making reference to her new clothes, new hairdo and new look, 'and a new interest in her family, being a mother and that kind of thing. But those of us who knew Mary Robinson in previous incarnations never heard her claiming to be a great wife and mother.'

According to Brian Cowen, Labour had raised objections about Flynn during talks with Fianna Fáil to form the 1992 coalition. The agreement hammered out in the talks at the end of 1992 was nevertheless that Flynn would be sent to Brussels as commissioner. If the coalition had backed Sutherland, then Flynn would have had to return to Ireland and domestic politics. At the time larger member states had two commissioners, whereas smaller member states such as Ireland had only one. If Sutherland had become president of the commission, that would have counted as Ireland's commissionership. That was not something either party wanted to deal with.

Modesty was not a character trait commonly attributed to Flynn, if ever. When asked about the possibility of Sutherland becoming president of the commission, he responded, 'I'm sure there will be a lot of people looking for the job of commission president and there may well be more than one Irishman. I am always available to serve in whatever capacity Ireland requires of me.'[3] Flynn's period as commissioner was, however, underwhelming.

There was speculation at the time that Dick Spring had his own reasons for blocking Sutherland. Ten years previously, in 1984, Sutherland had lobbied against the appointment of John Rogers to replace him as attorney general. Relations between Spring and Sutherland had been good up to that point, but Spring and Rogers had been very close since their student days in Trinity and Spring felt betrayed by Sutherland's move against Rogers.

Some believed that ten years later he still bore a grudge. Spring says that 'there is absolutely no truth in that. I remember there was an issue with the appointment of John Rogers but it did not affect my relationship with Peter Sutherland.'

Jacques Santer emerged as the compromise candidate to become President of the European Commission, although he was forced to resign in 1999 along with his entire team of commissioners following allegations of corruption.

*

Sutherland left public office in 1995 and went on to have a very rewarding career in the private sector, becoming chairman of Goldman Sachs International the same year. Sutherland told Eugene Regan that around the time he was making the transition from the public to the private sector, he went to his childhood mentor, Fr Joe Veale, for advice. Even though he was very tempted by the private sector, he had a deep commitment to public office. He also harboured a desire to land another international role. According to Regan, Sutherland took great enjoyment from Veale's response: 'I have the perfect solution. You take the job and give the money to the church.' Sutherland would make an estimated €120 million from the flotation of Goldman Sachs in 1999.* However, one of his close friends says it was never about the money. 'If he had a choice between Goldman Sachs and everything that brought him, or the president of the commission, he would have picked the commission every time.'

In 2004, Sutherland was back in the frame. This time it was a combination of domestic politics and his professional ties that scuppered his chances. At the time, Ireland held the rotating EU presidency. Bertie Ahern, the Taoiseach at the time, had been given the responsibility of finding a replacement for Romano Prodi. 'There were at least ten names floating around. Peter didn't figure early in the campaign. He came in around March when he saw

---

* According to the *Sunday Times* Rich List.

there was no strong runner. After a good bit of wheeling and dealing the frontrunner clearly became Guy Verhofstadt.' Ahern insists that the Fianna Fáil–Progressive Democrat coalition was firmly behind Sutherland's candidacy. 'I supported him both publicly and privately at the [European] Council. I had a very good relationship with him. Charlie McCreevy and Mary Harney were also very enthusiastic supporters.'

But, says Ahern, Sutherland failed to drum up enough support from other member states. '[Tony] Blair had a bit of interest in going himself, but he would also have been happy enough with Sutherland.' After Blair ruled himself out of the running, a period of negotiation, largely in Ireland, took place around the time of the enlargement ceremony in May which welcomed the accession of the so-called 'A10' countries, including the Czech Republic, Hungary and Poland. 'When the French and Germans rolled in behind Verhofstadt, everybody thought it was a done deal,' Ahern continues. 'I think we would have got a bit of support for Peter but everybody thought it was Verhofstadt. He had ten or twelve member states.' The problem for Verhofstadt was that he didn't have the backing of London, and the British government vetoed his candidacy. He was seen as an arch-federalist who would have taken the EU down a road unacceptable to British interests. Indeed, when Verhofstadt was the president of the European Parliament between 2014 and 2019, he would take a very vocal and critical position against the British government in Brexit negotiations.

'There was nobody else on the list strong enough. The process was suspended in June 2004 because of a lack of consensus. I was asked to see if there was anybody who wasn't on the list who would get sufficient backing. That's how José Manuel Barroso's name came into the ring. The problem with 2004 was that Peter's star had faded. It was a new generation. I wasn't supporting Verhofstadt for two reasons. I knew the Brits were going to veto him and he was far too integrationist. Peter was in there until the end, but it was a decade after he had been in the limelight.'

There were other reasons as well. David O'Sullivan, secretary general of the European Commission in 2004, was at a dinner in Paris for EU diplomats when a senior French official, whom O'Sullivan knew well, approached him and asked if he was working for Sutherland's presidential campaign. 'And I said no I'm not, I'm secretary general of the commission. He said yeah, but we all know that you are very close to Peter and you would like him to be president.' O'Sullivan replied that he thought Sutherland would make a very good president, but that O'Sullivan would probably lose his job if Sutherland was appointed. 'I'm Irish and if we got an Irish president I would presumably have to move. I don't know whether I'm working for my own career suicide.'

'We all know what you are doing,' said the Frenchman. 'I have a message for Peter Sutherland from President Chirac I'd like you to pass on.'

'I do speak to Peter,' said O'Sullivan, 'and I can give him the message.' France, he was told, would never accept that a chairman of Goldman Sachs could become president of the commission. It was utterly unacceptable and could never be acceptable under any circumstances; that was the absolute position of the French government, and Sutherland needed to know it. 'To which I replied, to the best of my knowledge Jean Monnet was an investment banker! But this didn't appear to change his mind very much.'

O'Sullivan believes that Sutherland's career trajectory after he left public office made it increasingly unlikely that he could be a credible candidate. 'I think Liam Hourican was probably right to say in 1989, that Peter Sutherland had to make a choice.' If Sutherland wanted to come back to a good European career, says O'Sullivan, he had to go back to the nitty-gritty of domestic Irish politics, become a cabinet minister again and be a national politician in order to have a springboard back to the European theatre.

Ahern met Tony Blair in London just before the decision was made to appoint Barroso, after which he sent a message through diplomatic channels to Sutherland. It said: 'Tell Peter it can't be done.' Barroso, the former Portuguese prime minister, was elected president in 2004. He would serve two terms. Ironically he would replace Sutherland as chairman of Goldman Sachs International when he retired from the commission.

Henry 'Hank' Paulson, the head of Goldman Sachs in 2004, and subsequently US Treasury Secretary under President George W. Bush, had meanwhile developed a close relationship with Sutherland. 'I remember that,' Paulson says. 'We all worked to try and make that happen for Peter and it would have been very good if it had happened. Peter talked to me a lot about how to make it happen. I don't know the extent that it was Goldman Sachs, because this was well before the financial crisis, so investment banks were not as discredited then as they are now. I think the French wanted an excuse and they did not want an Irishman running the European Commission. You could not have found someone who was more ecumenical when it came to Europe than Peter. The strange thing is that he helped France. We held a board meeting in Paris in 2004. We were one of only four firms that helped the government in a mega bond deal.'

Adrian Jones also worked with Sutherland at Goldman Sachs. 'He had no issues with the French response. He felt it was the rational response from the French. It was a power play. They saw what was happening and closed it down. He had no animus for them. I do think that he would have loved to have seen more support from Ireland [in 1994]. He felt we were unnecessarily tribal and petty.'

Niall FitzGerald, a former chief executive and chairman of Unilever, was another close friend of Sutherland. 'He deeply regretted he never became commission president. He could have made a difference. I think it was the single major disappointment of his life.' He would have been a great president, says FitzGerald. 'He was a consistent voice for a liberal market regime. He was one of the most persuasive voices for the ongoing integration of Europe. He was absolutely fearless and uninhibited.'

Cowen agrees that Sutherland would have made an excellent commission president. 'He had a track record and standing that was as good as any prime minister.' There are two approaches to running the European Union, he says: the Franco-German view, which means that Paris and Berlin hold the whip hand over legislation and the direction of travel for the bloc, and the communitaire view, which means a much more consensus-based approach and is obviously more amenable to the wishes of smaller member states such as Ireland. 'Sutherland had the independence of mind to stand up to the big guys and do the right thing. Look at Sarkozy, he tried to throw his weight around and tell everybody what to do, including the governor of the ECB. The commission is the originator of policy. Then it should be up to the communitaire system about what is implemented. It is the protector of the small member state if it is working properly. That is why you need a really good commission president. I don't think Prodi had it and I don't think Barroso had it.' Sutherland, says Cowen, would have been very good at arguing his case, in part because of his legal training. 'The president of the commission has to have political personality. Sutherland was in jobs that were sufficiently complex and still managed to get political backing. Also the Irish are generally seen as honest brokers. The Irish presidencies have generally been very good, including when we got the draft constitutional treaty through. It was a very proud day to see how the Irish pulled that together, particularly seeing as how much of a mess the Italians had made of it.'

Sutherland retained an intense interest in European affairs after his second failed attempt to become president. He didn't have to look far to find out what was happening in Brussels. After all, O'Sullivan and Day, who had been in his cabinet, were in charge of the European civil service between 2000 and 2015. Day says that Sutherland kept in frequent contact.

'He was frustrated with the commission. I would try to explain to him that the whole European landscape had changed since he had been commissioner, but of course he was too intelligent not to understand that. But emotionally he didn't want to accept it. He thought the commission should be much tougher with member states. Now I think that myself, but I had to accept that the member states had taken back a certain amount of power and that the commission, certainly in the post-Lisbon architecture, could never be the powerhouse that it was from 1985 up to 1989. But he was terribly frustrated by it.

'I think he thought the power of the argument and a sufficiently strong intervention could carry the day. Now he would say it's erosion by a thousand cuts or whatever, but I just think the landscape changed and there was much more collusion between member states.' This is in part thanks to innovations like the mobile phone, she points out: in the past member states didn't really talk to each other. It was necessary to pre-book a phone call, and have an interpreter standing by. 'Now they all have each other on speed dial.' The member states started setting up contact among themselves, away from the Brussels machinery, to the frustration of foreign ministers and ambassadors alike. 'So it changed, and I don't think the commission could or should have stopped that. And part of the backlash was because the commission was seen to be a relentlessly federal machine and I don't myself think that's the right direction. I think we have to be federal on a limited number of things but actually to give up on quite a lot of other stuff.'

That, she claims, frustrated Sutherland. On paper the commission had power to make proposals and get them through, 'but the mood had changed. Maybe it has gone too soft but also you can only force a certain number of things. If you keep forcing it there will be a backlash.'

10

BROKERING THE URUGUAY
ROUND AND SETTING UP THE WTO

ON 16 APRIL 1994, THE NOW DEFUNCT IRISH Press newspaper carried a prominent photo of Sutherland on its inside cover page. The reason was that the day before, Sutherland, as director general of the General Agreement on Tariffs and Trade (GATT), had presided over the signing of the Uruguay Round of multilateral trade negotiations. It was a significant landmark and deserved recognition. But what made the *Irish Press* photo different was that it featured a series of arrows, pointing to Sutherland's features. The intention of this particular physiognomical exercise was to highlight the characteristics that had helped him succeed at the summit of international relations. Perhaps the photo said more about the pervading mentality in Ireland at the time than anything else. With the dark shadow of the bleak 1980s still casting a pall over pre-Celtic Tiger Ireland, confidence was extremely low. It was almost as if this was proof that an Irish person could succeed at the very highest level through their innate ability. Just because we were Irish didn't mean that our rightful place was at the back of the queue.

When Sutherland took up the position the previous year, few people rated his chances of success. GATT was part of the post-war global economic architecture established under the Bretton Woods

Agreement, which established the rules and institutions needed to regulate the international monetary system. The aim was to break down barriers to international trade. Most countries agreed it was a laudable objective, although there was very little consensus on how to bring about the removal of those barriers. Each individual government pleaded that it needed to protect politically or economically sensitive sectors. By the 1980s, advancements in technology and transportation meant that cross-border trade had become logistically easier than ever before. At a ministerial meeting of GATT members held in Geneva in 1982, a decision was made to launch a major new negotiation on trade. The talks broke down because of a failure to reach a compromise on agriculture, but enough common ground was forged to lay the basis for what became known as the Uruguay Round. In September 1986, at Punta del Este, the 123 ministers in attendance were able to agree an agenda that covered most areas of trade.

The scope of the Uruguay Round was more far-reaching and ambitious than any previous attempt to broker an international agreement on trade. New areas such as services and intellectual property were included in the agenda, as were commitments to reform trade in areas such as agriculture and textiles. The original timeframe set by ministers for the conclusion of the round was 1990. While there was widespread hope that an agreement would eventually be reached, privately many ministers doubted that such a schedule was realistic.

According to an official account of events, ministers met again in Montreal, Canada two years later, in December 1988, for what was supposed to be an assessment of progress at the round's halfway point. The purpose was to clarify the agenda for the remaining two years, but the talks ended in deadlock that was not resolved until officials met more quietly in Geneva the following April. Despite the difficulty, ministers did agree during the Montreal meeting a package of early results. These included some concessions on market access for tropical products – aimed at assisting developing countries – as well as a streamlined dispute settlement system and the Trade Policy Review Mechanism, which provided for the first comprehensive, systematic and regular reviews of national trade policies and practices of GATT members. The round was supposed to end when ministers met once more in Brussels in December 1990. But they disagreed on how to reform agricultural trade and decided to extend the talks. The Uruguay Round had entered its bleakest period.

Despite the poor political outlook, a considerable amount of technical work continued, leading to the first draft of a legal agreement. This draft 'Final Act' was compiled by the then GATT director general, Arthur Dunkel, who chaired the negotiations at officials' level. It was put on the table in Geneva in December 1991. The draft became the basis for the final agreement: its text fulfilled every part of the Punta del Este mandate, with one exception – it did not contain the participating countries' lists of commitments for cutting import duties and opening their services markets.

Over the following two years, negotiations lurched between impending failure and predictions of imminent success. Several deadlines came and went. New points of major conflict emerged to join agriculture: services, market access, anti-dumping rules and the proposed creation of a new institution. The resolution of differences between the United States and the European Union became central to hopes for a final, successful conclusion.

In November 1992, the US and the EU settled most of their differences on agriculture, committing to reduce export and domestic support subsidies in a deal known informally as the 'Blair House Accord'. There are echoes of the Brexit negotiations in the final push to gain agreement on the Uruguay Round. Theresa May, the British prime minister, would spend most of 2018 telling anybody who would listen that 90 per cent of the Withdrawal Agreement had been finalised between London and Brussels, and that the only remaining matter was to reach a compromise on the backstop for the Irish border – when in fact the backstop may have been only one item in the overall framework, but it was hugely divisive and irreconcilable.

Arthur Dunkel was a chain-smoking Portuguese-born Swiss civil servant who had been director general of GATT since 1980. Over those twelve years he had been the right man for the job. He had a painstaking eye for detail, a necessary pre-condition for putting an agreement of such complexity together. He was also good at cajoling countries to accept that reaching an agreement would require all member states to give something up. But by December 1992 he had run out of steam. Efforts to get a deal over the line were desultory. The previous month Bill Clinton had won the election to become the forty-first president of the United States. He had an ambitious agenda, including trade.

Clinton appointed Mickey Kantor as the US trade representative. Kantor, who would later serve under Clinton as Secretary of Commerce, says, 'Clinton was deeply concerned about the lack of momentum in the Uruguay Round. There seemed to be a lack of energy to make it happen. I was under huge pressure to get a deal done. I had nothing against Arthur Dunkel, but I knew it needed a change of leadership.'

Kantor knew Brussels-based lawyer Ray Calamaro, a specialist in trade who had met Peter Sutherland when he was still a European commissioner. The two struck up a friendship. Kantor had held talks in early 1993 with Leon Brittan, the European Commissioner for Trade. Both men agreed that a change of leadership was needed to get the Uruguay Round moving again, but finding a replacement who would be acceptable to the most powerful blocs within GATT was not going to be easy. When Kantor rang Calamaro in February 1993 to discuss the dilemma, Calamaro told him Sutherland had all the right credentials. Kantor did some background checks on Sutherland. 'He had shown tremendous guts and resolve as the attorney general in Ireland and again as a European commissioner. This was the sort of person we needed,' Kantor says.

At that stage Sutherland had already become chairman of AIB in Dublin. One close friend said it was a role he enjoyed, but he was bored. His period in the commission had instilled in him a deep interest in international affairs, and he harboured desires to become president of the European Commission. The role of director general of GATT was therefore enticing, but there were obvious pitfalls. Sutherland had developed a close relationship with Richard O'Toole, his chef de cabinet at the commission, and trusted his judgement probably more than anybody. So he rang O'Toole when an initial approach had been made about the GATT position. 'I said well, it seems to be bogged down in a lot of nitty-gritty. There is no guarantee of success because this show has been going on now for nearly seven years.' The key people in making an agreement work were the EU and the US, O'Toole told Sutherland. It was they who had to make concessions to other countries in order get them on board, and they also had to be willing to make concessions to each other.

O'Toole advised Sutherland that if he was thinking of taking the position then he would have to decide how long he was willing to commit to the negotiations, as well as discovering what sort of commitment he was likely to get from the big players to make it work and figuring out a strategy for making it come together. Sutherland rang O'Toole a few days later to tell him that he was more than likely going to take the job. He also asked O'Toole to examine the existing negotiations more thoroughly. That meant a trip to Geneva for a meeting with Dunkel to investigate the state of play.

'So I said okay and I went down to Geneva. Dunkel was extremely secretive. We met at a hotel close to Geneva airport. I went through the whole negotiation with him, and it was apparent to me that from a technical point of view, the bulk of the work was done. There were about seven or eight big core issues that needed to be resolved. But they were resolvable. Dunkel himself was very tired, he was worn out. I don't think his health was great and he was rather depressed – he was very pessimistic about the whole thing.' O'Toole went back to Sutherland and said he should give Dunkel credit for the progress achieved to date in successfully putting together the technical aspects of a future agreement.

Sutherland agreed, and would publicly acknowledge the role played by Dunkel on a number of occasions.

'I told Peter I didn't think he [Dunkel] had either the energy or the political force to move it further. That was why, in O'Toole's opinion, Dunkel was bowing out. Nor did he think the member states would be able to get fully behind Dunkel, because he was associated with too many of the technical decisions that had already been made. The problem, continued O'Toole, was that the trade experts were talking to each other in technical jargon, while what they were fundamentally dealing with at home were political issues. The process had to be taken out of the technical morass and given a political dimension that people could understand; the politicians could then be persuaded to make a deal on that basis.

Sutherland saw it the same way. 'And so he took on the job, and he asked me to come and work with him as an assistant director general. He managed to persuade the general council that that would be okay. So we soldiered again for two years.'

Arthur Dunkel died at the age of seventy-two in 2005 – broken by the talks, those closest to him claim. The following is an extract from his obituary in the *Guardian* newspaper:

But he was always philosophical. He saw his role in part as carrying the can for political leaders. A tall, lanky man with permanently bent shoulders and pockets loaded with Gitane cigarettes, he gave the impression of bearing a burden. In some senses, that was the case; Dunkel had an almost papal presence in the Gatt. He was neither a manipulator nor a servant of spin. Yet he understood the power of words. When he spoke, delegates listened and analysed. That is how he provided leadership, direction and vision while endowed with almost no executive power. His essential humanity and decency were uncommon in public life. He had no pretensions to cut him off from those with whom he worked, at all levels: members of the Gatt staff saw him queuing for coffee in the cafeteria, print room workers with whom he checked documents and hard-pressed interpreters got equal attention.[1]

Sutherland met Mickey Kantor for lunch in Brussels in March 1993. It was a crisp Sunday in the Belgian capital. 'I knew about twenty minutes through that lunch that Peter was the person. I have rarely met anyone like him. He had only about ten days to prepare for that lunch but he was extremely well briefed,' says Kantor.

Rufus Yerxa, a former US ambassador to GATT and by early 1993 an assistant trade representative under Kantor, also attended the meeting. 'After the lunch, I remember this distinctly, Kantor and Sutherland went for a walk and it was clear they hit it off pretty well. But Sutherland had one question for Kantor which he had also asked Sir Leon [Brittan], which was I'm not going to take this job unless I'm convinced that you are politically committed to finishing the Uruguay Round.' He needed Kantor's assurance, said Sutherland, that he wasn't wasting his time, that the US was committed to reaching an agreement. 'Kantor said to him in no uncertain terms that the Clinton administration was committed to finishing the deal. And then after that Sutherland agreed to it and basically the member states of the EU supported him.' Interviewed at the WTO in 2011, Sutherland himself recalled that lunch. 'Kantor said, look into my eye. I know you don't make history unless you make agreements. I knew he meant it. I rang him once from South Africa and used some very undiplomatic language over a disagreement. I said to him, remember what you said in the restaurant, now is the time to deliver.'

Kantor then met Leon Brittan. With the Europeans favourably disposed to Sutherland, Japan and Canada, the other two members of the grouping of countries known as the Quad, quickly came on board, and Sutherland was offered the job of director general of GATT. Sutherland officially took up the role on 1 June 1993; with Clinton pushing Kantor to have the talks wrapped up by the end of the year, it was a daunting task in almost every way.

On his first day Sutherland met with British Prime Minister John Major in Downing Street. It was a meeting of minds. The two men got along very well and developed a good rapport. Major assured Sutherland that he would give him whatever support he needed.

Even though a good deal of progress had been made since the commencement of the talks in 1986, Sutherland knew that if differences between the Quad member states were not resolved then the process could be easily derailed. Agriculture had been one of the main sticking points since talks first got underway. There was a yawning chasm between the US and the EU on agricultural products. If Sutherland was to succeed, then he would have to find a way of reaching a compromise. The Blair House Accord, finalised in November 1992, was merely a sticking plaster – as Sutherland quickly found out.

The next head of state he met was Edward Balladur, the prime minister of France. Balladur raised a number of red flags. He and Helmut Kohl, the German Chancellor, had held a number of meetings on agriculture, and both men issued a joint statement. This was interpreted by the French as meaning the Blair House Accord would have to be renegotiated. If that were to happen then it would be a major setback for the talks. A separate meeting between Kohl and Sutherland, however, proved to be extremely useful; Kohl not only signalled a willingness to back Sutherland, but gave him a number of tips on how to deal with the French.

Sutherland knew that the relationship with Balladur would be critical. Notoriously protectionist when it was in their interest, the French had the ability to veto the EU position, which in turn could collapse the talks. As Sutherland explained in a subsequent interview, he requested a one-on-one meeting with Balladur. 'I told him I recognise your concern, I recognise there is huge political pressure on you at home, but there must be an agreement. There has to be compromise. Whatever drawbacks you perceive in an agreement, they are nothing to the potential chaos that would result if there is no agreement at all.'

Sutherland then went to Japan, where he had a number of fraught meetings with farming groups over rice production and quotas, and to India, where tricky negotiations took place over the issue of intellectual property rights. 'A lot of things could have gone wrong,' says O'Toole. 'But I think all of those parties did make advances in their positions as a result of the persuasive effort of Peter, sufficient to make the thing come together.'

Roderick Abbott, number two on the European negotiating team, had his first encounter with Sutherland just after he had been ordered by his boss to withdraw all of the EU's bilateral offers to Japan because it had offered no concessions on footwear. Footwear was a long-standing problem with the Japanese. They had quotas and enormous tariffs, and they were not prepared to compromise on either. The Japanese negotiators insisted that they could not afford to offend that particular segment of Japanese society, says Abbott. 'So we withdrew all our offers, including our offers on shoes because they didn't reciprocate. And that led to me being summoned by Peter down to a meeting of his negotiating committee.' Abbott had been called to explain himself because withdrawing the offer to the Japanese affected other countries – in particular the Brazilians, who also sold footwear to the EU and issued a protest. 'That was quite a daunting experience,' says Abbott of his meeting with Sutherland. 'We were in the largest negotiating room, probably getting on for a hundred people, all very senior, and I had to go and dare say, "Look I'm sorry. These were my instructions and I carried them out".' Sutherland noted Abbott's explanations and urged the EU and the Brazilians into bilateral discussions, which eventually led to an agreement. The EU and Japan also settled their differences.

Abbott remembers that his main focus at the time was to ensure that the EU-Japan-Canada-US quadrilateral maintained progress in moving towards zero tariffs across a number of different sectors. 'We ended up with something like twenty different sectors where we all agreed to go to zero tariffs,' he adds.

The process entailed an extremely punishing schedule for Sutherland, who visited five continents during that period. He was also commuting from Dublin, as his family had not relocated to Geneva.

Sutherland was asked in 2011 what lessons from the Uruguay Round would help move along the Doha Round, which had hit an impasse after ten years of negotiations. He responded that the success of any negotiation hinged on ensuring that people in the right places were persuaded by the right arguments. 'People say I was a bit of a bully. I hope I did it with a smile on my face. I don't think I would have done anything differently. I had the right people around me. You have to get the right people. If you have a trade minister spitting bile into the ear of a prime minister you have a problem.'[2]

The skills picked up by Sutherland in the Law Library, probably more than any other factor, were key in getting the negotiations over the line: the cajoling, the gentle persuasion, the inability to take no for an answer. Mickey Kantor describes him as a 'force of nature. He was very charming, but I always knew where I stood with him. He was incredibly tough.' Rufus Yerxa says there were a few times when Kantor felt he was being pushed too hard by Sutherland on certain issues. 'But I don't think they ever really accused Sutherland of having a bias towards the European approach. Sutherland was willing to be really hard on the Europeans, particularly on some key issues like agriculture. And in those days we had fought out a lot of the US–European fights earlier in the round, so there wasn't really a problem in the closing stages – for example industrial market access, where the US insisted on a request offer approach rather than a Swiss formula.'*

---

* The Swiss formula is a harmonised mathematical approach to tariff cutting. The US wanted this replaced with customised agreements

The US eventually prevailed with that argument, while many of the market access negotiations were done on a strictly bilateral basis. 'My recollection of how Sutherland handled things is he didn't get involved in taking sides between the US and EU where we had differences, but he pushed us along to a solution and said it would be the US–EU blockage which was holding things up. And so he encouraged both sides to get over their differences.'

Yerxa says that as the December deadline approached there were many showdown meetings between Kantor and Leon Brittan. 'A lot of issues were still unresolved – a lot of agriculture issues, a lot of issues related to fights between the US and EU over aircraft subsidies and audio-visual, financial services, a number of other things.' Sutherland, says Yerxa, played a key part in several high-level, intense negotiating sessions. But his main task was keeping things rolling in Geneva, finalising the text in areas other than those where the US and the EU, and sometimes maybe Japan and Canada, were fighting.

Finally, after months of resolving issues in Geneva, while high-level bilateral negotiations simultaneously took place between the US and the EU, a basic deal to approve the text was reached in December 1993. 'Sutherland gained a reputation during that short period for being a very effective closer. He pushed everybody in the direction of a deal. He played hard ball with the Japanese, he played hard ball with the Europeans, he played hard ball with us. And eventually we got a deal.'

According to Abbott, Sutherland was very effective at ensuring that the core countries – the US, the EU, Japan and Canada – were all going in the same direction. By talking to their people, he would find out who was blocking what. After months of hard bargaining and compromises, the December deadline was fast approaching. It was inevitable there would be a few last-minute roadblocks. This, says Yerxa, was when Sutherland really burnished his credentials.

'He was a very persuasive speaker and a great advocate. He was also a very good lawyer, by the way.' He recalls one incident in the very closing hours of 15 December, there was still a deadlock between the US on the one side and India and Pakistan on the other over some language in the textiles agreement. The US chief textile negotiator Jennifer Hillman and the chief US negotiator John Smits were refusing to move, and so were India and Pakistan. Both were threatening to veto the whole deal after the US and the EU signed off on it. 'It was very late in the night. It was actually the night before we were all to meet in the International Conference Centre to sign off on the deal. I got a call at something like two in the morning to come down to Peter's office. We had a session to sort this stuff out. Kantor had gone to bed up at the InterContinental Hotel thinking the deal was completely done.' Kantor had refused to budge on the textile agreement and presumed that Sutherland would push it through.

But India and Pakistan would not move from their position and were demanding changes. 'Sutherland finally came up with the language during that session. He crafted some language himself with his legal reasoning and skills that he thought was a good compromise. And then he kind of forced me to say yes to it, but I told him I couldn't say yes to it until I talked to Kantor. I had to call Kantor at three thirty in the morning and wake him up.' Kantor was impressed with the final language, only asking if Yerxa thought Washington would find it acceptable. The consensus was that they would, and the deal was done. 'I make that point because it showed Peter's skill with crafting compromises and legal reasoning. He was a very good lawyer and he had a force of personality.'

As Brendan Halligan noted, Sutherland's ability to draft documents had been picked up during his early days in Fine Gael, learned from people such as Jim Dooge, Garret FitzGerald and Alexis FitzGerald. It certainly stood him in good stead at this crucial moment in his career.

Every country seemed satisfied. Most importantly, the US and the EU were willing to sign the draft agreement. A historic deal was in sight. Then, at literally the last minute, the Japanese ambassador raised a red flag that had the potential to collapse the entire talks. Seven years of intense and difficult negotiations were on the line. The US had insisted that anti-dumping regulations had to be very strong. The Japanese wanted to weaken them. There was a greenroom adjacent to the main negotiating room. Sutherland requested a bilateral discussion with the Japanese ambassador.

According to those present, what happened in that room would not be recommended in too many diplomatic handbooks. Sutherland pinned the Japanese ambassador against the wall. There was a lot of screaming and shouting – all coming from Sutherland, it should be noted. He demanded the phone number of the Japanese prime minister, threatening to ring him, even though it was the middle of the night in Japan, and tell him that his ambassador was about to wreck the first multilateral global agreement on trade ever achieved. When the ambassador declined to pass on his prime minister's number, Sutherland went ahead and announced at the main press conference that the deal would be signed by every member state. The stakes for the Japanese had been dramatically raised. The ambassador would have to publicly veto the deal if he wanted to follow through with his objections. He didn't. That was it. The deal was signed.

The main points that were agreed: the richer industrialised nations agreed to cut tariffs on industrial goods by 40 per cent. Over 40 per cent of trade would now be done on a duty-free basis. In the sensitive area of agriculture it was agreed that domestic farm subsidies would be cut by 20 per cent and subsidies on exports by 21 per cent. In terms of intellectual property, patents would be protected for twenty years and copyright for fifty years, while trademarks would be given stronger protection. New rules were introduced as to what constituted dumping, which is the practice of a country lowering the price of its exports to get an unfair market share. It made it much harder for a country to claim that products were being dumped so that they could unilaterally impose tariffs.

After each of the 125 countries that signed up to the agreement in December 1993 had gone back to their governments to sign it off, Sutherland banged the gavel at a lavish ceremony in Marrakesh on 15 April 1994 to officially conclude the Uruguay Round. Each country's representatives were requested to come to the stage when it was their turn to sign. As the Americans' turn came, they made no movement. Sutherland went down to the US delegation, which included Kantor and Al Gore, the vice-president. Kantor said, 'Peter, we have a problem and we can't sign.' Sutherland replied: 'No, you don't have a fucking problem. Get up there and sign or I will drag you up there.' Kantor laughed and turned to Gore, saying: 'I told you he would react like that.'

The agreement was 22,000 pages long and weighed 385 pounds. 'I'm tempted to do an Irish jig on this table to show what I think,' Sutherland told reporters at the ceremony. 'No one got everything they wanted, but that is the nature of these negotiations.' Sutherland was now in the league of international big hitters.

*

One of the more intriguing questions that arises is whether the Uruguay Round would have happened anyway. Was a consensus forming on the benefits of global trade that would have pushed the deal over the line?

Pascal Lamy says it was a combination of factors. 'It's a mix of circumstances, luck and Peter's own personal input in a very, very complex chemistry. The talks started in 1986, so there had been quite a lot of water under the bridge, but the experience of the negotiations, which I know well, doesn't tell us that having talked for so long the negotiations would succeed. I'm pretty sure Peter's input was pretty substantial. And that's the sort of memory he left in Geneva. Many people in Geneva think he came to the WTO to push his career and was not committed enough to the institution to stay much longer, which probably could have been the case. But again Peter was very ambitious – moving forward, taking one more bit of the ladder and then looking to another ladder was something which was substantial to him.'

Kantor, however, says it is unlikely that the Uruguay Round would have concluded without Sutherland's input. 'He was absolutely critical. I really don't think it could have been done without him. He was absolutely relentless. He had the right mix of charm and heft. Look at the Doha Round, it started in 2001 and there is still no deal.' John Major agreed at the time that in his opinion, the success of the Uruguay Round owed everything to Sutherland.

But the drama was not yet over. Later that year, when the trade deal was due for ratification by the US Congress, Sutherland got a call from the White House to say there was a problem. The Republican Party looked set to block it. Sutherland arranged to meet Newt Gingrich, the Republican Speaker of the House.

'He told me he had two problems. Agriculture and sovereignty. Agriculture was dealt with. I told him sovereignty had stopped the US from creating the ITO [International Trade Organisation] in the late 1940s. Sovereignty is not something you should be concerned about. I drew the distinction between the WTO and the EU. In the EU national courts can be invoked to support international agreements against their own governments. That is a degree of supranationalism beyond what we have asked for. But what we have done is ensure there are enough sanctions in trade so that if you don't comply with the adjudicating body of the WTO, there will be repercussions. So I said it is a major step forward and you should go with it. At the end of the interview he said, "I will". And that was how we got it over the line.'[3]

11

GLOBALISATION AND ITS DISCONTENTS

THE EFFECTS OF GLOBALISATION BECAME EVIDENT from the late nineties onward. It initially became a catch-all phrase for any type of economic, social and cultural changes. Sutherland was one of the early and most prominent defenders of globalisation, which made him a convenient bogeyman for critics across the political spectrum. Very often he was attacked for views that he never held. It is therefore apposite to put in context the type of globalisation that Sutherland favoured and why. One of the most significant achievements of the closing stages of the Uruguay Round was getting the US to accept the creation of the World Trade Organisation. It was something that Sutherland was immensely proud of. In an interview many years later he said: 'Like Jean Monnet, one of my heroes, I believed that creating an institutionalised legal system is key to creating an institution that will survive. I think that dispute settlement mechanism was the key advance. That is the huge success of the WTO.' He became the first director general of the WTO in 1994, before leaving a year later.

According to Pascal Lamy, Sutherland's departure from the WTO so soon after taking up the role, caused disquiet among his former colleagues. 'And who are we or am I to judge. But for quite a number of people, the fact that he then went to Goldman

142

Sachs and BP – one an investment bank and the other one an energy company, with all that happened with the environment that came to light – is something that, for many people, suggested that he changed sides in a way. I wouldn't say that, but I think this is the way it was seen by some. And the reason for changing sides was for the money.' But Richard O'Toole insists that Sutherland made it very clear when he took up the role in 1993 that he would do it for only two years. 'That was the commitment he gave.'

According to Mickey Kantor, Sutherland's career path after the WTO is not open to legitimate criticism. 'He did a magnificent job in public service. Why shouldn't he go to the private sector? I think it was a perfectly natural move.'

David O'Sullivan says Lamy's comment is a 'very French view . . . But I think you can regret Peter's departure from public service.' He wonders how Sutherland would have made his way back, even supposing he had served in the WTO for four years: 'What comes next? If you were French or German or Italian you could go back and be a minister. As a minister you could become a commissioner again. But there was no path back for Peter, once he chose not to stand for election, in Irish terms.'

Sutherland may have left the WTO and forged a very successful career in the private sector, but just as in the EU, trade was never far from his thoughts. He remained a tireless advocate of free trade, which he saw as one of the most effective ways of lifting people out of poverty. His views certainly resonated with the times. Bill Clinton was the US president, while in 1997 Tony Blair would become the British prime minister; the two leaders would champion the so-called 'third way'. In the 1990s, globalisation became the commonly accepted description of what was happening at a wider level in trade, commerce, finance, media and technology.

According to Roderick Abbott, who went on to become deputy director general of the WTO, the internet and the internationalisation of finance were more important than trade in pushing the globalisation agenda. However, a very interesting institutional dynamic that became evident during the Uruguay Round would later, he says, have much more profound effects on the political landscape. Up to that point, the political system had been primarily organised around the idea of the nation state. Political accountability resided at the level of national governments, because that was where the decisions were made. But during the Uruguay Round, Sutherland engaged directly with civil society and lobby groups. 'He started dealing much more with civil society because the nature of a trade negotiation had changed. Now you had all of these separate things like environment, like climate change, like health and education – all of which you could claim were impacted to some degree by a tariff cut or by a decision to eliminate a non-tariff barrier of some kind. Peter's legacy is that the whole nature of trade negotiations and trade agreements was going through this kind of change. And the stakeholders were absolutely changing.'

The changing dynamic between governments and civil society would have complex and unintended consequences. Most importantly, it changed the concept of political accountability. Key decisions that had very real consequences for the citizens of nation states were no longer the preserve of national governments, but were taken by people like Sutherland, at the helm of multilateral organisations. The rationale for European integration is that by pooling sovereignty, countries can better deal with issues such as climate change; or that, by negotiating as one bloc, the twenty-seven EU member states can strike much better trade deals than if they all individually pursued the same objective.

In the good times, and when the benefits were shared widely, most people were happy to go along with the new global order. After all, globalisation, particularly in the area of trade, greatly increased prosperity. But there would also be losers in this increasingly globalised world. Some industries in the developed world could no longer compete with cheaper imports from developing countries. The deindustrialisation of many developed countries devastated communities, which inevitably prompted a backlash.

Nina Pavcnik is Niehaus Family Professor in International Studies for the economics department at Dartmouth College, a US Ivy League university. Widely regarded as one of the world's leading experts on trade and globalisation, she says that trade on the whole can be beneficial for a country, but it generates winners and losers; the question then becomes how a government compensates the losers so that they benefit from globalisation as well. 'People knew that trade would have consequences for income inequality in a country, but the assumption was that a rising tide would lift all boats, i.e. those who were losing out might be lifted.'

After the Second World War, most international trade was between developed countries, but from the 1980s onwards much more trade took place between developed and developing countries. Trade between developed countries tends to be a win-win situation: companies benefit from economies of scale and innovation, while consumers benefit from cheaper goods. In general, says Pavcnik, this creates a lot of benefits and has no stark downsides.

But trade between a developed and a developing country creates a lot more conflict. The downsides are much more pronounced: some industries contract if there is no comparative advantage. Following the Uruguay Round, says Pavcnik, there was a lot more trade between developed and developing countries. 'And while everybody knew that trade has distributional consequences, I don't think anybody realised how hard some people would be hit by this. Countries like the US are not well equipped to deal with those made worse off by globalisation. This didn't become obvious until later on, in the late 1990s, 2000s and now. If you look at how much China impacted the US, it didn't become obvious until the last decade.' The effects, she points out, are also geographically concentrated, while the people who are most affected tend to be less well educated and older. It is much harder for them to adjust. 'Trade from a country's perspective is still a good thing, but there are also losses, and these are hard to address.'

Because the people hurt by trade are geographically concentrated, moreover, this undermines the tax base of the regions affected. And this has obvious consequences for the next generation, because there is less revenue available to pump into areas such as health and education. In other words, it can lead to a downward intergenerational spiral.

The politically loaded question then was, how would discontent with globalisation manifest itself? National governments were no longer in control of the forces shaping the everyday lives of their citizens. In one sense globalisation has created huge tensions and helped lead to a resurgence in nationalism. This is most obvious in the backlash against the EU. Indeed, the idea of losing sovereignty threatens to unravel decades of European integration of the kind Sutherland so assiduously promoted. Brexit was in part a response to globalisation. Another obvious manifestation of the backlash was the election of Donald Trump as US President. Trump campaigned on a platform of economic nationalism, while his presidency has been punctuated by frequent threats to start a trade war, particularly with China. He has even threatened to withdraw the US from the WTO. It would seem that Trump is an implacable opponent of any form of multilateralism.

Niall FitzGerald, the former chief executive and chairman of Unilever, says open markets are economically desirable, once they are properly managed. 'Brexit and Trump were not a direct rebuke of what he [Sutherland] stood for in terms of free trade and open markets. They were a rebuke of the political systems in the UK and the US which didn't ensure that the benefits of those had been more evenly distributed.'

FitzGerald attended Boston University in 2011 'to receive an award of some sort'. The title of his acceptance speech was, 'What happened to the American Dream?'

'I told the audience that I should probably address them from the door as they may want to punch me afterwards. I am a great supporter of the US. The economy has done many things: it is open and welcoming. The American dream was that each generation would do better than the one that preceded it. Within each generation, if you work hard you can move through the social strata. That was true until twenty years ago. This is the second generation that will be worse off than their parents: 90 per cent of the growth of the total economy has gone to 1 per cent of the population.'

His message to the audience that night was that even if their only motivation was to keep what they had, then they had better play a part in restoring the American dream. 'Because if you don't it will come back to bite you and destroy you. If you don't make a large body of society feel that they are participating in this in some way, then eventually your system will be rejected. That is what we have seen in the US, and that is what happened with Brexit.'

According to FitzGerald, Sutherland's work on migration was motivated by a desire to ensure that the benefits of globalisation were distributed evenly. 'Where Peter was less understanding was that one of the consequences is that there was a growing cohort in the developed world who were beginning to suffer. It behoved politicians in the developed world to ensure that the case for global free markets was not damaged by the growing disparity in the sharing of the rewards. Poverty might have been erased at an unprecedented pace in the third world, and that is what Trump has played to. It didn't need to be like that – that cost to blue-collar workers in the US and the UK.'

Assessing Sutherland's legacy is almost as complex as assessing globalisation itself. Klaus Schwab is the founder of the World Economic Forum (WEF), perhaps most famous for its get-together every January of the world's most powerful political and business leaders in the Alpine retreat of Davos. Schwab first met Sutherland at Davos in 1988 when he was European commissioner, while Sutherland was on the board of the WEF between 1995 and 2014 and attended every Davos meeting between 1988 and 2015. He was often depicted in profiles as 'Davos Man'.

Schwab claims that people tend to conflate globalisation and globalism, even though they are two distinct entities. Globalisation is a process that describes global linkages in trade and other areas.

Globalism is a philosophy which believes that everything should be submitted to the neoliberal forces of the markets. 'In my opinion it is a populist argument to mix up globalisation and globalism,' he says. 'Let me be very clear, I do not support globalism and neither did Peter.' Schwab says that over his close to thirty-year relationship with Sutherland, the two extensively discussed trade and related issues. 'Peter was the most sophisticated and deepest thinker on trade and globalisation I have ever met. I have never met anybody of his general intelligence. What mainly brought us together was our common philosophy, which was the stakeholder concept. Business should not only serve shareholders. It should also serve society. As a former head of the WTO, Peter was very much in favour of a rules-based, open system. But what I liked so much was his social responsibility. He believed in responsible globalisation, not unfettered globalisation.'

Following his career with the US government, Rufus Yerxa was deputy director general of the WTO for eleven years, and is now president of the National Foreign Trade Council in the US. He says that the globalisation Sutherland helped to create has been 'remarkably successful': 'The Uruguay Round and the World Trade Organisation is only a part of it, obviously. The vast majority has to do much more with technology, technological change, the information revolution and automation, and the remarkable changes that created in the ability to trade things. The interesting thing about the backlash against globalisation is that once people see the stark reality of the alternatives which are now coming out under Trump's version of economic nationalism, they will start realising how absurd that notion is and that a lot of globalisation is inevitable.'

According to Yerxa, the challenge for societies is not how to stop globalisation but to ensure that domestic policies, in terms of taxes, education, training and infrastructure, are calibrated for living in a more globalised world. 'I'm not sure that holding all the old structures in place with an old infrastructure of highly restrictive trade norms, in a world of expanding technology, would have worked. I certainly don't think it would have worked any better than what we have today. If we hadn't had the Uruguay Round, I think a lot more people would have been poorer. I don't have any doubts in my own mind that this was the correct direction to go. I do think that governments have been very, very slow in reacting to changing technologies and patterns of trade, and in making it easier and facilitating it rather than fighting it or not adapting to it.'

He accuses the US of being guilty of this more than most countries. 'I think Europeans have actually done a better job, but my own country is a classic example. And it has obviously led to greater wealth disparity and a certain segment of society that hasn't adjusted well at all. But that shouldn't mask the fact that millions of people have adjusted well. That's the ironic thing, millions and millions of Americans have adjusted well and are doing pretty well. But there is a segment of society that is doing less well than they were, partly because they were so highly protected in the past.'

According to Pavcnik, one of the most tangible benefits of the WTO is the dispute settlement mechanism: 'The WTO has been very good at focusing on trade-related issues.' A lot of the bilateral deals agreed over the past two decades, she says, have contributed much more to income inequality and the other downsides of globalisation than anything that was a consequence of the Uruguay Round. She cites the North American Free Trade Agreement (NAFTA): 'While NAFTA did have clauses that would protect workers' rights, ultimately they were just there to acknowledge those issues. They were in effect in the agreement to enable multinationals to gain access to those markets. You can't really say that with the Uruguay Round. There was a backlash, but Brexit was more about migration than trade. In European countries there is a better safety net and they are better able to cope with displaced workers. I think the backlash in Europe has more to do with migration, and by that I mean a clash of cultures. There is less of a backlash against trade. In the US, where there is much less of a safety net, there is a bigger backlash against trade.'

She says that neither Bill Clinton nor Barack Obama made enough provisions to cushion US communities against the downsides of trade when they negotiated NAFTA deals. 'The interesting thing is that the jobs are being outsourced to lower cost countries, but if that wasn't the case then these jobs would have been displaced by technology.' The problem of what to do with the displaced workers would have remained. 'The difference is there is a much bigger political backlash against trade. I don't view this as a failure of the Uruguay Round. I view it as more of a failure of a developed country's social safety nets.'

The backlash against globalisation did not start with Trump, however. From the late 1990s onwards, G8 summits (gatherings of the eight largest industrialised world entities to discuss current issues) were more often than not hijacked by anti-globalisation protesters, and the protests were often violent. The anger might have been inchoate, but it has become increasingly destabilising in political terms. The immediate effect of the backlash was to derail the Doha Round of trade talks.

Doha was supposed to be the follow-up agreement to the Uruguay Round, and it kicked off in 2001 with a much more ambitious agenda. Pascal Lamy was head of the WTO when Doha was launched. But it got off to a difficult start and never gathered the momentum needed for talks of this scale to succeed, generally lurching between crisis and standstill.

The first politician of international significance to publicly attack Doha was Hillary Clinton, who in 2007 was a US senator and had just declared her intention to seek the nomination of the Democratic Party for the 2008 US presidential election. In an interview with the *Financial Times*, she raised questions about whether it was worth reviving the stalled Doha Round if she were elected US president, and said that theories underpinning free trade might no longer hold true in the era of globalisation. She called for the US to take 'time out' on new trade agreements: 'I agree with Paul Samuelson, the very famous economist, who has recently spoken and written about how comparative advantage, as it is classically understood, may not be descriptive of the 21st century economy in which we find ourselves. I want to have a more comprehensive and thoughtful trade policy for the 21st century. There is nothing protectionist about this. It is a responsible course. The alternative is simply to pick up where President Bush left off and that is not an option.'[1]*

Shortly after Clinton made those comments in 2007, Sutherland took issue with her, also in the *Financial Times*, saying 'I was deeply worried by that intervention. It seems to me that the Doha Round is very, very important; it also seems to me that it is in deep difficulty at the moment.' First of all, he noted, it was often forgotten that the discipline brought by the WTO into trade negotiations, especially the integration of China into the global trading system, had been crucial in providing rules for the world-wide liberalisation of economies, which had led to years of sustained growth and had been very important in the development of the so-called BRICs – Brazil, Russia, India and China. 'If the Doha development round fails, and at the moment one cannot be confident at all that it will succeed, then this clearly has an effect on the global trading system. One aspect of that effect clearly will be the proliferation of regional, or inter-regional, bi-lateral trade negotiations, which I think is a bad thing. The so-called "spaghetti bowl" of agreements brought about thereby created confusion and undermined global intra-dependence. So I am very worried about the present situation.

'So, the way that the Doha Round seems to be taking second place in political discourse, the way that it seems to have been referred to by Mrs Clinton – and others, it should be said, in the United States are adopting a similar line – it seems to be a line that is popular amongst many in Congress – a somewhat more

---

* When Clinton finally ran against Donald Trump in the 2016 presidential election, Trump owed much of his victory to relentless tirades against free trade deals, particularly the NAFTA agreements. He blamed Clinton and the Democrats for previous trade deals that had allegedly damaged America's industrial base.

protectionist approach – and we've had evidence of it here in Europe as well, is quite the wrong way to proceed.'[2]

The last time Rufus Yerxa saw Peter Sutherland was at a conference in Salzburg in 2011. By that stage, the Doha Round was in deep trouble. Sutherland, he says, had taken the view that it was a mistake to launch the round because there was too little common ground between the major players. 'His view was now that it was started, it had to be finished. He was a strong supporter of finishing it. If he had still been director general of the WTO he would not have launched it that quickly.'

The commencement of Doha just seven years after the conclusion of the Uruguay Round was in part a misjudgement, felt Sutherland, on the part of the WTO's Pascal Lamy. 'He felt that Lamy was not very politically adept at finishing things. And I think he was critical of some of Lamy's decisions. On the other hand I think he didn't blame Lamy completely for the deadlock. I mean everybody knows it was more a function of deadlocks among the major players. And at the point we were in 2011, he gave a pretty dismal presentation to the Salzburg Seminar about the prospects for finishing the round and the embarrassment that it was creating for the WTO.'

In 2011, Sutherland was invited to write a report on the state of the Doha talks and what could be done to break the impasse. Titled 'The Doha Round: Setting a deadline, defining a final deal', the report was commissioned by the governments of the UK, Germany, Turkey and Indonesia. When Sutherland gave an interview to the in-house TV channel of the WTO in 2011, just after the report was published, he said again that the Doha Round was in real trouble.

'We find ourselves ten years into this round, even though in 2008 we were within a whisker of striking a deal that would be very important for the global trading system. Why this has happened is that the political will in vital areas has been absent. If this goes on then the round itself is doomed. I think it is a truly dangerous state of affairs. There is only a small distance left to travel. The fear is that multilateralism as an instrument in bringing countries together will be irrevocably damaged – there will be an absence of political will. I have spoken to a number of heads of government over the past number of months. They all express desire to conclude, but are they going to grasp the opportunity? It is insane if it is allowed to fail. Because it is a lose-lose situation if it fails, particularly for developing countries. The gains are incalculable. Putting figures on market access is extremely difficult, but we have seen figures of €360 billion as the minimum that could be expected from increased trade flows. That could be up to €750 billion with additional flows.'

Sutherland continued to say that significant benefits for consumers can arise from a multilateral trade deal – but because the process is as complex as it is opaque, it is hard to get public backing for these talks and that is why fatigue can set in.

'Businesses which were the motors behind previous rounds have backed away. I think this is tragic. After the war the World Bank and the IMF was created. The one piece that was missing has been the great institutional achievement since that is the WTO. We created a brave new world, which allowed us to integrate China, for example, in a rules-based global system. I remember going there and seeing plans they had which show a move away from a command economy to a market rules-based system. And that is what they have done. If you remove that and go back to the law of the jungle, to bilateral deals, where it is the powerful against the weak, then we are saying something that is very damaging to mankind. I know that might seem like a hyperbolic statement, but it isn't. What we have here is a demonstration of countries working together with a legal system at its core.'[3]

Sutherland concluded the interview by drawing lessons between where Doha was in 2011 and the Uruguay Round. The deadline system had been very effective in focusing minds in 1993, he said. 'I think it is needed again, because people are willing to go on negotiating forever in this city. But history will remember them because they can be identified.'

In the event, the Doha talks broke down irretrievably. Globalisation is now at a crossroads. The sort of multilateralism that Sutherland advocated is out of political favour. In fact, Donald Trump is openly hostile to the concept.

The context has changed considerably over the past two decades, says Klaus Schwab; those who support globalisation need to be mindful of the new landscape. 'We have to be much more aware of our eco-system. Things have to change if we want to leave a world that is still enjoyable for our children and grand-children. We need to change the structure of globalisation to make it more sustainable.' He argues too that although, from the 1980s to the early part of the current century, open markets created both winners and losers, there were mainly more winners than losers. Because of this governments found it a lot easier to remove trade barriers, and globalisation lifted hundreds of millions out of poverty. Today it is different, he says. 'The losers who are left behind have a voice. They are rightly looking for much more social justice and not being left behind. We have to maintain a rules-based open system, but at the same time every government has a responsibility to protect the social cohesion of its countries, so there is a fine balance that has to be made because social cohesion is needed for the functioning of a society.'

Sutherland, with his belief in a rules-based system, never argued for unfettered globalisation, says Schwab. 'But what we see today is that not everybody plays by the rules, and the rules have to be updated. The WEF has argued that we need international rules on things like artificial intelligence and blockchain. What is missing are two things. I think Peter would agree. We continue to need a rules-based system but we have to update those rules for today. I am a big believer in the Scandinavian model. We need to renew the social contract to look after those who have been left behind.'

Pavcnik says it is impossible to determine the direction of travel for the global economy. Citing the Trans Pacific Partnership (TPP), she doesn't expect that too many trade deals will be struck over the coming years. Donald Trump pulled the US from the partnership in 2017. Japan and Canada are exploring whether a trade agreement can be reached without the US.

'I'm hopeful that what is happening between the US and China in terms of a trade war is an isolated incident. In most cases globalisation has gone so far. We have interlinked supply chains and because of that globalisation won't take a step back. But it's just so hard to predict what will happen with Trump at the helm. It is very easy to criticise international trade. We have learned a lot from trade policy and the biggest lesson is that people get hurt. Because of this I'm hopeful that countries will spend more time addressing social safety nets in trade agreements.'

The area of corporate taxation and fairness, she says, will become a hugely sensitive political issue as it feeds into the perception of inequality. 'There was hyper globalisation over the past decade. Looking back now, most economists and policy makers still support free trade, but financial liberalisation is much more questionable. And the most political area of globalisation is migration.'

Corporate Career

12

ALLIED IRISH BANK: THE DIRT SCANDAL

TAOISEACH CHARLIE HAUGHEY'S REFUSAL TO OFFER
Sutherland a second term as a commissioner in 1989
meant he had some choices to make. In his four years at
the European Commission he had gained a reputation as a very
formidable operator. His stock was high both in Brussels and in
other European capitals. He had gained a taste for public life,
and according to those closest to him, if he had been offered
another prominent role he would have embraced it with both
arms. But there was no suitable vacancy.

Instead Sutherland returned to Dublin in 1989 with his family.
He resumed his career at the Bar, but only for a matter of
months. There can be little doubt that if Sutherland had stayed
at the Law Library, he would have ended his career as a senior
member of the judiciary. There is a long-running series in the
Financial Times every Saturday called 'Lunch with the FT'. The
conceit is that a journalist from the paper interviews a high-
profile figure every week, the details of what they eat and how
much it cost being an integral part of its enduring appeal.
Sutherland's lunch was the eighth most expensive in a series
that dates back to 1994. After an hour at Wiltons, Jermyn Street,
London, spent ruminating about Europe, globalisation, big business and migration, the bill came to £211.50. Sutherland

concluded the interview with a most interesting observation: 'I always saw myself as a jobbing barrister.'[1]

There is no doubt that Sutherland retained a passion for the law, but after four years of intrigue, brinkmanship and EU high jinks, the narrow confines of the Law Library would never satisfy his ambitions. Childhood friend Tony Spollen, visiting Sutherland just before Christmas 1988, asked what he was going to do next. 'He said: "I have to provide for my family".' In fact, says Spollen, Sutherland was offered some big directorships, allowing him to gain a good understanding of business. 'He knew his limitations. He wasn't a financial guy, he wasn't into reading profit and loss accounts or balance sheets, but when he needed advice he would consult the best. He was a very good chairman: he never spoke too much but he would never allow anybody else to speak too much either. He was able to defuse any situation with humour.' Paddy Kevans, another close friend, agrees that when Sutherland came back from Brussels he decided that business was the logical next step.

Ireland in 1989 was not exactly a bustling hive of corporate activity. The International Financial Services Centre in Dublin's docklands had recently opened and would go on to become a huge success, but there was little evidence of that yet. Political moves were being made in government circles towards the economic reforms that would presage the Celtic Tiger. For the most part, however, the economy in 1989 remained mired in recession, although the country had been enlivened by the heroics of the men's soccer team at the European Championship the previous year, and further success at *Italia 90* was to come. Indeed, some people attribute the first awakenings of modern Ireland to the heroics of Jack Charlton's team. It was no longer heroic to be a failure. But for anybody embarking on a career in business, there were slim pickings.

The banking sector in Ireland was small and underdeveloped, but although not free from controversy, it was generally trusted. The same year he returned from Brussels, Sutherland became chairman of Allied Irish Bank (AIB). At the time the sector was essentially a duopoly, with the Bank of Ireland the other dominant institution; the only other significant player was the arriviste Anglo Irish Bank, set up in 1986 and headed by executive Seanie Fitzpatrick, a relative unknown determined to break into the big boys' club.

AIB had been formed in 1966 through the merger of three banks: the Provincial Bank of Ireland, and the Munster and Leinster banks. For most of its life it had been a well-run and conservative bank. That would change in the 1980s, when it became embroiled in its first major controversy. It emerged in the mid-1980s that the London office of the Insurance Corporation of Ireland (ICI), a subsidiary of AIB, had been concealing heavy losses that could have potentially toppled the entire group. ICI had been underwriting a lot of new business, which made it look like a lucrative member of the group, but had not been putting aside enough reserves to cover its potential exposures. The revelation that there was a hole in its capital base created a political crisis. In March 1985, two months after Sutherland had taken up the role of European Commissioner for Competition, John Bruton, the Minister for Finance, announced in the Dáil that the government would take control of AIB's shareholding in ICI.

By the time Sutherland took over the chairmanship of the bank in October 1989, the ICI scandal had faded under chief executive Gerry Scanlan.* Sutherland would be at the helm of AIB for roughly three years. During that period, the group reported profits of IR£237 million in the year to 31 March 1990. In 1991, its reported profits were IR£178 million.

Con O'Callaghan was AIB's company secretary from 1988 until 1994. 'I liked him very much, he was very easy to work with. He wasn't into detail. He was into the bigger issues, not the nitty-

---

* The other board members included Maurice Abrahamson; Tom Cavanagh; Liam St J. Devlin; Patrick M. Dowling; Dermot Egan; Padraic M. Fullon: Peter Froggatt; John F. Keogh; John B. McGuckian; Raymond J. McLoughlin; Diarmuid Moore; Douglas Morpeth; Denis J. Murphy; Miriam Hederman O'Brien; Michael J. O'Keeffe; and Seamus J. Sheehy.

gritty. But that is the role of the chairman. I think at times he felt he didn't have enough to do.' They were quiet times, says O'Callaghan. 'There were no really stand-out moments. Sutherland was very popular among his colleagues, but he would not have been close to the executive on a personal level. His relationship with Gerry Scanlan, the chief executive, was business-like, but again they wouldn't have been friendly.'

To the outside world, nothing much may have happened during Sutherland's time as chairman. But internally there were developments that would have significant repercussions for the bank later that decade.

Deposit interest retention tax (DIRT) was a government tax on bank deposits introduced by Garret FitzGerald in 1986, during the Fine Gael–Labour coalition. At the time, tax evasion was a national pastime. The 'stroke' culture (that of being deceitful for personal gain), prevalent throughout Irish society, had taken on a life of its own when it came to tax evasion. Politicians, businesspeople, members of the clergy, prominent sportspeople and other pillars of society saw nothing particularly wrong with avoiding their tax obligations. The more complex the tax avoidance strategy, the more elevated the sneaking regard for it. Almost as soon as DIRT was introduced, people were looking for ways to avoid paying it, and the banks proved very useful in this respect. DIRT applied only to resident accounts, but physically moving out of the country to open up legitimate non-resident bank accounts was a step too far for most people. That is when banks had a Eureka! moment. Resident accounts could simply be reclassified as non-resident, which would take them out of the tax net.

Obviously this was not exactly above board, as it didn't require the account holders concerned to move abroad. As with a lot of things in Ireland back then, however, most people – except apparently for the revenue commissioners – knew it was happening. What was more, all the banks were at it, although AIB and ACC, the state-owned bank, were particularly aggressive. The other banks complained that AIB was attracting a lot of their customers because of its willingness to offer bogus non-resident accounts.

That began to change at the start of 1991, when a Revenue official called Tony McCarthy contacted Jimmy O'Mahony, the head of taxation at AIB, about the issue of bogus non-resident accounts. Exactly what was discussed and what was agreed at those meetings would subsequently become the subject of a parliamentary inquiry – but Donal De Buitléir, O'Mahony's deputy head at the AIB taxation department and previously a Revenue official, claimed at the time to have had extensive discussions with O'Mahony about his meetings with McCarthy.

'He said Revenue had made a proposal. It became known as "the deal".' Although De Buitléir had been in the Revenue, he claimed never to have been aware of the extent of the problem, but every bank had been involved. 'There were offers made to other banks at the same time.' De Buitléir says he had a meeting at the time with Revenue official Sean Moriarty. 'I said to him, "We [AIB] did a good clean up." He said "Yes you did, we checked." So we thought the problem was sorted.' As AIB understood it, the deal was that they would pay the Revenue IR£10 million to settle past DIRT liabilities, and they were to reclassify all bogus non-resident accounts as resident accounts that were subject to the tax.

Around the same time, the relationship between Sutherland's boyhood friend Tony Spollen, now head of internal audit at AIB, and the chief executive had become strained to the point where there was open hostility between the two men. Invited to a meeting at the end of January 1991 with two senior AIB executives, Spollen was advised that he was being transferred to a new role within the bank. Unhappy with the proposed move, which he viewed as a demotion, Spollen put together a dossier of potential liabilities facing the bank. He included the issue of bogus non-resident accounts, estimating that AIB's exposure was potentially IR£100 million. Crucially, in Spollen's view, the meetings between O'Mahony and McCarthy had concluded with a verbal handshake.

AIB had nothing in writing. Spollen said this could not be considered an amnesty. The dossier was intended for Scanlan, although he refused to take it, insisting that Spollen report directly to his line manager. Eventually a sub-committee, headed by Douglas Morpeth, was set up to look into Spollen's claims. It reported that there were no issues.

Spollen's future at the bank had, however, become untenable. Peter Sutherland was in an invidious position. He had been friends with Spollen since childhood and was loyal to him, but he was also chairman of the bank, and that conferred responsibilities. The last thing he wanted was for the dispute to end up in court. He brokered a deal between Spollen and AIB which involved a pay-off for the former.

John Blake Dillon, at that stage a partner with PwC, was in Sutherland's AIB office in February 1993 when the call came through from Mickey Kantor. According to Dillon, Sutherland was immediately flattered and interested by Kantor's proposal – to become the next director general of GATT. De Buitléir says the feeling in the bank was that it was only a matter of time before Sutherland moved on. 'When he was in the bank, a lot of the senior executives felt he was too big for the bank. He spent a lot of time there but he would be ringing Jacques Delors. That was his base. He would be operating at a global level.'

In 1998, Liam Collins, a journalist with the *Sunday Independent*, was given Spollen's dossier by one of his sources. (Spollen says he was not himself the source and has never met Collins.) Among the various issues contained in the dossier, Collins homed in on the DIRT liability. When, having done some digging, he eventually published his story in April 1998, it was the scoop of the year, triggering a chain of events that would shape the country's political landscape for some years.

Collins' story prompted the Public Accounts Committee (PAC) to examine the chairman of the Revenue Commissioners on the issue at a meeting on 28 April 1998. As a result of further substantial reports in the media, the PAC requested the chairman of the

Revenue Commissioners to attend a meeting of the committee on 13 October.

At that meeting the chairman said that Revenue had been unaware of the alleged scale of bogus non-resident accounts in AIB until the media disclosures in April 1998, and that no deal had been done with the bank in respect of unpaid DIRT. Representatives of AIB were then invited to attend a meeting of the PAC to respond to the chairman's statement. The meeting took place on 15 October 1998, with a delegation from AIB headed by Tom Mulcahy, now its chief executive, and including De Buitléir. At the meeting Mulcahy insisted that the issue of bogus non-resident accounts was an industry-wide problem rather than one specific to AIB. He added that Revenue had agreed with the AIB in 1991 that there would be no retrospective liability to DIRT in respect of interest on accounts wrongly classified as non-resident.

The governor of the Central Bank also gave evidence to the PAC on 15 October, and on 21 October the Dáil passed a resolution asking the PAC to examine any alleged settlement between the banks and the Revenue Commissioners in relation to undeclared DIRT and the use of bogus non-resident accounts. The inquiry began hearings in September 1999 that lasted for six weeks. They were televised daily on TG4 and dominated the news headlines for the entire period. The plot unfolded like a soap opera, only far more interesting. The animus that had existed between Scanlan and Spollen was laid bare. Revenue stuck to its line that there had been no amnesty, verbal or otherwise, in February 1991, while AIB insisted that there was. The tone was set by Fine Gael TD Jim Mitchell, chair of the PAC, whose questioning of AIB executives, including Sutherland, was unsparing. Even pre-crisis, bashing bankers played well with the electorate, and it was not unknown for rhetorical flourishes to be timed for the news bulletins. Sutherland's last interaction with the PAC had been during the Arms Trial when he defended Captain James Kelly. This time he was in the witness box.

Sutherland had moved on both from AIB and from Ireland itself by the time the DIRT scandal erupted. Nevertheless he was sensitive to ongoing developments. He was now at Goldman Sachs, which was due to float at the beginning of 1999, and stood to become a very wealthy man. If he were to be embroiled in a scandal at home, then it could potentially force him to resign from his Goldman Sachs role.

Called before the PAC to give evidence, Sutherland said that the bank had acted on Spollen's dossier. 'We did everything possible to examine the situation and concluded that there was no past liability, on the basis of what the bank believed had been agreed with the Revenue Commissioners. In terms of liability we were looking at the future.' Sutherland said he had relied on the word of De Buitléir, a tax expert, that the issue had been settled with Revenue. But the PAC in its report eventually came down on the side of Revenue, and AIB was forced to pay over €90 million in back taxes and fines. The Revenue Commissioners collected €859.2 million in total, including €225 million from the banks and €634.2 million from depositors who owed back taxes on the money held in the accounts. It had been the largest fraud ever perpetrated on the state – though those involved for AIB have never admitted liability.

The PAC also made an adverse finding against De Buitléir, who nevertheless says, 'I had contempt for the process because it was so nakedly political. Peter gave his evidence. I don't think he was tarnished. He was by some media people who didn't like him anyway.' According to De Buitléir, Sutherland had no role in the internal handling of DIRT in AIB. 'The whole thing was dealt with. It was a very good piece of public administration but Revenue didn't stand over it.'

*

In Spollen's view, Sutherland was unfairly maligned because of his chairmanship of AIB. 'The big thing that hit AIB was the investment in the Insurance Corporation, and that was before his time.' The bank had since had further problems; it emerged in 2002 that John Rusnak, a currency trader at Allfirst Bank, a wholly owned subsidiary of AIB, had concealed $691 million in trading losses. He was sentenced in 2003 to seven and a half years in prison. Rusnak, says Spollen, was nothing to do with Sutherland. 'The property lending happened way after his time.'

Spollen had left AIB in 1991. When the leak to the *Sunday Independent*'s Liam Collins took place in 1998, he says, 'I sat down with Peter and I explained that I didn't know Collins. I didn't leak it. In the middle of the PAC hearings we went out for dinner. Peter was not the chairman of the audit committee when I was there, and I suspect it was because of me. He told the PAC exactly as he saw it. Even during the hearings we would have gone for dinner quite a bit. He made it clear that he was representing the bank. Only once did we discuss the hearings and that was when Peter told me he knew that I didn't leak. He was completely fair to me and very nice. He was a barrister, so he looked at the facts.'

Sutherland would return to the AIB board after leaving the WTO, but he severed all ties with the bank in 1997. Having, like the other banks, embarked on a reckless property-lending binge in the early 2000s, in 2011 AIB would require a €21 billion bailout from the Irish government during the financial crisis. The upfront cost to the exchequer for bailing out the six domestic banks was €64 billion. The state rescue of the banking sector was partly responsible for forcing the country into an EU/IMF bailout programme in November 2010. Sutherland, who had close links to the finance sector, would get caught in the backlash.

13

FLYING HIGH –
THEN CRASHING – WITH GPA

ALONGSIDE THE CHAIRMANSHIP OF AIB, Sutherland held another high-profile directorship when he left the European Commission. Little did he realise, however, when he took up the position with Guinness Peat Aviation (GPA), that it would become one of the most colourful sagas in Irish corporate history.

Ireland is now one of the top centres in the world for aircraft leasing. Its success is largely due to one man. Tony Ryan, who was originally from Tipperary, had started his working life with Aer Lingus in 1955 at the age of nineteen. He held a number of positions with the fledgling airline, including postings to the UK and the US, before returning to Ireland in 1972 to take up a role in its aircraft leasing division. Tasked with leasing out Aer Lingus's surplus aircraft to other airlines, Ryan quickly discovered he had a talent for making deals. In 1975, he formed a joint venture between Aer Lingus and London-based investment bank Guinness Peat. With his headquarters in Shannon, he held a 10 per cent stake in the new company, Guinness Peat Aviation, with the remaining 90 per cent split evenly between Aer Lingus and Guinness Peat.

GPA became among the biggest of the few Irish business

success stories of the 1980s, and Ryan set up an airline named after himself along the way. His style – he was teak-tough and a very skilled negotiator – became legendary in Irish business circles. Denis O'Brien and Michael O'Leary are just two of the businessmen who started their careers under Ryan's wing. In 1990, when Sutherland joined the board, GPA made a profit of $242 million through lease agreements on 240 planes to 68 airlines in 41 countries, but it needed more capital if it wanted to expand. Ryan eventually agreed that the company would float on the stock exchange.

Sutherland even set up a meeting for David O'Sullivan with a view to joining the company. 'So I had a few conversations with them. I even had an interview with Tony Ryan. My wife and myself flew over.' There was talk of flotation on the stock market within a few years, which would have been extremely lucrative for employees had it been successful. 'I was honestly not convinced,' says O'Sullivan. 'I kept saying to Peter, so what happens with all these shares you loan me money to buy? What happens if something goes wrong? And he said, no, no, nothing can go wrong. I remember Peter Ledbetter saying to me over dinner that there were almost no circumstances in which he could imagine GPA going bankrupt. Now I had no business acumen whatsoever, I just had a kind of gut feeling that this wasn't quite for me. So I turned down the offer and came back and told Peter. And it was the first time I think I saw Peter clearly not happy with me. He harrumphed and said, "Well it's your future, but I think you are making the wrong decisions. You're turning down a huge opportunity, I think you are being timid."'

In 1991 Michael Lillis, after his secondment from the Department of Foreign Affairs to the European Commission, was back in Dublin on a break when he made contact with Sutherland. The two men had lunch in Ballsbridge, close to the headquarters of AIB. That afternoon Sutherland called Tony Ryan. 'I was told to go down to Tony for an interview, which was very interesting,' Lillis says. He gave up his career in the civil service and joined

GPA. Richard O'Toole also left the civil service to join GPA. Both men worked on plans for the company's initial public offering (IPO) – its launch on the stock market.

The GPA board was packed with heavyweights. As well as Sutherland, its directors included Garret FitzGerald, Nigel Lawson, the former British Chancellor of the Exchequer, and Sir John Harvey Jones, the former chairman of ICI. The flotation, planned for 18 June 1992, was the most ambitious offering ever undertaken by an Irish company. GPA shares would be floated on the London and New York markets as well as in Dublin. During 1992, the GPA management team went on a roadshow to meet investors. The feedback was generally positive, but this was a misreading of the general backdrop. The global economy and in particular the aviation sector were in a slump. If it had been successful, then GPA would have accounted for 20 per cent of the Irish stock market. Instead it was a spectacular flop. The shares collapsed as soon as they were put on the market.

Tony Ryan took responsibility for setting the share price. This was a fatal mistake; he had set the price far too aggressively. When institutional investors largely shied away from GPA shares on the day of the flotation, the management team took a decision to abort the IPO. It was both humiliating and financially disastrous. On 17 June, GPA had looked like a company that would dominate the Irish business landscape for the foreseeable future. On 19 June it was facing bankruptcy, with unsustainable debts and a shortage of funds.

Michael Lillis is in no doubt what went wrong. 'Tony [Ryan] made some big mistakes in the run-up to the flotation, in particular that it should float at a certain price which was just not possible. The flotation would have squeaked through if it had been floated at 60 per cent of what Tony was insisting on. Tony was a smart guy but he got that wrong.'

Attempts to rescue GPA were as colourful as the crash. Lillis, who was friendly with the son of the Emir of Kuwait, was involved in one such effort. 'They were interested but they backed off.

Then we went to Mexico, where there was a guy of Irish ancestry called Rómulo O'Farrill, whose ancestors had gone to Spain in the seventeenth century from Longford. Like many families they did very well.' O'Farrill, who had extensive holdings in telecoms and the media, was the richest man in Mexico at the time and held a position as Irish honorary consul. He came to Ireland, to Ryan's place in Tipperary. 'He owned four Gulf Stream Fours. He brought all of them over.' Brown Thomas, the upmarket department store on Dublin's Grafton Street, was opened for a private shopping session for the O'Farrill family on a Saturday morning. According to Lillis, it required two trucks to ferry the shopping to the airport.

'Rómulo, who was eighty-two, piloted his own plane. We arrived that night in Mexico City. The customs guys came out to unload the plane,' Lillis says.

Next day, recalls Lillis, he, O'Toole and Ryan had lunch with ten of the richest men in Mexico. 'The most spectacular lunch I have ever seen in my life.' Towards the end of the lunch Lillis turned to Ryan with a simple injunction. 'I told him, "For fuck sake would you say something".' It was not an unreasonable request, as the Mexicans were willing to put up $1 billion to rescue GPA. 'He just couldn't do it. It offended his dignity. Don't ask me to explain. The deal was there to be done. The documentation was ready. All that needed to be done was for Tony to say, great that you are interested, now let's sign the papers. He just wouldn't do it and he lost his company.'

*

General Electric picked up most of GPA and Lillis went to work for the US firm. But there was a sting in the tail. Most of GPA's senior management team had taken out loans to buy preference shares in the company. The shares were worthless, which left many of them nursing heavy losses. Sutherland had bought 34,000 shares, which put a dent in his wealth, but he had sufficiently deep pockets to absorb the losses; Garret FitzGerald, who had taken out a loan of IR£170,000 from AIB to buy his 45,000 shares, repaid IR£40,000 of the loan, and AIB – still under Sutherland as chairman – wrote off the balance. There were accusations of a sweetheart deal between Sutherland and FitzGerald. But when the deal was scrutinised by the Moriarty Tribunal, it was revealed that FitzGerald had sold his home and used the profit to pay down his AIB debt. He had no other assets. Confronted with the choice to bankrupt him or write off the debt, it had chosen the latter. There were no findings against either the former Taoiseach or Sutherland.

14

GOLDMAN SACHS

'THE FIRST THING YOU NEED TO KNOW ABOUT Goldman Sachs is that it's everywhere. The world's most powerful investment bank is a great vampire squid wrapped around the face of humanity, relentlessly jamming its blood funnel into anything that smells like money.'[1]

These are the opening lines of a 2010 article written by Matt Taibbi for *Rolling Stone* magazine. The piece chronicles how many Goldman alumni have seamlessly made the transition to running the world's central banks and getting their hands on other levers of power. The article struck a chord with many. The vampire metaphor had been deployed with dizzying frequency during the financial crisis. It is not hard to imagine why Goldman Sachs has become a lightning rod for disaffection on both the left and right. Founded in 1869, it is by far the most successful bank in the history of finance. In 2018, it had over 36,000 employees worldwide, and global revenues of $36.6 billion.

September 2008 was the inflection point in the global financial crisis. The collapse of Lehman Brothers in the middle of that month threatened to bring the entire banking edifice down with it. When the US government stepped in and launched the $700 billion troubled asset relief programme (TARP), Goldman Sachs received €10 billion in TARP funding, and the suspicion has always been that Goldman's alumni on Capitol Hill intervened to ensure its survival. It is one of many accusations that have mired the firm in controversy over the past decade. For example, it emerged that Goldman Sachs had made profits of roughly $4 billion by shorting the US sub-prime market, even though the bank had helped put together the underlying assets, and it was fined $550 million by the Securities and Exchange Commission (SEC) in 2010. It was also revealed, when the sovereign debt crisis erupted in Europe and Greece was forced into an EU–IMF bailout, that Goldman Sachs had helped the country manipulate its national accounts so that it could qualify for membership of the European Monetary Union.

But Goldman Sachs is not the only financial institution to have been found guilty of misconduct. What is now obvious is that in the decade leading up to the 2008 financial crisis, light-touch regulation fostered an 'anything goes' culture. The majority of investment banks were guilty of misdemeanours of varying gravity. Goldman Sachs was far from the worst offender.

There is another reason why Goldman Sachs is a lightning rod for widespread disaffection. The British Labour Party, under the leadership of Jeremy Corbyn, has been engulfed by an anti-Semitism scandal over the past few years. Leading members of the party have been accused of condoning abuse directed both at the Jewish community and at Jewish members of the Labour Party itself. Corbyn was embroiled in the scandal in March 2018 when it emerged that in 2012 he had liked a Facebook post of a mural in east London that was replete with several anti-Semitic tropes. He subsequently apologised. When David Baddiel, a British Jewish comedian, went on the BBC's *Daily Politics* show a few days later to discuss the incident, his argument was that there is a belief system among the hard left that equates Jews with finance and secret plots to rule the world. Goldman Sachs has become a convenient shorthand for this narrative.

*

It was a line of attack that was often used against Peter Sutherland, particularly when he became UN special representative for migration in 2006. However, Sutherland's relationship with Goldman Sachs goes back to a different era. Having joined the bank in the early 1990s as a regional adviser, he left when he became director general of GATT. Then, after the success of the Uruguay Round and the establishment of the WTO, he returned to Goldman Sachs when Gene Fife, based in London as chairman of Goldman Sachs International, recruited Sutherland as his successor – a choice backed in New York by Steve Friedman, the global head of Goldman Sachs, who had developed a friendship with Sutherland during the latter's first stint with the bank.

'The first period of association was very important. He [Sutherland] got to know us and we got to know him,' says Richard Gnodde, current vice-chairman of Goldman Sachs and chief executive of Goldman Sachs International. 'Obviously the role of adviser is quite different to the second role. In the advisory role he had no legal governance issues. He wasn't a full-time employee. But he would have got to know the firm well. He had a very large network and understanding of Brussels. He knew everything about Europe. He had banking experience with AIB. He wasn't a businessman, but he had networks and he had bundles of energy. GATT and WTO enhanced his reputation and he seemed like the ideal candidate.'

Before Sutherland accepted the most senior role in London, he went to the US to meet Goldman Sachs' top brass. Among them were some of the most exalted names in the world of finance, including Henry 'Hank' Paulson.

'1994 was a terrible year for Goldman Sachs. We had significant losses. Steve Friedman came in after Labor Day and said he was having heart problems and he needed to leave immediately,' says Paulson.

Friedman, according to Paulson, was going through a personal crisis at the time. 'His son had come to him and told him he wanted to be a writer.'

'Steve has got a son who is a real talent. If you follow the TV programme *Game of Thrones*, his son is the screenwriter on that show. He goes by the name of David Benioff. Peter [Sutherland], even though he had only been in Goldman Sachs for a short while, took great pride in getting David into Trinity College Dublin.' Benioff studied Irish literature at Trinity for a year from 1995. While at TCD, he met D. B. Weiss, who would become co-creator of the *Game of Thrones* TV programme.

'Decisions had to be made immediately,' continues Paulson. 'I had spent my career in Chicago. I had run investment banking from Chicago. I had turned down various promotions because I wanted to stay in Chicago. I also ran Asia and Private Equity. We picked Jon Corzine, but nobody was comfortable with Jon Corzine running Goldman Sachs by himself, so he was chairman and I was vice-chairman and chief operating officer.' As Paulson explains by way of context, Corzine remained chairman while Paulson was elevated to president. The deal was stitched together very quickly, and it was not to last. Corzine was eventually forced out – he became a Democratic senator for New Jersey and then governor of the state – and Paulson ended up running the firm.

Before he left, Friedman informed Paulson and the rest of the managing partners that he was working to bring Sutherland to the firm. 'He told us he would be a great addition to Goldman Sachs,' says Paulson. He was 'a very special guy', Friedman had said; the youngest ever attorney general in Ireland, with impressive achievements at the European Commission and the WTO. Friedman was sure Sutherland would do a great job and was keen for Paulson and Corzine to meet him.

Corzine gathered the Goldman Sachs management team for a weekend in the Hamptons at the end of 1994. 'He said that he would ask Peter to meet us all,' says Paulson. 'So Corzine said, as only Corzine could, "I want to meet Peter before you do. I am going to ask him to come on the Thursday and I want you to come on the Friday." So that was my first introduction.

'My first impression of Peter was that I liked him. He had very good people skills. I was sceptical about what role he could play at Goldman Sachs. I knew he had been a very good politician with very good experience of government.' Paulson himself had some small experience of government in his youth, having worked at the Pentagon immediately after leaving business school and going on to work in the White House, and he remained sceptical as to what Sutherland might be able to offer.

Friedman told him that Sutherland's expectations would have to be managed. He had plenty to offer to Goldman Sachs' culture and would be a great asset in Europe, but he would not immediately understand the business. He would not be a member of the management committee, a situation Paulson would have to find a way of managing. 'We were a partnership, he would be a partner, which had some very significant economic benefits. People worked very hard to become partners. I met him and liked him and said he is somebody who is going to be good. I think Goldman Sachs does it better than anybody else. We did it later with Mario Draghi and Mark Carney.' Draghi was president of the European Central Bank between 2012 and 2019, while at the time of writing Carney is governor of the Bank of England. 'A good number of former partners have gone back and forth.'

When senior political people go to banks, says Paulson, they very often make a lot of money but they are unhappy because they are relegated to secondary roles. 'And they find that people would hit them at the knee if they acted like they did in the political world. So I met him [Sutherland] and I liked him and I thought I sure hope it goes well because this is a real talent. But how would the integration work?'

John Thain and John Thornton were the two executives underneath Gene Fife in Goldman Sachs' London office.* When Fife left the London office, says Paulson, he had concerns about the future of the operation. '[Fife] was the cultural glue. John

---

* Thain would subsequently become the head of the New York Stock Exchange between 2003 and 2007 and then chief executive of Merrill Lynch before it was taken over by Bank of America in 2008. Thornton left Goldman Sachs for academia in the mid-2000s as his chances of becoming chief executive of Goldman Sachs receded.

Thornton and John Thain were really arrogant. They were really bright and really young and they really knew how to offend people. I bonded with Peter because he had an expectation that he would go on the management committee.' But the management committee was not intended for people in senior positions or with senior titles. It was for the people who were running the businesses day-to-day – the heads of equities, fixed income, investment banking, for example. There was no role for Sutherland in that equation, and somebody would have to go to London and explain this to him. 'I said I wanted to do it. Jon Corzine said he wanted to do it. I called one of my contacts in London and said how did things go, and he said I wonder did Corzine tell him, because I have never seen Peter look so happy.' When Paulson asked his contact to find out what Corzine had said, it turned out that he had told Sutherland he would join the management committee the following April.

Paulson approached Corzine and asked why the offer had been made. 'It keeps him happy,' was the reply; anything might happen before April. 'He'll figure out he isn't going on it by then,' said Corzine. 'I just want to keep him motivated in the meantime.'

Paulson was appalled: 'It was part of the reason I ended up not working with Jon.' He was left with no option but to meet Sutherland and explain the situation. When he did so, 'I became a huge fan of Peter Sutherland. Corzine had offended him beyond belief and made sure he was never going to be a fan of Jon. But Peter is a very unique man. He could be blunt but do it in a very eloquent way. He wasn't the sort of person who told people what they wanted to hear. He was straight. He had great people skills and great judgement about people.'

Sutherland officially took up the role of chairman of Goldman Sachs International in September 1995.

*

Adrian Jones is probably one of the most senior Irish-born executives on Wall Street. The former Irish army cadet is the managing partner of the Principal Investment Area of Goldman Sachs, having joined the firm in 1994. 'Peter came to New York in 1996 for an internal conference. I saw him and introduced myself. I had read about him and I was very proud that he was joining the firm. He spoke to me for about ten minutes and wanted to know how somebody from Roscommon could end up working for Goldman Sachs in New York. He was very interested in people. A few weeks after that, he called me and said he wanted to hire a new chief of staff in London and would I be interested.' Sutherland carried out a background check on Jones through Josh Bolton in the New York office, who would become George W. Bush's White House chief of staff in 2006. Sutherland and Bolton remained good friends.

'I went over to London in late 1996,' Jones says. 'I knew I wanted to do it. It was an opportunity to work with Peter Sutherland for a year. I moved over in April '97. The formal part of the job was to make Peter as efficient as possible in impacting the firm's strategy. He had been at the firm for a year. He had a golden Rolodex.' Having been a big name and a big presence, Sutherland was coming into a firm with a very strong culture and a very narrow hierarchy. Jones's job was to make the transition as seamless as possible, to ensure he had a chief of staff who understood the firm and made sure they got the best out of him.

Sutherland now had many outside interests. He was already on five international boards, and in April 1997, when Tony Blair won the UK general election, David Simon, chairman of BP, went into government. Sutherland stepped up to take over. 'He had a lot of plates in the air and I needed to make them steady,' Jones added.

According to Adrian Jones there were real consequences for what Sutherland could do at Goldman Sachs. 'For me over the next year it was managing that balancing act. He took a role chairing one of the UK's biggest PLCs. It probably created challenges in terms of how much he could be integrated into Goldman Sachs. It may have caused tensions higher up.'

Gnodde, though, says there was never any tension at Goldman Sachs about Sutherland's role at BP. 'He was a workaholic. He had more than enough energy to do both.' Goldman Sachs used Sutherland both internally and externally. 'Externally we used him for government relations and navigating Europe. We were a much smaller organisation at that time. That guidance and access and ability to develop relations was extremely helpful.'

'He had great intellect and intuition and knowledge about people and structures. He understood politics extremely well. I think it is fair to say he was unlike anybody else at Goldman Sachs, either in London or New York.' Sutherland's history, says Jones, was very different from that of the bank's other employees. 'People in Goldman Sachs usually joined in their twenties. He was used to dealing with heads of state. He could get on with and disarm different types of people. That is a challenge for people who don't understand public life. He could navigate that public–private realm very easily.' If seasoned politicians in their late sixties or seventies in a country that was important to Goldman Sachs were confronted by a group of aggressive bankers thirty years their junior, that could create difficulties. Sutherland would be extremely important in navigating such situations. 'He was European to the fingertips. The firm at the time was more international than global. He was able to shape issues that were sensitive to Europeans and Asians, able to make sure there were no cultural misunderstandings.'

Sutherland became a mentor for other Irish people at the bank. Gnodde recalls his first encounter with Sutherland, just after he became chairman. 'I got an invitation to a gathering. I was quite junior. I thought this was really nice of him. I got there a few minutes after everybody else, there were about fifteen people in a huddle with Peter in the middle and then the penny dropped. He had obviously asked human resources for a list of Irish people.

I carry an Irish passport, and so my HR file would have me down as an Irishman.'

Basil Geoghegan joined Goldman Sachs a month before Sutherland. He had trained as a solicitor and worked with Slaughter and May in London for the previous two years. The two had first met in 1991, when Geoghegan was doing a master's in European competition law at the European University in Florence, and they quickly developed a good working relationship. 'Peter was a very intelligent man. He could master a brief very quickly. I used to write up memos for him when we were going to see clients. When Peter joined Goldman Sachs it was not the behemoth it is now. It was very much the challenger bank. It was not part of the establishment. His address book was clearly important. He was a very quick thinker. He had opinions that counted. People wanted to hear what he had to say about world trade, about European integration. One of the internal sayings in Goldman Sachs was that important people liked important people to be important. He embodied that.'

Hugo MacNeill, who had played full back for Ireland in the Triple Crown-winning team of 1982, was yet another high-profile Irishman at Goldman Sachs. In 2000 he made the decision to leave the firm and move back to Ireland. Sutherland asked him why he didn't consider opening a Goldman Sachs office in Dublin. 'I said if we are going to do this, I am going to need your support. And he always did. We ended up working with C&C, Smurfit Kappa, Aer Lingus, Eircom. He understood Europe. He was very passionate about Europe. To have somebody like Peter and his judgement was a tremendous asset. He spoke his mind. He would tell it straight. He was a great ambassador. He was also a great mentor and was a great counsel.'

Adrian Jones explains that Sutherland's role didn't entail getting involved in the nuts and bolts of the business. 'It wasn't that he didn't have the intellect to understand what we were doing. He was an extremely intelligent guy and could bring tremendous focus. But there were big swathes of what we did he just didn't find interesting.' One of Jones's roles, he says, was to figure out which meetings it was useful for him to attend – and if he did, what parts of the meeting were relevant to him. 'He was a terrific salesman and ambassador for the firm, but he could not get interested about shaving a few basis points off borrowing costs and he wasn't going to sit there and talk about that. Peter didn't want to be in a room with a client who was just interested in the finer points of finance. He learned to focus on the stuff that matters.' Sometimes, when Jones asked Sutherland if he wanted him to go over a certain subject in more depth, 'his eyes would roll and he would say maybe I should dig a little deeper into this, but we have thousands of quantitative analysts who are paid to understand this. Peter wasn't hired to be an additional smart quant guy. He was hired to help in the areas where we weren't strong.'

Sutherland's focus in his work for Goldman Sachs most often related to geopolitical matters. 'There was tremendous focus on about a dozen countries, mostly in eastern Europe, but the dynamic was also changing in Russia and Turkey – countries where there was huge sensitivity around the western mindset and sensitivity about being patronised, and a wariness about the Anglo-American banker just fetching up in town. This was low-hanging fruit for Peter. Through the WTO he understood these countries. Being Irish was very important because he understood empathy. He was also very important in terms of privatisation mandates in India.'

Gnodde says the two men never discussed Sutherland's lack of executive experience. 'He had strong executives underneath him at all times. The complexity of the business was such that he was never going to master all of it. He drove the firm forward on reputational issues, governance issues.'

Paulson says Sutherland was important in terms of developing the culture and identity of Goldman Sachs in London. 'He had a real mature presence who looked at Europe the way it should be looked at, as a major power centre. He was somebody whose

February 1960 Gonzaga Junior Cup team. Sutherland can be seen at the front, kneeling, second from left.

The 1969–70 rugby season, Landsdowne Football Club. Sutherland can be seen on the back row, third from the right.

Called to the Bar, 1968. Sutherland can be seen on the back row, second from the right.

The attorney general in his office, 1982.

Meeting of the first Delors Commission, 1985. Sutherland is seated at the front of the picture.

The EU Commissioner cabinet. From left to right, David O'Sullivan, Eugene Regan, Richard O'Toole, Peter Sutherland, Colm Larkin, Catherine Day and Michel Richonnier.

The EP President awards a medal to Commissioner Peter Sutherland in December, 1988.

Sutherland, then chairman of AIB, with the bank's then chief executive, Gerry Scanlan, 1991.

A press conference after BP and US oil giant Amoco announced plans for their merger. From left to right, Sir John Brown, Laurance Fuller and Peter Sutherland.

Sutherland as head of GATT at the Uruguay round of global trade talks. Richard O'Toole is to the left of Sutherland.

Peter Sutherland as General Director of the GATT shows one of numerous documents on the final act of the Uruguay Round, 15 April 1994.

Secretary-General Kofi Annan meets with Peter Sutherland, Special Representative of the Secretary-General for Migration, in Davos, Switzerland.

A joint press conference at the conclusion of the Global Forum on Migration and Development. From left to right, Esteban Conejos, Undersecretary for Foreign Affairs of the Philippines, Secretary-General Ban Ki-moon and Peter Sutherland.

Sutherland addresses the Security Council meeting on cooperation between the United Nations and regional and subregional organizations in maintaining international peace and security.

Sutherland visiting a refugee camp in Athens, 12 May 2016.

Sutherland with Angela Merkel and Martin Schulz at the Valletta Summit on migration, 2015.

Sutherland with Pope Francis at the Vatican, 26 June 2015.

Peter Sutherland and his family at the 2007 Business & Finance Awards in Dublin.

judgement about reputational risk and what Goldman Sachs should or shouldn't be doing was great. He was a cultural glue. All sorts of people who were on the way up could go and talk to him in a way they couldn't talk to other people.' Paulson said that when the time came for him to decide what to do with his career, he realised Jon Corzine wasn't the right leader for Goldman Sachs – because of their poor working relationship. Also, when he was making decisions about John Thain and John Thornton, neither of whom in his opinion were the right people to run Goldman Sachs, Paulson added that Sutherland had been an enormous help. 'So that relationship evolved to the point that I used him as a real partner. He never became a real expert on any part of our business, but he learned about every part so as to have good judgements on how to keep the firm out of trouble. He had a terrific nose for risks and reputational risks.

'I loved the fact that he lived in Britain, but neither he nor I could abide the upper-crust Brits who had all gone to Oxford or Cambridge; the sort who looked down their nose at the rest of us; the sort who smiled while they dissembled. I think Peter's legacy is that. Goldman Sachs International became a big international bank. It became a big European bank. Gene Fife gets a lot of credit for that and Peter Sutherland gets a lot of credit for that.'

*

The flotation of Goldman Sachs in 1999 made a lot of people extremely wealthy. Sutherland himself made $120 million from the initial public offering; according to the *Sunday Times* Rich List in 2017, he had a personal fortune of €153 million. Sutherland had only been with the bank in an executive capacity for four years before it floated, making him very much the exception among the partners who had cashed in. The vast majority of them had spent their careers at the bank and worked their way up through the ranks. 'There was probably a lot of people looking at Peter saying where did this guy come from,' observes MacNeill. 'But when people got to know him that put an end to any question marks.'

Hywel Jones, who had worked with Sutherland on the Erasmus programme, developed a friendship with him after the European Commission. Every year they would meet for the Ireland v. Wales match in the Six Nations rugby tournament. When it was played in Cardiff Sutherland stayed with Jones; when it was played in Dublin, Jones with Sutherland. Jones recalls the first such match after the flotation. 'I never understood why he went to BP and Goldman Sachs.' Finding himself in a car with Sutherland on the way to Cardiff, Jones was shocked by how much money he had. 'I told him he had to do some good with it. That was just after he got a cheque.' Jones told him to set up a foundation. 'He was generous. He gave me some money for the European Research Centre. I thought he should have given us more. He saw his children right. He gave money to the Sutherland Centre in UCD.' Sutherland did give away a sizeable chunk of his windfall, but it was done privately.

Perhaps unaware of this, Jones feels he could have done more. 'I don't understand why he stuck with it. He had a good period with BP and Goldman Sachs. He could have pulled away and his voice would have been stronger. People knew what he was earning. He reacted calmly. He didn't mind me saying it. We were good friends. But he wasn't listening.'

Sutherland won the lifetime achievement award at the Business & Finance Awards in 2007. He was among the cream of Irish business that evening, but his speech was quite a departure for such an occasion; he felt 'a bit of a fraud', he said, for being the recipient of such a prestigious award as he was not a businessman in the orthodox sense. According to friends he was acutely aware that he had moved to the private sector relatively late in his career and lacked the executive experience of some of his peers.

*

When Hank Paulson left Goldman Sachs in 2008 to become US Treasury Secretary, he would have to preside over the bailout of the US financial system. 'I called him a couple of times when I left. When I left I went to the Treasury, so I was cut off from Goldman Sachs.' Sutherland provided significant assistance for the Irish government when it was caught up in the sovereign debt crisis. 'I was not one of the people he contacted. Ireland got into trouble in the backend of the crisis. I was dealing with the big European countries. I knew that he was doing that on behalf of Ireland.'

Aware of the backlash Sutherland faced when the economy turned in 2008, Adrian Jones says it wasn't all about Goldman Sachs. 'There was BP as well and RBS. He became a piñata.'

Gnodde emphasises Sutherland's loyalty to Goldman Sachs. 'He did his public service, in Ireland, Europe and at the WTO. He had built up a great reputation. But all of his wealth came from Goldman Sachs, it didn't come from anywhere else. It gave him a remarkable platform.' Alongside the BP chairmanship, the two roles were critical pillars of his business career. 'He was a partner when the firm went public and he did very well. He did very well for the firm, so he deserved to do well. Peter wasn't someone who ran away from a scrap if there was a bit of difficulty or controversy. He believed in the firm and he believed in the values of the firm, and he saw some of the negative commentary for what it was, which was a cheap shot at the leading institution in what over time became an unpopular industry. That sort of thing did not bother Peter. I'm not saying he liked it.'

Gnodde says that he and the other Goldman Sachs executives were very aware of the assistance Sutherland gave the Irish government when the economy hit the buffers. 'The thing about Peter was he would be very supportive and always had your back, but he would also be very direct with you. I say that because it was the same for Ireland. Publicly he was very supportive, but he was also very straight with the finance minister about what had to be done. He would have relied a lot on our bank experts about what needed to be done in terms of recapitalising the banks. He was very engaged and we spoke about that frequently. Peter was a man of enormous breadth and covered a lot of ground.'

*

Sutherland's Goldman Sachs role was sometimes called upon in the most unlikely of places. Just before Easter 2007, he joined his good friend Nicholas Kearns and a few other men on a pilgrimage to Mount Athos in Greece, through a mountainous region in the north-east of the country that is famous for its monasteries. The pilgrimage took them on foot between one monastery and another, where they stayed overnight in sparse conditions.

After a few days, Sutherland was struggling with the walking and the limited food. When Kearns shared a room with Sutherland on one night, he noted in his diary that Maruja deserved to be canonised. Sutherland's snore reached volcanic proportions as the night unfolded.

Finally the group arrived at their third and final monastery. Soon after they checked in, a monk invited the men to meet the abbot. 'The abbot used the monk as his interpreter, asking if this was our first visit, how we had heard of Athos – polite formal questions.'

Kearns spoke on behalf of the group. 'When I finished my little account, the abbot delivered himself of a homily to our group, all of which was translated for him by the monk, and we nodded sagely and gravely at the right moments, which were largely focused on prayer, doing God's will and good deeds. He gave us a form of blessing at the end of what seemed for him a familiar routine and then murmured something to the monk.

'The latter eventually spoke: "The abbot is wondering if Meester Sutherland, who has much experience, would advise the Vatopedi Monastery about its assets and investments on mainland Greece." We kept straight faces with some difficulty as Peter blustered out some reply.'

15

CLIPPING GOODWIN'S WINGS AT RBS

O N 6 FEBRUARY 2009, SUTHERLAND AND SIX other directors stood down from the board of the Royal Bank of Scotland. The previous October, the British government had pumped £45.5 billion into RBS in return for 82 per cent of its share capital in order to prevent the bank from collapsing. It had all been so different when Sutherland joined the board in 2001. Formed in 1727, for most of its history up to the early 2000s the bank had enjoyed a reputation for being conservative, dependable and most of all prudent.

That had all begun to change in the 1990s. In the Anglo-Saxon world, the precept adopted by most governments at the time was that markets were efficient and largely self-regulating. There was a logical progression from this belief towards a model of light-touch regulation. For well over a decade, it was a creed that served many countries well, at least fiscally. The financial sector, a marginal component of the economy for most of the twentieth century, dwarfed most other industries from the 1990s onwards. But the rise of RBS from a stalwart of the UK banking sector to a global behemoth cannot be separated from the controversial career of one man.

Even though the financial sector is a complex industry, it is still driven by human emotions. Take for example Richard Fuld, the chief executive of Lehman Brothers at the time of its spectacular demise in September 2008. Fuld, a man with both an innate inferiority complex and a superior sense of his own strategic nous, had spent the previous decade pursuing an aggressive growth agenda so that Lehmans would be taken seriously by the blue bloods of Wall Street. Meanwhile in Ireland, Seanie Fitzpatrick, stung by the slights heaped on Anglo Irish Bank by Bank of Ireland and AIB, spent most of his time as chief executive of Anglo Irish trying to put it on a par with the big two. He eventually succeeded, but again with disastrous consequences.

Fred Goodwin came from working-class roots in Glasgow. He was the first member of his family to go to university and subsequently trained as a chartered accountant. Goodwin, who had gained a reputation early in his career as a ruthless cost-cutter – earning him the nickname 'Fred the shred' – joined RBS in 1998 as deputy chief executive at the age of forty.

In the BBC documentary *The Bank that Nearly Broke Britain*, made to mark the tenth anniversary of the near collapse of RBS, a former executive of the bank recalled how he got a telephone call from a former colleague at Clydesdale to say they had been partying for four days following the announcement of Goodwin's departure. A charitable interpretation of Goodwin's management style was that it was uncompromising. Former RBS executives described how his morning meetings became known as 'morning beatings'. But his stock was rising within RBS. A seminal moment in the history of the bank is the 2000 acquisition of NatWest. The move was initially viewed with suspicion in the City of London, and was depicted as an attempt by Scottish insurgents to prise away a key pillar of the English establishment. Some analysts nevertheless doubted whether the deal would have been successful without Goodwin. Whatever the feelings about his management style, he had a formidable command of numbers, and was able to lay out in forensic detail how the deal would work, where the synergies would be achieved, and most importantly why it made sense from a shareholder perspective.

RBS took over NatWest in June 2000 for £23.6 billion. Through the deal, it would also acquire Ulster Bank in Ireland. Goodwin became chief executive of RBS in 2001, with Sir George Mathewson moving from chief executive to chairman. That same year Peter Sutherland joined the board, inaugurating what would prove to be an eventful eight years.

*

RBS then embarked on a massive acquisition spree. A series of mini-deals over the next couple of years was followed by its next sizeable acquisition in 2004, when Charter One, a US bank with its headquarters in Ohio, was procured for $10.5 billion.

The Charter One deal provided RBS with its first big bite of the US market, but the consensus among analysts was that the price was too high. 'The feeling was that Fred had done a duff deal and spent far too much on that business,' says Katherine Griffiths, banking editor at *The Times* in London. 'And the speculation at the time was that there was unhappiness on the board.' A view was forming in the City of London that Goodwin was going after deals for the sake of making RBS a much bigger bank rather than creating value for shareholders. 'I remember being told that Peter Sutherland was out to get Fred,' Griffiths says. 'The view was that Sutherland was a real heavyweight on the board who was critical of Fred. But ultimately they did not get rid of him and they went on to do a far bigger deal.' The feeling, she believes, was that Sutherland was among those most opposed to Goodwin, but they took no action. Only when the credit crisis came along was he exposed. 'There were misgivings before the crisis but nothing was done about it.'

Griffiths's account is backed up by Ian Fraser in his book *Shredded: Inside RBS*.[1] According to this account, Sutherland was one of three directors who became wary of Goodwin in the wake of the Charter One deal. At the beginning of 2005 Sutherland, who was a member of the chairman's advisory group and head of the nominations committee, commissioned Brunswick, a major London public affairs firm, to compile a report. Its brief was to canvass influential analysts, investors and other stakeholders about the difficulties facing RBS, and in particular the role played by Goodwin. The report was delivered in June 2005, just prior to an RBS board meeting at the Gleneagles Hotel & Golf resort in Scotland, and Sutherland made a limited number of copies available beforehand.

Excerpts of the report which Sutherland read out in front of Goodwin and the rest of the board can best be described as unsparing. Among them were: 'Fred is out of touch'; 'Fred is arrogant'; 'Fred doesn't listen to shareholders'; 'Fred treats all shareholders like they are idiots'; and 'Fred is a megalomaniac.' In the *coup de grâce*, Sutherland turned to page 48 and read out the succinct contribution from one City analyst: 'Fred is a complete cunt.' Sutherland then turned to Goodwin and asked him to respond.

According to people in the room Goodwin remained calm, although visibly shaken. One board member said it was the only time in their life they 'felt sorry for Fred'. But the episode brought about a change in RBS's strategic direction. Goodwin took more of a backseat in terms of public appearances while heads of the key divisions within RBS became more prominent, particularly when it came to representing the bank in the media.

Sir Tom McKillop took over as chairman of RBS in 2006, but many questioned the rationale of the move. 'When McKillop came in, there was a question, why does he have to be a Scot? He was a chemist and the feeling at the time was it wasn't necessarily a bad thing to have somebody from outside the sector,' says Griffiths. But it was felt, she explains, that RBS thought it was more important to get a Scottish businessman for the role than look across the landscape for the right person for the job. McKillop was at the time the chief executive of pharmaceutical company AstraZeneca. Like Goodwin, he had come from a humble background, reaching Glasgow University thanks to a series of scholarships. Described as being exceptionally intelligent, he graduated with a Ph.D. in chemistry.

McKillop has not spoken to the media since he stood down as chairman in 2009. He broke his silence for this book to explain: 'Peter [Sutherland] was on the nomination committee that persuaded me to become chairman. When they came looking for me as chairman, one of the things they wanted was somebody who would be strong and hold Fred to account. We were certainly doing that.' There had been speculation at the time that Sutherland was looking to replace Goodwin with Cormac McCarthy, the chief executive of Ulster Bank. 'I remember Cormac very well,' says McKillop. 'He was one of the people who was on a succession list. The board discussed succession plans a couple of times a year, including a potential successor to the chief executive. We would look at fallback positions if somebody was hit by a bus, as any good board would do. We would also be looking at younger people whom we thought might have the potential to be candidates for other positions. It is certainly true McCarthy was on that list. We had conversations with him about how he saw his future going, but to my memory he was happy to stay in Ireland. Cormac was one of the people we followed very carefully, but there was never a plan to put him in Fred's role in the short term. It may have been a long-term plan.'

After the bruising encounter with Sutherland and the contents of the Brunswick report, Goodwin seemed to develop a sense of humility. But by 2005, the die had been cast. There is an adage among investors that whenever a company moves to a shiny new headquarters or acquires a corporate jet, then it is time to dump the stock. In 2005, RBS moved into a new 72-acre campus outside Edinburgh at a cost of £350 million. In 2002 it had acquired a private jet. When the jet was eventually offloaded, the following piece appeared in the *Guardian*:

November 2008: For sale: Executive jet, 14 seats, satellite TV, rear lounge with two side-facing sofas, full service history.

Private registration number G-RBSG (just possibly 'Royal Bank of Scotland Goodwin'). Bought 2002 for $32m. Asking price $25,950,000 (£18m).

May 2009: Sold at a knocked down price. The Dassault Falcon 900EX jet used by Sir Fred Goodwin, the disgraced former chief executive of Royal Bank of Scotland, was sold last week by the new management team at the loss-making Edinburgh-based bank. RBS bought the top-of-the-range jet in October 2002 when the bank was in the midst of cutting 18,000 jobs as a result of the NatWest takeover. Based in Paris, it could fly Goodwin and other senior RBS executives 4,500 nautical miles non-stop, allowing them a one-hop trip from their Edinburgh headquarters to Beijing, where RBS was trying to expand after buying a stake in Bank of China.[2]

In 2005 Goodwin still had his fans on the board and in the City of London. It wasn't long before he regained his swagger. The final, and fatally flawed, acquisition of his reign was Dutch bank ABN Amro. Barclays, another UK bank, had been pursuing ABN Amro in 2007 and came close to striking a deal, but ultimately it fell through. RBS immediately seized on the opportunity. Compounding the problem, they paid for the bank entirely in cash, rather than meeting any of the asking price with shares.

That year, 2007, was the peak of a global financial bubble that had formed early in the new millennium. Asset prices had become inflated to levels that had no compelling rationale. To buy any company at this time was freighted with huge risks; to buy a bank that was heavily exposed to the US sub-prime market was fatal. ABN Amro had been a very enthusiastic purchaser of collateralised debt obligations (CDOs), the nifty piece of financial engineering popular in the US, whereby tranches of mortgages were pooled together and sold off as bonds. With so much money sloshing around the economy, house prices were seen as a one-way bet.

But what goes up an escalator usually comes down a mineshaft. The first signs that US house prices had reached hopelessly unsustainable levels appeared in 2007. House price growth stalled. Prices then began to fall. Soon there were widespread foreclosures. CDOs put together using bonds from the US housing market soon became toxic, and ABN Amro was heavily exposed. It became a minefield sitting on the balance sheet of RBS.

McKillop rejects the popular narrative that RBS's woes were caused by an autocratic chief executive and a compliant board. 'I hadn't been chairman for very long before the acquisition of ABN Amro, and then the financial crisis happened and I found myself chairman of a bank that had huge problems with the merger of ABN and RBS. We had probably the biggest balance sheet in the world, when asset prices were collapsing.

'The ABN Amro acquisition, contrary to the public portrayal of it all, was not Fred driving the board to do something against its wishes. The board had been interested in ABN Amro for a number of years and had followed it closely. It was a natural fit with RBS. When Barclays reached an agreement to merge with ABN Amro, it was debated up and down many times by the board. Fred was very clear to the board that this wasn't a deal that we had to do, because the bank was going very well at the time. But it did fit the overall strategy and the decision to go ahead received the unanimous backing of the board, even though elements of the deal were challenged.

'Fred led that consortium, but it wasn't a case of Fred doing this against the wishes of the board. This kind of public portrayal that the media love is completely erroneous. Fred was a strong chief executive. You can't run an organisation that size without being strong.'

While Sutherland challenged Goodwin at boardroom level, says McKillop, there was no personal animus between them. 'Peter was a very good colleague – he balanced real challenge with appropriate support. Intellectually he was always interested in analysing problems. Peter contributed to a very vigorous debate about what to do. In the end we agreed to go ahead as a consortium. The strategy at the time was to turn RBS into a big universal comparable to JP Morgan.

'We had weaknesses, we were not strong in Asia or emerging markets. ABN Amro was and the fit was very good. The fit in North America was very good as well. RBS did not have a strong global payments system, ABN did, so they were the kind of factors that drove the deal. The numbers looked good. If the financial crash had not happened it would have been seen as a brilliant move. It would have led to an even stronger RBS. But because the crash came so soon after the merger and we had this huge balance sheet, then we took a hammering.'

Following the collapse of Lehman Brothers on 14 September 2008, governments were faced with two choices: orchestrate politically toxic bank bailouts or let the financial system collapse. Most governments chose the former. Alistair Darling, the British Chancellor of the Exchequer at the time, made a very angry phone call to Dublin following the Irish government's guarantee of its banking system on 29 September. Rightly concerned that if there was an outflow of deposits from the UK to Ireland, he would be left with an even more vulnerable financial sector, he bowed to the inevitable on 8 October and announced a £500 billion rescue package for UK banks. A series of calls between senior officials in his office and RBS executives the previous day had focused Darling's mind. If the British government had failed to make a very public and convincing intervention, then RBS would have collapsed. It had run out of money and the markets were unwilling to lend it a penny more.

The recriminations started almost immediately. Goodwin was forced to resign on 11 October and quickly became the public face of the unfolding banking crisis. Sutherland and the rest of the board followed four months later, amid heavy criticism that they had failed to do their job.

McKillop says this criticism is misplaced. 'I would disagree with the notion that the board did not do its job. It was a very experienced board; we had people with 350 years' aggregated experience of financial services. They were all strong individually. There was plenty of questioning. That was found to be the case when the FSA did its investigation of RBS. There was no evidence to suggest that the board was not doing its job in providing challenge. The difficulties were associated with the financial collapse when we had massive assets.

'You might ask, did we not foresee that was possible? No we didn't. There was always a chance that a systemic collapse of the financial system would occur, but it was seen as a very very small chance. We were a significant casualty of these timing elements. I have been on many boards. You do deals, you make investments. There is always a risk with them. If you are afraid of a tail risk, a low-probability risk of something going wrong, you will not do anything and the company will atrophy.'

This viewpoint is not widely shared. Katherine Griffiths says, 'I remember McKillop at the time saying there were no patsies on the board. There were patsies on the board. Fred was massively dictatorial. He was the guy driving the ABN Amro deal. A lot of people at the time thought that the deal was absolutely crazy. RBS became this banking conglomerate over time that Mathewson did not necessarily understand. He was part of the Scottish establishment.' There was also a feeling that Goodwin did not necessarily understand all of the bank's operations, particularly the investment banking side. Griffiths continues, 'A big problem with RBS is that the board lacked the requisite skills. I think that Sutherland had the nous. He was obviously a very smart person and could see Fred for what he was. He was not scared of him like other people. He probably surveyed the landscape.'

According to former associates, Sutherland was receiving feedback through his role at Goldman Sachs that Goodwin's RBS strategy was flawed and that the deals he had struck were not very good. But Sutherland was in the minority on the board.

'It is probably true to say that RBS's board was third rate, but to put it in perspective most banks' boards were third rate at the time. It is very much a post-crisis thing that regulators thought that boards should be made up of people who understood banking,' says Griffiths. There is no single culprit for the RBS debacle, she adds. 'Fred bears a lot of responsibility. He created a dysfunctional culture. I do think the board was really poor. For the ABN Amro deal, they could have set a price limit. The Barclays deal was all shares. RBS paid cash. But nobody can find much evidence that the board challenged Fred.'

*

Ulster Bank, also owned by RBS, racked up roughly £14 billion in losses during Ireland's property boom. There had been speculation over previous years that RBS would look to ditch its Northern Ireland subsidiary as it sought to repair its own balance sheet. Much like RBS itself, Ulster Bank had been a well-run and conservative bank for most of its existence. That changed around the time of the RBS acquisition. A number of former Ulster Bank executives revealed the pressure they had come under from RBS head office, and from Goodwin in particular, to increase the bank's exposure to the property market during the Celtic Tiger years. Probably the one deal that summed up the irrational exuberance of the period is Sean Dunne's acquisition of the Jurys Hotel site in Ballsbridge, Dublin 4. He paid €380 million for a 4.5 acre site. Ulster Bank competed aggressively against the other banks to fund the deal, and ended up nursing heavy losses when the market collapsed and Dunne filed for bankruptcy.

Sutherland gave an interview about Ulster Bank in 2011. It was never published, but the sound files have been provided to this book by a journalist who wished to remain anonymous. Sutherland said he was never on the board of Ulster Bank. 'Therefore what precisely was discussed or how the regulator dealt with the issue of risk in Ireland, I have no direct knowledge of. I can only say that – I don't know how the relativities in lending arose in Ireland, but every bank in Ireland as far as I know lent too much on property. For example Danske Bank and RBS through Ulster lent into what turned into a property bubble which was very substantial, and of course all of the Irish banks without exception were in the same situation.

'I don't think that Ulster was leading on this. I think the leader was Anglo Irish Bank – there has been a report into the Irish banking issues and how it happened. There is no doubt that lending and the availability of finance was a significant element in the problem, but it's the cause of that lending that is the issue. There was no inhibition, or suggestion that it should be inhibited – quite the reverse in government policy, which was probably reliant excessively on tax revenue. I'm not saying that they did it for this reason – stamp duty and so on – and I think everybody was living with a sense of delusion of how sustainable this was, but it's the exact same thing as what happened in Spain and to a significant extent here in Britain.'

At no time, said Sutherland, was a report submitted to the RBS board about whether the Central Bank had made any attempts to rein in Ulster Bank's lending activities. 'I certainly don't remember, nor do I expect that there would ever have been a direct report at the board of what the Irish Central Bank was saying to Ulster. But one would assume that the Irish Central Bank was not saying anything different to Ulster compared to the rest of Ireland – which can't have been very much, as everyone was lending in the same way.'

Sutherland was one of the more high-profile members of the board and received more media attention than the others. It would be one of the most controversial roles in his life, and one of the least financially rewarding. In 2004, he received a director's fee of £53,000; £60,000 in 2005; £88,000 in 2006; and £97,000 in 2007. While these sums would be a good salary for most people, they were insubstantial for somebody of Sutherland's wealth.

'I think he is a bit tarnished, but not massively,' says Katherine Griffiths. 'He did so many other things. In the business world people think of his role in Goldman Sachs. In the RBS thing, he bears some culpability. If people knew what happened they would be more likely to point the finger at other non-execs.'

*

Just as in Ireland, the regulatory system in the UK was heavily criticised in the aftermath of the financial crisis. Under the Financial Services Authority (FSA), which was responsible for the supervision of RBS at the time, the bank operated with wafer-thin capital ratios, which act as a buffer against losses when the bank hits a bout of turbulence. Goodwin was open about this: his argument was that it was expensive to hold capital and therefore he could get it from the markets any time he needed it. It should be noted that RBS was not alone in this approach; it was common throughout the industry. But it would prove to be a foolhardy strategy which deprived the bank of a last line of defence when it needed it.

16

THE LONGEST SERVING CHAIRMAN

WHEN PETER SUTHERLAND BECAME CHAIRMAN of BP in 1997, it was the UK's largest public limited company. BP was at the heart of the British establishment. Formed in 1908 as the Anglo-Persian Oil Company, in 1935 it became the Anglo-Iranian Oil Company and in 1954 its name was changed to British Petroleum. The British government began the process of privatisation in 1979 and completed its divestment in 1987.

Sutherland had originally joined the BP board in 1990, after he stood down from the European Commission. As a commissioner, Sutherland had taken action against oil companies based in the EU after the industry was accused of concerted practice behaviour in its chemicals businesses. David Simon, finance director of BP in 1988, went to Brussels with deputy chairman Peter Cazalet to meet Sutherland and present BP's defence.

'We pleaded our case,' Simon says. 'On our way back, Peter said, "What did you think of Sutherland? I thought he was excellent." I particularly liked him because I was a well-known Europhile. I thought he was terrific. He was open, relaxed, political but jolly. Peter said, "Would you think of him for the BP board?" I said if we were to get non-Brits on the board, he would be the ideal candidate.'

Sutherland would be a perfect fit for BP's European plans, thought Simon. He would be a great help in telling the company what it could and could not do. After BP paid the fine for its misdemeanours, he joined the board. 'That is how I got to know him.'

When Sutherland joined the board of BP in 1990, his role was split into two parts. First, he was to work on the integration of its European businesses; second, he was to help its international expansion. It was a turbulent period. A collapse in the oil price in the early 1990s, combined with high levels of debt, had plunged the company into a doom loop. Simon, a BP lifer, took over as chief executive in 1992 and steadied the ship. Having left the BP board in 1993 when he joined GATT, Sutherland returned in 1995 when he stood down from the WTO, and was elevated to the role of deputy chairman. The same year, Simon became chairman and John Browne, another lifer, stepped up to the role of chief executive. Browne would do more to shape BP than any of his predecessors.

When Tony Blair won that thumping majority in the 1997 British general election to become the first Labour prime minister since the 1970s, Simon left his post at BP to become Minister for Europe (following an objection from Robin Cook, the title was changed to Minister for Trade and Competitiveness in Europe). Simon joined the Blair government, he explains, because he wanted to confront the issue of how to get markets to behave responsibly. 'At the time we were coming out of the ravages of Thatcher.' He found that his worldview chimed with Sutherland's. 'We were more socially minded than your average business leaders.' The two men were both passionate Europeans and had developed a close relationship. When Simon pointed to Sutherland as his replacement, the idea was broadly welcomed by the rest of the board. 'I had absolutely no reservations about him becoming chairman.'

According to another BP executive, it was very obvious where Sutherland's strengths lay. 'Peter by his own admission was much stronger on strategy and politics than he was on business. He never struck me as a person who would get a lot of commercial advice. If you wanted a view of the politics of a region, then he was excellent. On the development of relationship with Europe, he was excellent.'

So it was that Sutherland, having never considered himself a businessman, took on one of the most powerful roles in the British corporate world. His relationship with John Browne was generally good in the early years. People close to both men say that while they never developed a close personal bond, they both respected each other. Sutherland was sociable and charming, with many interests. As had been described on a number of occasions, he brought the might of a front-row forward to everything he did. While not confrontational, he was not afraid of confrontation and favoured an open approach to professional relationships. Browne lived with his mother Paula, a Hungarian Jew who had survived Auschwitz, and to whom he was devoted. Apart from BP he had few outside interests, and he avoided confrontation as much as possible. But he understood the oil markets intimately and he had an ambition to make BP the biggest energy company in the world.

A year after Sutherland became chairman, Browne completed the biggest deal in BP's history. He merged the company with Amoco, a US oil major, in a $48.2 billion all-stock deal that catapulted BP into third place in the world's largest oil companies, behind only Exxon and Shell. At that stage the largest deal ever to involve an American company and a non-US corporate, it was supposed to be a merger, but it was effectively a takeover. A joke doing the rounds at the time was:

'How do you pronounce BP-Amoco?'

'BP, the Amoco is silent.'

It was a hugely successful and transformative deal for BP and Browne. In fact, it was transformative for the industry. It presaged a wave of mergers and acquisitions: Exxon took over Mobil; Total took over Fina and Elf; Chevron merged with Texaco; and Conoco merged with Phillips.

Sutherland's first few years as chairman involved a steep learning curve. It was certainly very different from his role at Goldman Sachs, a position that played more to his strengths. At BP he had to become infinitely more aware of the nuts and bolts of the business. Oil companies have three main divisions, known as upstream, midstream and downstream. Upstream, the exploration and production division, is responsible for ensuring that the company has enough oil and gas reserves to sustain robust levels of production. Midstream is the division that controls refineries, converting the oil into different products. The downstream division is an extensive network of petrol stations to sell the end product. Over the past couple of decades, increasingly punitive government levies have weighed on the profitability of the midstream and downstream divisions. Indeed, some oil companies have exited these operations altogether.

The problem companies such as BP face is that oil is running out in places that are well disposed to western energy companies. For decades, the North Sea was a rich source of oil production. There was an abundance of reserves in geophysical terrain that was relatively easy to access. Most important, it was located in a country that had a stable business regime. But when basins such as the North Sea and similar areas in OECD countries started running out of oil and gas reserves, oil companies were forced to look at physically and politically more challenging areas. In 1999, BP made a $27 billion move for Arco, another US company, and one that owned extensive exploration acreage in Alaska. The problem for BP was that it already had extensive exploration assets in Alaska, and as a result the US Federal Trade Commission (FTC) opened an investigation into the deal. There was a feeling at the time among industry analysts that Browne had never been likely to get a free run at acquiring a second major US energy firm in the space of a couple of years. The FTC investigation took a year, testing to the limit the patience of the executive team at BP.

Roddy Kennedy retired as head of BP media relations in 2009

after a thirty-year career with the energy giant. By the time he stood down, he was a legendary figure in the City of London and beyond, his prowess as a spin-doctor unparalleled in the British corporate world. Originally from Toomevara in north Tipperary, he had emigrated to London at the age of thirteen. He trained as a journalist and eventually became the series editor of the *Sunday Express*. One of the first Fleet Street journalists to move to a gatekeeper role, he was close to both Sutherland and Browne.

'I think Peter was concerned [about the Arco deal] because the process was a long one. Most of the senior people working at BP backed the deal because they didn't think there would be a huge hold-up. I thought we would be in some trouble taking a second bite – the US can be protective of its energy assets. If the deal had been allowed to go ahead, then it would have been great, but it didn't. It was ultimately a political decision. Peter was not in a position to argue with it. Nobody on the outside was saying it couldn't be done.'

Browne wanted to be more adversarial towards the FTC and a press release taking a very strident approach to the stand-off was put together. Sutherland ensured that it never saw the light of day. 'He didn't want to go into fisticuffs with the FTC,' says Kennedy. The commission eventually cleared the Arco deal, but with the proviso that BP divest itself of the Alaskan assets. It was a pyrrhic victory. Getting control of those assets had been the rationale for the deal in the first place.

Around this time Sutherland confided in a colleague at BP that he was considering resigning as chairman. 'He said "I'm just not a businessman",' says the colleague, who spoke on the basis of anonymity. 'Anyway, I persuaded him not to. It didn't take him long after that to really bed down in the role.'

At the time, Sutherland's reservations about his chairmanship were not shaped by his personal relationship with Browne. People who were there say the two men got on well. And even though the senior management team at BP conceded that the Arco deal was a setback, it was presented to the outside world as a positive and logical step in the company's growth strategy. But there could be no papering over the fallout from Browne's next, and ill-fated, strategic decision. When in mid-2000 he announced a series of ambitious production targets, cracks appeared for the first time in the relationship between himself and Sutherland. Over the next three years, Browne declared that production would grow annually by 5.5 to 7 per cent, targets that were well above the prevailing industry average at the time. Some BP executives privately had concerns about the strategy. There was the obvious risk that the company would end up taking production decisions based on volume rather than quality. Sutherland had a very good network inside the organisation who kept him abreast of what the wider management team was thinking. The feedback he was getting about the production targets was that they were a bad idea. And the further BP advanced into the three-year timeframe, the more unease grew.

'There was a feeling he [Browne] bludgeoned it through,' says one former BP executive. Browne's rationale was that if you wanted the share price to grow then you needed a performance metric that investors could understand. At the time Browne was on the board of Intel. Former colleagues would describe how he would come back from quarterly board meetings enthused by the heroic targets the tech industry was setting at the height of the dotcom bubble.

While Browne was publicly committing to ambitious production targets, BP embarked upon a quixotic marketing campaign. A US marketing agency was retained, at considerable expense, to make the company's image more attractive to the outside world. The idea was not to make it more appealing to investors, but rather to potential employees. After all, BP was in competition with numerous other sectors to hire the brightest and the best. By the early 2000s, the problem of climate change had become a much more prominent social issue. It was starting to shape the political agenda, with many parties keen to highlight their green credentials, and that would inevitably have consequences for the corporate world. For the first time big businesses had to include tackling climate change in their corporate social responsibility programmes.

For a company such as BP this presented a Schrödinger-style dilemma. One of the most effective ways of tackling climate change is to reduce the world's reliance on fossil fuels; BP's profits were made from selling fossil fuels.

There was internal dissent about the marketing campaign. It was impossible to reconcile the lofty goals of the campaign with a strategy of raising production targets to appeal to investors. The campaign, and its tagline 'Beyond Petroleum', was quietly dropped, but many were left questioning Browne's judgement.

In 2003, the production target wheeze became a fiasco. The targets were missed three times before they were scrapped. The first real tarnishing of Browne's reputation, it had a big impact. At the next BP board meeting, held in Seville, Sutherland was absolutely furious with Browne; for the first time, simmering tensions spilled over into a boardroom-level confrontation. People close to the situation say that it was the first time the chairman began to question whether the chief executive should continue in the role he had held for eight years. Sutherland and Browne would travel back separately from Seville.

The relationship between chairman and chief executive is complex, a point of creative tension. The problem for Sutherland was that even though BP was the third largest energy company in the world and the largest British PLC by market capitalisation, it was becoming synonymous with its chief executive. The klaxon had been sounded in 2002 when the *Financial Times* published a profile of Browne, then fifty-four years old, which was titled 'Sun King of the oil industry'.[1] The piece was laudatory and focused on Browne's meteoric rise through the oil industry and the traits that had helped him become, when the profile was written, the most admired business leader in the UK for the third year in a row. But the last few paragraphs were prescient:

A former senior director of BP and long-serving contemporary of Browne's says there are worries about 'his huge power. The longer he is there, the more of a feeling of a court develops. Think of it this way: a whole generation of managers who grew up in the business with John has been progressively removed in order to make way for the next generation. We felt ourselves his equals in a way. Now, with everyone around him being so much younger, there is no one to challenge him.' Browne rejects this, but mainly by stressing his willingness to seek advice from outsiders including academics such as John Gray, the London School of Economics professor, and Daniel Yergin, the US author and oil expert. Nevertheless, a former BP manager says: 'The question we have to ask is: Is he still learning? People like him are, even if they have the best intentions, surrounded by people who are terrified.' His willingness to stay on for another six years may offer comfort to those who worry that there is no one around to fill his job. However, it also raises the spectre of a company growing ever more dependent on the abilities of one man. The Sun King, some fear, will become even more dominant than he is now, while his court could turn ever more subservient. Ultimately, Browne's legacy may depend on whether he can groom a successor capable of taking over this vast and sprawling corporation. History does not look kindly on the ruler who leaves behind an empire only he himself can govern.

One former executive said that even though the FT piece seemed to cement Browne's reputation, in hindsight it just made him a target. Anybody on a pedestal is always liable to come a cropper.

Thanks to his track record of transformative deals and pushing the share price, Browne nevertheless had a sizeable fan base in the City of London. If the production targets debacle left him vulnerable and exposed, he was soon able to deflect any unwanted attention with another transformative deal. Oil prices had risen steadily through most of the 1990s from the trough of $10 per barrel at the start of that decade. Although the market temporarily slumped in 2001 after the implosion of the dotcom bubble and the 9/11 terrorist attacks in New York and Washington, prices quickly recovered. In 2003 Goldman Sachs published a research paper which suggested oil prices could hit €100 per barrel. Initially met with some scepticism, in the event it was a conservative assessment; prices would peak at €150 per barrel in 2008.

A spiralling oil price is obviously good news for any oil major. The problem for BP was whether it could access new reserves to take advantage of the buoyant market conditions. Global oil reserves were increasingly becoming concentrated in a handful of regions, such as Russia, the Middle East and deepwater Africa. In the Middle East, reserves were controlled by national oil companies and it was hardly in the interests of the ruling royal families to open up access to the source of their wealth. Deepwater Africa, meanwhile, was extremely challenging terrain, and therefore costly. Profitability hinged on oil prices remaining at elevated levels, and in 2003 there was no guarantee that would happen.

Finally, Russia had an abundance of reserves, but was politically risky. In 2003, President Vladimir Putin was stripping the assets of the sixteenth richest man in the world. Mikhail Khodorkovsky, the head of Russian oil giant Yukos, had a personal wealth of $15 billion, but he made a fatal error. He questioned Putin's authority and pledged to pump money into opposition parties in Russia. He would spend the next ten years in prison and the ownership of Yukos would be transferred to a number of Putin allies. That was the backdrop against which Browne formed a joint partnership with a number of Russian businessmen.

At the end of 2003 BP set up a joint venture with the Moscow-headquartered AAR consortium. Called TNK-BP, it was initially a great success. Indeed, overall it was a great success, making the company about $8 billion in profits over its relatively short life. Although Sutherland made no public comment on the deal, however, former colleagues say that even then he had reservations. He did not trust Putin and his view was that the separation between the public and private realms in Russia was paper thin. Nevertheless, in the immediate aftermath of the TNK deal, the sheen had been restored to Browne's reputation. It was generally seen as a brilliant strategy, even though it was going to be a rough ride.

Allied to this strategy of topline growth was an aggressive programme of cost cutting. Browne replaced BP engineers with sub-contractors. But then disaster struck. On 23 March 2005, an explosion at BP's oil refinery in Mexico City killed 15 workers and injured more than 180 others. A number of investigations found evidence of widespread health and safety failures at the site, which had come with the Amoco acquisition. BP paid over $70 million in fines, and paid out $1.6 billion in compensation to victims of the tragedy.

It was what Browne did next that really put him on a collision course with Sutherland. Browne had setbacks during his ten years as chief executive, but his nose for a good deal had bailed him out in the past. He was quickly on the lookout again. He didn't have to look very far. Royal DutchShell was reeling from the worst corporate crisis in its history. In April 2004, Phil Watts, its chief executive, was forced to resign amid a huge reserves scandal. Watts had headed the exploration and production division in the late 1990s and early 2000s. His track record was remarkable and helped him secure the post of chief executive when it became available. He had not only managed to significantly reduce costs, but had also vastly improved the success rate of the exploration division.

It seemed too good to be true, and so it turned out. Oil companies break down reserves into different categories. Proven oil reserves – those that have been located and tested and whose fields are ready for production – are the most lucrative. In the next category are reserves that have been located but still have to be tested to see how many barrels can be recovered. Watts had moved vast chunks of the second category into that of proven oil reserves to inflate the performance of his division. When the reclassification emerged, Royal Dutch was plunged into a period of deep trauma. The company announced that it was cutting its estimates of proven oil and gas reserves by 3.9 billion barrels, equivalent to 20 per cent of its total reserves base.

In 2005 Browne made contact with Watts' replacement, Jeroen van der Veer, with the intention of doing a deal. 'John thought he could rescue his reputation with the Shell deal. He had some very opaque conversations with Jeroen van der Veer. But I think John's motive for doing it was to overwhelm everything else. The way these mergers work is that they create so many synergies that it is usually a great boon for the share price,' says one former BP executive. Having previously been European Commissioner for Competition, Sutherland knew that a merger between BP and Shell would not get clearance. The companies were number one and two in most EU member states. More importantly, Sutherland heard via feedback through private channels from the Shell board that they would never agree to a merger. It was dead. Sutherland soon put an end to any tentative discussions.

*

Browne was scheduled to retire on his sixtieth birthday – which fell on 20 February 2008 – according to company policy and a succession plan agreed with the board, which it had been agreed would be put into operation in 2006. Sutherland's nose for spotting potential trouble was alerted by an article written by Patience Wheatcroft, business editor of *The Times*, who suggested that Tony Blair should become the next chairman of BP and that Browne should stay on until Blair was ready to take up the position. Sutherland sensed that Browne was in full agreement with Wheatcroft, and his suspicions were justified when Browne refused to say he would go at the specified date. Things came to a head in July 2006, when Browne was invited to Anji Hunter's wedding to Adam Boulton. Hunter had been one of Tony Blair's chief advisers and had moved to BP as Director of Communications in 2001. Boulton was the Political Editor of Sky News at the time. The BP chief executive sat next to Andrew Neil, the former editor of the *Sunday Times*. When Neil asked Browne how he was, the answer was surprisingly blunt, according to two people familiar with the situation: 'Not too good. I am being bullied out of my job by Peter Sutherland.'[2]

The *Sunday Business* newspaper carried a paragraph the following morning saying that Browne would not be standing down. Roddy Kennedy was in a car with Browne on Sunday 23 July, the day after the wedding, on their way to a televised interview at Bloomberg, when a call came through to Kennedy's phone. It was Sutherland, who asked Kennedy in very blunt terms whether he had seen the *Sunday Business* piece. Kennedy replied very politely that he was in a car with Browne, travelling to the Bloomberg studios. 'You can tell him from me he is not staying and this has to stop,' said Sutherland.

'I spoke to John that afternoon and said that Peter would ask him to confirm at the results press conference the following Tuesday that he intended to stand down,' Kennedy says.

Kennedy received a phone call that evening from a journalist at the *Financial Times* who was working on a front-page story to say that Browne would not be standing down. Kennedy persuaded her that this was definitely not the case. The same reporter rang Kennedy on Monday to say that she had it on very good authority that, on the contrary, Browne did not intend to stand down. According to media reports at the time, a series of showdown meetings were held between Sutherland and Browne. Having ensured that he had the full backing of the board, Sutherland insisted that Browne confirm he would be standing down on his mandatory retirement date. Sutherland prevailed. On Tuesday 25 July, BP issued a press release stating very clearly that Browne would be leaving his position in February 2008.

Around this time a rumour began circulating in media circles in London that the reason Sutherland had taken such a hard-line approach with Browne was because of his sexuality. It fitted a convenient narrative: after all, Sutherland, an Irishman, was a practising Catholic. Browne was not the source of the rumours.

Nevertheless, Sutherland was stung by the accusation. He had invited Browne and his partner to his daughter Natalia's wedding in Dromoland Castle in 2004, while the pair had also stayed with Peter and Maruja at their house in Spain. What was more, Sutherland's brother David, who had died in February 2006, was gay and had a long-term partner. Sutherland had always been very close to his brother, whose sexuality had never been an issue. There is no doubt that some perceived Sutherland as a conservative, but those closest to him said this was far from the reality.

Even though the relationship between the chairman and the chief executive had been strained, the two men settled back to a more peaceful coexistence once the matter of Browne's retirement had been resolved. That situation would soon unravel. Kennedy received a phone call from the *Mail on Sunday* in early January 2007, to be told that the newspaper was in possession of a 12,000-word affidavit from Jeff Chevalier, Browne's Canadian-born ex-partner. Even though Browne's sexuality was an open secret in BP, he had never publicly come out. The affidavit was mostly inconsequential, but the paper was able to invoke the public interest thanks to one line which involved Chevalier having dinner with Tony Blair in Browne's flat, an occasion at which gossip was exchanged.

If Browne wanted to stop the publication of the story, his only hope was to seek an injunction under EU privacy laws. Those close to Browne advised him against such a move. Injunctions rarely end well for the applicant; they invariably ensure that the story flares up into something much bigger. The *Mail* story was heavy on tittle-tattle but short on anything that would compromise Browne, his friends reasoned. But the BP chief executive was resolute. He was intent on stopping the story and was prepared to commit as much money as necessary to employ the best legal defence. He retained top London law firm Schillings, as well as Alan Parker, the managing partner of PR firm Brunswick, and secured an injunction to prevent immediate publication of the story. Then the process began of killing it off completely.

When Kennedy went to Sutherland to inform him of the developments, Sutherland's advice was that all legal and other expenses must be borne by Browne: this was a personal matter, not BP business. Kennedy had to give a full statement to Schillings based on what the *Mail on Sunday* had told him and what it intended to report. Browne said in his witness statement that he had met Chevalier out jogging in Battersea Park. Among the information Chevalier had shared with the *Mail* was that he and Browne had first met through an escort agency called Suited and Booted.

The truism that it's the small things that trip you up is certainly apposite for Browne. A BP employee all his working life, he had enjoyed one of the most gilt-edged careers in British corporate history, but it was all about to crumble because of one lie that exposed all-too-human frailties. Even with the stakes as high as they were, he could not bear to admit the transactional nature of his relationship with Chevalier. When it emerged that his statement had been misleading, the injunction was lifted and the judge said that he had considered bringing contempt proceedings against Browne. As soon as Sutherland saw the judgment he said that Browne had to go.

Browne left in May 2007. He has been busy in retirement and has taken on many roles, including chairman of the advisory board at Schillings. When he released his memoir, *Beyond Business*, in 2011, Sutherland wasn't mentioned once in the 344 pages.

*

Until 2007, the chairman's office had been on the sixth floor of BP's headquarters in St James's Square, whereas the chief executive was on the fifth floor with the rest of the senior executives. As soon as Browne left, Sutherland moved the chairman's office to the fifth floor. Browne was replaced by Tony Hayward, a popular figure in BP whose management style was very different from Browne's – much more affable and accessible. Sutherland agreed to stay on while the new chief executive bedded in, but by this stage he had been at the helm for ten years and was considering his own position. According to Tom McKillop, Sutherland was ready to go in 2008.

But then the joint venture with TNK hit a bumpy patch. The Russian shareholders were allegedly playing fast and loose with corporate governance standards. Robert Dudley, chief executive of TNK-BP at the time, was forced to leave Russia temporarily in 2008 as a result of the Russian authorities' strong-arm tactics; after BP's offices were raided by the Russians, the company was forced to pull staff from the country.

Sutherland took a very public stance in defending BP's interests. 'It saddens me to say that nowhere in our recent history have we been treated as we are currently being treated in Russia, where our fellow shareholders – called AAR – have been orchestrating a campaign of harassment in order to gain control of our joint venture TNK-BP,' he said in an interview with the *Irish Times* on 25 July 2008. In reference to Sutherland's robust defence of the company, Hayward added that 'we can park our tanks on their lawn as well'.

'Sutherland was fearsome. There was a weight, energy and intellect that could all be brought to bear on you at any one time,' says one former BP executive.

For most of Sutherland's twelve years as chairman of BP, his only public outing had been at the annual general meeting. 'Which he turned into a performance art,' one former colleague says. 'You could certainly see the barrister coming out. He could really master a room and ensure it never got unruly.' The 2009 AGM was different. In the immediate aftermath of his forced resignation from the board of Royal Bank of Scotland, a number of investors at the AGM turned their attention to Sutherland. By then a successor had been announced, but it was not the ending that Sutherland would have wanted.

A few short months after Carl-Henric Svanberg took over from Sutherland came the Deepwater Horizon disaster. The explosion in fireballs of a BP-owned oil rig in the Gulf of Mexico on 20

April 2010 not only killed eleven men but caused the biggest pollution incident ever to occur in US waters. In response Hayward made one of the most inept public appearances by a chief executive in history, pleading for an end to the crisis so that he 'could get his life back'. When the seemingly callous injunction drew the ire of President Obama, among others, Hayward was forced to resign.

*

Sutherland had been in his role at BP for twelve years, making him the longest-serving chairman of the company. The modern BP was shaped by Browne and Sutherland, but views are mixed on Sutherland's time as chairman.

Niall FitzGerald, former chief executive and chairman of Unilever, has chaired a number of boards. 'Peter was a very good chairman of BP but they weren't sufficiently hands-on to get the best out of him. He needed more of a frontline role. Did he rein in John Browne when he needed to be reined in? Peter and I talked about that a lot.' FitzGerald explains his view of the chairman's role: 'You should not interfere with your CEO if the CEO is the right person, because you can't have two people doing the same job. But you need to be sufficiently engaged to know when to intervene.' In every company he has chaired, he says, 'my contract with my CEO is that you have my 100 per cent support until you don't. And when you don't have 100 per cent it is time to change the CEO.' He thinks Sutherland let Browne have too much autonomy; Browne had pulled off two very good deals, but Sutherland allowed the cult of John Browne to develop too much. 'Had he intervened a little earlier, he might have moulded it differently.' Having joined as chairman with no real corporate experience, Sutherland would have found it difficult to impose a view on his CEO because he lacked the relevant background.

'I've chaired from the perspective of being a long-time CEO,' says FitzGerald, 'so I know how to get inside the veins of a company. At RBS, I think, there was partly the same problem. If you look at the board, there were very few with hands-on executive experience, so it was very difficult for them to know when to intervene.' Being chairman, he says, is a non-executive role, but it is not a part-time role. 'If you want to take it seriously, you have to put in the time to get to know the business and the people and you have to spend time outside being an advocate for the business. You can't do that and do a half a dozen other things.' Others might disagree, he continues, and say that by becoming too involved a chairman risked losing objectivity. 'I suppose it would be fair to say that Peter was on the opposite end of the spectrum to me on this. He believed you could do a lot of other things at the same time.'

While stating that Sutherland was a very effective chairman of BP, Tom McKillop adds that he 'recognises' questions about whether Sutherland ever saw himself as a businessman. 'Peter was very realistic about the experiences any individual brought to a board table, including himself. He had huge experience of chairing things. He was very good at using the broad array of talent around a table. He was never loath to ask opinions from people with the kind of experience that he didn't have. And that is the sign of a good chairman. No individual has it all and the most important quality of a good chairman is they bring out the whole diversity of talent and experience around the table. Peter was very good at that.

'He had a fine analytical mind. He had a very good sense of geopolitics. He knew what was going on in the world, and that is very important for large companies, particularly companies such as BP. He had a great ability to work with people. You could trust him, but he was very challenging.

'He never once got involved in game-playing. He was very open and direct, but he had all the skills of a politician. As far as standing down in 2008, he was always planning to do that. We had conversations about who would replace him, so it wasn't a surprise to me. After 2008, anybody who had any experience of the banking world was getting a torrid time. To some degree that affected Peter. But BP was going through its own problems.'

According to one former BP executive, however, Sutherland's time at the helm was ultimately a mixed bag. 'The problem was we did too many deals too quickly and we grew it [BP] out of its natural skin. For a board that is a very commercial decision. You have to have a commercial nose about the other companies: is it a good fit, will it add value, what do the numbers look like? The board will get data which shows what a good idea an acquisition is. What you really need is commercial nous. Peter was not the person to judge a good deal.'

Sutherland, he says, should have challenged Browne much earlier on the risks of the acquisition strategy. 'The fact that he didn't intervene earlier was a mistake. It all fell apart with the proposed Shell deal. The Arco deal was a disaster. Shell was a bridge too far and it should have been killed at the very start.'

As a result of the Amoco deal, BP had taken several Americans onto its board. 'The one thing we discovered is that you didn't really want too many top US executives on a UK board. It tipped the board against Peter and towards John, because everybody knew John in the US.' Sutherland's forte was dealing with Europe, Asia and Russia; he was less comfortable with the US. 'By 2005, what needed to be done was to concentrate on the business and not go after Shell. Someone should have said, "John, that is madness. You can't do that." But because of the board's composition, Sutherland could find no way of challenging Browne. 'He had an extremely effective political and strategic period, but the sharp commercial edge that would be required to control a chief executive hellbent on an acquisition strategy was not his best feature.'

But Roddy Kennedy rejects the criticism that Sutherland should have kept a tighter rein on Browne: 'It is easy to say that. John was not an easy guy to be in charge of. He had enormous support in the City and that was something that Peter had to be cognisant of.'

On a professional level, meanwhile, he says that a lot of the criticism of Sutherland is misplaced. 'One of the great weaknesses of UK corporate governance, in my view, is that the non-executive members of boards, such as Peter, have only limited access to what's happening further down the company chain. The system is deliberately designed to give the executive management the freedom to run the business. So the non-execs have a key supervisory role but can't readily poke their noses into day-to-day management. Nor do they generally have any staff of their own to give them expert independent advice.'

Sutherland had a raft of other directorships over his business career, including Allianz, Koc Holding, BW Group and membership of the advisory board of Eli Lilly. But according to Kennedy, there were never any tensions at BP about Sutherland's other roles. 'He always worked extremely hard. He was brilliant at mastering a brief. Before AGM, we would brief Peter on every conceivable angle. He would sit down on things he thought would come up. He was brilliant at doing that.'

A Sense of Duty

17

MIGRATION: UN SPECIAL REPRESENTATIVE

THE IMAGE OF ALAN KURDI'S LIFELESS THREE-year-old body washed up on a beach in Turkey on 2 September 2015 brought worldwide attention to the refugee crisis in the Mediterranean. Thousands of asylum seekers primarily from Syria and North Africa had already lost their lives making the same perilous journey, but it was this young boy's tragic end that would force the world to take note of the scale of the human tragedy that was unfolding.

Migration thrust Sutherland back into the international spotlight after a long spell of relative obscurity. His chairmanships of BP and Goldman Sachs, as well as his board membership of the Royal Bank of Scotland, occasionally put him back in the public eye – sometimes for the wrong reasons – but overall he maintained a low profile. Migration would change all that.

Migration has always been politically sensitive, particularly for sovereign states. It has been one of the issues that has fuelled the rise of populism and caused the political axis in many developed countries to shift to the right, sometimes to the far right. The United Nations, from its foundation in the aftermath of the Second World War, has shied away from the subject of migration. It has been bandied around between different UN agencies like a political football.

Kofi Annan, secretary general of the UN between 1997 and 2006, tried to change that. Harvard-educated Irish-American Michael Doyle is currently a professor of international relations at Columbia University in New York, having served between 2001 and 2003 as assistant secretary general and special adviser to Annan. On migration, he says, 'I had written a report for Kofi in 2002 on the challenge migration posed to the multilateral system of law and organisation and how the UN could respond to it. We have treaties for trade and bilateral investment, but migration tended to be unilateral.'

At that point, Annan was looking at ways of developing a framework that would provide for the better regulation of migration. Doyle's report led to the establishment, on 9 December 2003, of a global commission on international migration. But, against the international backdrop of the second Iraq war, it was hardly a propitious moment for UN member states to discuss the matter, never mind reach agreement. It was a hugely divisive issue that bitterly cleaved developed countries. The commission gained very little traction.

In 2005 Annan had the idea that he needed a powerful personality to put migration on the international agenda. He consulted a number of people, including Ed Mortimer, his speechwriter and a former journalist with the *Financial Times*, as well as Doyle, who by then had returned to Columbia University. Both men say that Annan thought of Peter Sutherland, but as soon as his name was mentioned there was an immediate acceptance that he was the right candidate. 'He had enormous credibility in the business community as well as in the EU, but at the same time Kofi knew him as a humanitarian, and that he cared deeply about the human face of globalisation,' says Doyle.

Annan referred to Sutherland as a 'romantic pragmatist'. 'He [Sutherland] cared about the human dimension of globalisation but he was also practical and knew how to cut a deal. He had enormous influence,' Doyle adds. By now, in the days before the financial crisis of 2008, Sutherland was closely associated with BP and Goldman Sachs. 'One of the factors that led Kofi to want him to be a special representative was his business background. Previously he had human rights campaigners. The advantage of Sutherland is that he knew how the world operated. He was not a starry-eyed idealist. He had practical capability. Yet at the same time his heart was on the side of the vulnerable people, the refugees who were driven from their own countries or the very poor who were forced to seek work to feed their families. So he was deeply sympathetic.'

Mortimer agrees that Annan was aware of Sutherland's general view on migration. 'Kofi thought if he could get him to take the role then it would be taken seriously.' Mortimer had encountered Sutherland a decade earlier when the Irishman was setting up the WTO. As a journalist with the *Financial Times* he had attended a conference where Sutherland was the headline speaker; Sutherland had told the audience half-jokingly that he would not let the UN near the WTO.

The UN's reputation in the 1990s was not good. To many it had become an ineffective talking shop. 'Technically the WTO is still outside the UN,' said Doyle. 'Thanks to Kofi, the UN's reputation had improved in those circles. Peter had taken a very tactical line of keeping it away from the UN when he was setting it up.' Annan then went about persuading Sutherland to take a job with the UN. The big question was in what capacity.

A position had opened up unexpectedly in 2005, when Ruud Lubbers, head of the United Nations High Commission for Refugees (UNHCR), was forced to resign because of sexual misconduct allegations. Annan asked Sutherland if he would be interested in replacing the former Dutch prime minister. For the second time, Sutherland and Lubbers were being linked to the same position, although in very different circumstances from the occasion twelve years earlier when they had both gone for the presidency of the European Commission. Sutherland said he would be interested in becoming commissioner of the UNHCR, but he would not be able to disentangle himself from his corporate roles within the period of time needed to take up the position.

Determined to get Sutherland on board, Annan came up with the idea of a UN Special Representative for Migration. The role of special representative is created at the discretion of the secretary general; it has no executive functions within the UN. Sutherland agreed immediately to accept.

At the time it seemed like a Sisyphean endeavour. When Doyle finished his report at the end of 2002 Annan asked the UN membership if they were willing to take on the issue and create a better regulatory regime for migration. There was a very clear and unambiguous response: no. 'There was so much scepticism about international co-operation on migration that we knew we would need a major campaign to educate the public about the value of orderly and safe migration,' says Doyle. 'Sutherland took on that role and set up the global forum on migration and development to think about migration problems and how they could be addressed.'

Interestingly, when the role was first created, it was called the UN Special Representative for Migration and Development. 'It was a way to smuggle it into the UN agenda,' says Mortimer. It was felt that if the focus was solely on migration, then member states would not accept the role, and so development was tacked on. Mortimer remembers a meeting in New York between Sutherland and Annan. 'He approached me and said, I'm not going to be able to do this by myself. I need somebody. I will pay them.' So Mortimer introduced him to Gregory Maniatis.

Maniatis had grown up in Boston and New York until his early teens, when his Greek parents returned home. He went to high school in Greece but returned to the US for university, studying European and International Affairs at Princeton before a stint at the Paris Institute of Political Sciences (familiarly known as Sciences Po). In his early twenties he founded a magazine called *Odyssey* in Greece, selling it a decade later. He went on to become an international journalist, coming into contact with Mortimer when he started writing about the aftermath of the 9/11 attacks for *New York* magazine at the turn of the century, focusing on the role of Kofi Annan and the UN, and subsequently became an expert on Europe at the Migration Policy Institute, a Washington-headquartered think tank. Maniatis flew to London to meet Sutherland in January 2006, and would serve as his number two at the UN for the next eleven years. Sutherland also relied throughout his tenure on the counsel of a former senior UNHCR official, François Fouinat, who was based in Geneva.

There has always been much speculation about why Sutherland took the role. Mary Robinson was the United Nations High Commissioner for Human Rights between 1997 and 2002. 'Peter saw his appointment as give-back time. Maybe it was to compensate for the fact that he had made a lot of money in ways that even he may have had a private judgement on at times,' she claims, although admitting that he never said as much. 'He was a Jesuit, so he could be a good capitalist when he wanted to be. He had a very strong moral conscience. What I felt about him in his passion for migration, it was in part driven by the need to give back for a life that he had lived very successfully.'

Such a view is not widely shared. Dáithí Ó Ceallaigh, who knew Sutherland during this period, says he was very committed to his corporate roles; he felt no shame or private reservations about his association with BP and Goldman Sachs. Maniatis, who developed a very close relationship with Sutherland over the decade they worked together, meanwhile bristles at the idea that Sutherland accepted the migration role as payback for his hugely successful career in the private sector. He says the role was consistent with Sutherland's worldview. 'He believed in global free trade, and the freer movement of people is part of that story.'

Mortimer says he gained the impression that migration was something Sutherland had felt passionately about for a long time: 'This was bound up with his Irish identity and that Ireland was a country that survived for many decades by exporting people. During the Celtic Tiger it started receiving people. Ireland therefore had an obligation to get it right because of its history, he felt. He applied that at a broader level. It chimed with his WTO liberal philosophy. He was in favour of the free movement of goods and persons.'

Michael Doyle says that from the many conversations he had with Sutherland, he gained the impression that Sutherland's business career 'was never the essence of his life'; the EU, WTO and UN was what gave him satisfaction. 'If it was just about the money he would not have taken on the migration role. It gave him a lot of grief. Peter thought that the WTO was a good thing. That doesn't mean that all trade is good. But the world is better off with well-regulated trade because it produces prosperity.' Sutherland felt, says Doyle, that the question of how that wealth was distributed was a matter for national authorities to deal with; it was their responsibility to make sure that the burdens of adjustment to trade were not borne by the poor or the lower skilled. He saw migration as one more aspect of globalisation that needed regulation if it was to deliver on its positive potential. 'Migration is good if you are a refugee because it can save your life; it is good if you are a labour migrant because it allows you to become much more productive for you and your family. And if it is well regulated it has benefits for the host country.'

Annan used the role of special representative to get around the political and bureaucratic constraints of the UN. In other words, Sutherland had no budget and the position carried a $1-a-year salary. He knew, though, that if he was to achieve anything significant in the role, then he would need resources. One of his first acts as special representative in April 2006 was to meet the president of the philanthropic organisation the MacArthur Foundation, Jonathan Fanton, for breakfast at the Ambassador's Grill in New York, as a result of which he received a pledge of $250,000. Over the years he raised funds from other donors; Maniatis nevertheless estimates that Sutherland put well over $1 million of his own money into the office over a decade.

Sutherland's initial brief was to ensure that migration did not turn into a source of conflict that pitted countries in the northern hemisphere against those in the south. When migration was discussed at the UN back then it was in archly political terms. While migration was already a sensitive issue in 2006, it was less contentious than it would become over the next decade. For the first few years, Sutherland's role took up a modest amount of his time. He went to the UN in New York or Geneva roughly four or five times a year and would spend up to three days there, although he would get weekly updates from Maniatis and Fouinat. From 2009 onwards that would change.

From the moment he took the role, says Maniatis, Sutherland went about persuading Annan that migration would become one of the key issues 'of our time' and that the UN had to take a leadership role. According to his former colleagues, Sutherland could see a problem a mile in advance. He was certainly right on migration; his argument was that migration was transnational in nature, that the numbers involved were increasing, and that it was politically important. If the UN could not take a lead role with migration, it would be diminished overall. 'He felt that strongly at the start. He thought it should be on the front burner. Kofi also felt that way,' Maniatis adds. But Annan knew that it would be very hard to get political support.

Sutherland had two main objectives when he took the role. The first was to put migration on the international agenda in some sort of coherent framework. The second was to get the International Organisation for Migration into the UN. Set up in 1951 by European countries as an intergovernmental body to help with the resettlement of millions of refugees displaced by the Second World War, the IOM had expanded its international reach over the subsequent decades, but it remained an organisation that offered member states services and advice on migration.

Sutherland came up with the idea of a Global Forum on Migration and Development (GFMD). In UN terms, a forum is relatively neutral; it has no institutional footing, so it is unlikely to arouse the suspicion of member states. According to Maniatis, this was Sutherland's signature achievement in his early years at the UN, and it set the stage for all his later achievements. The aim of the forum was to establish common understanding and trust on migration among member states, as well as between states and civil society. 'The GFMD was a total act of creation and will. Such a body hadn't been proposed before and there was no similar institution in the UN system to serve as a template.'

According to a memorandum Sutherland sent to Annan in 2006, the GFMD had very specific goals:

The Global Forum on Migration and Development is:
1. Open to participation by all Member States of the United Nations, although participation is voluntary.
2. Non-decision-making, non-policymaking, operating under Chatham House rules, with no recordings, no written transcripts, no attribution of statements; it will never become a decision-making body; put another way, the UN will be a stage, not an actor.
3. Organized by and for governments; governments oversee the Forum and its support services through a Board; other stakeholders attend by invitation only.
4. A place where governments go to learn the state of the art in managing the many linkages between migration and development, and to engage with each other on possible ways to voluntarily cooperate on policies of mutual benefit.
5. Built at the global level on existing regional and other consultative processes, without duplicating them.
6. Focused on migration and development issues, not on migration issues writ large; and based on a shared commitment to practical learning and cooperation.[1]

The main aim was to create a space for discussions of migration to take place between member states in ways that were practical and not overtly political. Sutherland saw the forum as a year-long process that would engage senior policymakers, rather than as a one-day-a-year showcase for politicians. Until it was created, there had been little space at the UN to discuss migration. The problem was how to establish the forum. In the era of the George W. Bush presidency, the US opposed it and was rallying other countries to oppose it too.

Maniatis recalls that in the entire time he worked with Sutherland, he saw him 'visibly shaken' on just three occasions. The first of these was a 2006 meeting with John Bolton, the US ambassador to the UN. An implacable opponent of multilateralism, Bolton would find a soulmate in Donald Trump, who took him from the political wilderness to appoint him his national security advisor in 2018. When Sutherland travelled to New York in the spring of 2006 to begin testing whether the GFMD could generate traction, one of his first meetings was with Bolton. It didn't go well. Bolton ripped into the idea of a forum and declared that the US would go all out to oppose it, since it risked, in his words, becoming 'the seed of a UN Migration Agency'. Sutherland knew that this was a setback but he moved on. In the months ahead he held dozens of bilateral meetings with member states. 'His obvious closeness to Kofi certainly helped the cause,' says Maniatis.

The second time Sutherland was visibly shaken was following a meeting at the Russian embassy in New York. The Russians displayed an equally resolute approach to migration as Bolton; in other words, they were implacably opposed to multilateral co-op-eration in the field.

Consultations that spring with member states, says Maniatis, gave Sutherland enough confidence to include the GFMD proposal in the UN secretary general's report informing that year's first ever High Level Dialogue on Migration and Development, scheduled to be held at UN headquarters in New York in September 2006. 'This was released in June and we spent the summer continuing to define the GFMD and campaign with states and UN agencies, many if not most of which were wary of the endeavour,' said Maniatis.

At the start of September 2006, Sutherland and Maniatis had a meeting with the assistant secretary general of the UN at his office in New York. The assistant general, Bob Orr, was a 'staunch supporter' of Peter's work, according to Maniatis. The idea of the meeting was to put flesh on the bones of the GFMD. 'We were trying to create a space around the forum. We were trying to create an institution that was state led. We had a constant incantation that it was state led, non-binding, and Peter was the only link to the UN. And the secretary general [of the UN] would attend the forum every year.' If the GFMD was not included in the secretary general's speech in September 2006, then it would be a huge setback. Even if it was included, it was necessary to get a critical mass of member states to back it.

'The reality was what we were proposing was so inoffensive,' Maniatis says. The GFMD would be outside the legislative architecture of the UN, its management run by member states. The idea was that three countries would have responsibility for the GFMD at any one time: the current host country, the country that ran it the previous year and the country that would host it in the following year. Alongside this so-called troika of member states, it would be governed by the 'Friends of the Forum' and a steering group, which between them would debate the GFMD's objectives. The only link to the UN was Sutherland. The US was still opposed, and a number of other countries were initially reluctant, including Australia and South Africa. The UK were also reluctant but in the end, it supported Sutherland.

'If you want to manage migration then it is a legitimate viewpoint that it should not be done on a unilateral basis. It is much better if countries develop a framework between them. However, from a country's perspective it is also legitimate that you do not give up control of your border. For many people, who controls who comes into your country and becomes a citizen is the essence of sovereignty. If you want to blow up that fear about who is responsible for rescuing migrants at sea or migrants in crisis countries, and if you suspect that at some stage this leads to somebody telling you who comes into your country, then that is the basis for opposition. The spectre of losing control of sovereignty is what motivates people not to do the basic things that can be done to make migration safer,' explains Maniatis.

The Refugee Convention of 1951 had established a right for persecuted people to cross borders to seek safety. That was the one category of people to whom UN member states were not permitted to refuse entry. But apart from this, there was little legislative framework setting out the rights of migrants outside of broad human rights frameworks.

A number of different agencies within the UN each had some responsibility for migration, and they were all initially suspicious of Sutherland and what he was trying to do. According to Maniatis, Brunson McKinley, then head of the IOM, was also resistant to the concept of a GFMD because it was not led by his organisation. In the early years, moreover, NGOs and civil society groups in the field of migration were deeply suspicious of Sutherland, partly because of his business background. He was seen as an outsider. That would change over time.

Over the summer months of 2006, Sutherland had met a number of governments about his idea for a forum on migration and development. He gained reasonably positive feedback, particularly among some EU member states, and secured a provisional agreement from the Belgian government that it would host the first forum. With the intention that by the time of that year's High Level Dialogue the forum would be a fait accompli, Sutherland enlisted the help of Mortimer, who wrote it into Kofi Annan's speech. But there was a last-minute hitch. On 12 September, two days before the dialogue, the Belgian government told Sutherland it was having second thoughts about hosting the forum. He rang the Belgian foreign minister from New York. 'It was really late at night in Belgium. Peter sounded like an outraged red-faced Irishman on the phone. He told him it was unacceptable. All the time, he was sitting across from me smiling,' recalls Maniatis.

UN member states turned up at the dialogue on 14 September expecting a debate about holding a forum. At 9.15 a.m., however, Annan announced that the first forum would be taking place in

Belgium. 'It was classic Peter,' Maniatis says. It was the same playbook Sutherland had used on the Japanese in the final day of the Uruguay Round talks, when he announced they had been concluded and put it up to the Japanese government to publicly spoil the party. They didn't, and neither did the Belgians.

The first GFMD was held in Belgium in 2007. It has grown in currency ever since, and the next meeting is scheduled to take place in Ecuador in November 2019. That initial forum was the first stake in the ground in terms of institutionalising migration in the UN. In some ways, John Bolton was right to be worried. Initially Sutherland in those early years had been focused on establishing the institution, finding countries to host it and figuring out how to fund it. Then he had to figure out its relationship with civil society groups.

The US did not show up in the forum's first few years. Then Barack Obama won the presidential election in November 2008. That changed everything. In the person of assistant secretary of state Eric Schwartz, the US attended at a high level for the first time in 2010, when the forum was held in Mexico. Schwartz was succeeded by Anne Richard, who developed a close relationship with Sutherland that would be responsible for one of the big institutional shifts in migration.

Sutherland was insistent that the forum would have a practical focus, identifying a number of areas that it was necessary to address. For example, there was a very significant issue with remittances. In 2006, every $100 a migrant sent back to their home country could cost up to $15. If the forum could reach agreement on reducing the cost of remittances, then it would increase the overall amount of money migrants were able to send their dependants at home. Another area that needed addressing urgently was the regulation of recruitment. Migrants going from Asia to the Middle East were in some cases paying up to 40 per cent of their earnings to recruitment firms.

In 2011, when the Libyan civil war broke out, 100,000 migrant workers were stuck in the country, including an estimated 60,000 Bangladeshis. There was no protocol at the UN or any other level to deal with migrants in these situations. When Sutherland raised it as an issue and went in search of a solution, he got help from the Obama administration. Migrants in Countries in Crisis (MICIC) is a government-led effort co-chaired by the United States and the Philippines, aimed at improving the protection of migrants when the countries in which they live, work, study, transit, or travel experience a conflict or natural disaster.

Sutherland and Maniatis went about identifying further crucial matters relating to migration that needed to be addressed. For example, what happens to migrants stranded at sea when their boat capsizes? Who is responsible for rescuing them? This would become one of the crux issues of the Mediterranean crisis, and it remains unresolved. Climate change, moreover, has the potential to make the Mediterranean crisis look like the mere prelude to a more intractable phase in the migration saga. If a village becomes uninhabitable as a result of climate change and 10,000 people are left without a home, they are not refugees under the UN Convention. But what happens to them? How can the UN go about co-ordinating an effective response? There are those like John Bolton, says Maniatis, who reject any proposal that impinges on sovereignty and don't believe in multilateralism. How do they react if somebody tells them they have to take climate change refugees? 'I think that was a big part of the backlash in Europe; the spectre of tens of millions of Africans being displaced because of climate change. That is an extremely politically sensitive issue.'

*

By 2009 the global financial crisis had erupted, and the world faced the worst economic downturn since the 1930s. Migration had never been at the forefront of the international agenda, and never would be as long as countries grappled with existential issues such as national solvency. But the aftermath of the financial crisis would form a toxic backdrop to the migration debate.

The Arab Spring in 2010 was the klaxon that heralded the subsequent migration crisis.

Migration started edging centre stage in 2012. Sutherland unintentionally played his part in fanning the flames of discontent when he appeared before a House of Lords EU home affairs sub-committee in June 2012. Even though he gave extensive testimony, news outlets reported just one line – that the EU should 'do its best to undermine the homogeneity of its member states'. The line generated acres of coverage; although taken out of context, it would be used repeatedly against Sutherland for the rest of his life. The right-wing British press were the first to turn on him. A week after his appearance in the House of Lords, this withering profile appeared in the *Daily Mail*:

On 21 June Peter Sutherland, KCMG, SC, UN Special Representative on Migration, sat massively opposite a House of Lords EU affairs sub-committee, a soft-faced man who has done very well indeed out of the culture wars. His erstwhile rugby-playing physique may be collapsing in on itself, but still he faced forward, safe in an armature of absolute self-belief and the certainty that he is on the side of History. His has been the life of a man of parts, one who walks and talks with the great, reminiscent of one of Holbein's Ambassadors, surrounded by measuring instruments and all the external signs of extreme cultivation, peering down on human affairs from a great height. Yet Mr. Sutherland's manicured machinations could prove calamitous for what remains of the West – just as Holbein includes a distorted skull to remind the viewer that all rational hopes are in vain. That is why he was peering at the House of Lords sub-committee like some well-fed but still peckish bird of prey, looking at the parochial parliamentarians from their dusty old-fashioned legislature – perhaps contrasting them unfavourably with the big-picture bureaucrats of his Global Forum on Migration and Development. He was there to answer questions about the government's immigration policies – and from the outset it was plain that he disapproved. And not just of the policy – but Britain's whole political structure, culture and national identity – all now, he broadly hinted, overripe for replacement.[2]

This shrill and personalised attack on Sutherland was tame in comparison to his portrayal across the fledgling alt-right movement on social media. He was depicted as a Jewish banker intent on dismantling the nation state. The fact that Sutherland was a member of the Bilderberg Group and the Trilateral Commission was grist to the mill for the keyboard warriors. The Bilderberg Group, in particular, holds a special place for conspiracy theorists. It is an annual meeting, held in private, for top business people, politicians, academics and the media. Sutherland was on the steering committee for a number of years.

However, Sutherland's House of Lords testimony was far more nuanced than the reports suggested. He said migration was a 'crucial dynamic for economic growth in some EU nations, however difficult it may be to explain this to the citizens of those states'. An ageing or declining native population in countries like Germany or the southern EU states was the 'key argument and, I hesitate to the use the word because people have attacked it, for the development of multicultural states . . . It's impossible to consider that the degree of homogeneity which is implied by the other argument can survive because states have to become more open states, in terms of the people who inhabit them. Just as the United Kingdom has demonstrated. The United States, or Australia and New Zealand, are migrant societies and therefore they accommodate more readily those from other backgrounds than we do ourselves, who still nurse a sense of our homogeneity and difference from others. And that's precisely what the European Union, in my view, should be doing its best to undermine.'[3]

In other words, Sutherland believed that most EU member states were facing a demographic timebomb that threatened future economic growth, and migration formed part of the solution. These countries would therefore have to live with diversity. It was not a call to destroy English culture or the culture of any country. Sutherland did not believe in open borders. What he wanted was much greater co-operation among countries in order to manage migration. He wrote at the time:

> Let me be clear: I am not making an argument for more or for less migration – although I do make the case for OECD countries to resettle more refugees. I am arguing for putting in place policies that will allow migration to occur in a safer, more orderly manner, and that also improve development outcomes. If we can achieve this, I am confident that the public will be on our side.

18

THE BIGGEST CRISIS OF OUR TIME

WITH THE START OF THE SYRIAN CIVIL WAR IN March 2011, the resulting displacement of millions of people would have immediate consequences for its neighbouring countries – and eventually for Europe. Sutherland knew that unless the UN and the EU had a comprehensive contingency plan in place, then the region was facing a migration crisis that would have profound humanitarian and political consequences.

Sutherland stood down from his role as chairman of BP in June 2009, and at the same time cut back on his corporate activity to focus on the migration role. His acute political antennae sensed that migration would be the geopolitical lodestone of the coming decade. He was correct. Along with Gregory Maniatis he set out a list of priorities for what he wanted to achieve.

The first of these, launched in autumn 2012, was to make migration one of the UN's 2030 Sustainable Development Goals. Over the next three years Sutherland lobbied intensively to put migration, immigrant integration and refugee protection on the agenda. In 2015 his efforts were to pay off through his close work with key governments such as Sweden and Switzerland, as well as key agencies and civil society partners. It was an important victory – but, in view of the scale of the escalating crisis, only a small step.

When Sutherland took on the migration role in 2006, the NGOs and civil society groups focused on migration hadn't trusted him because of his background. They viewed Sutherland as lacking either experience or the right motives, and sometimes both. That had now changed. Civil society groups had themselves been trying, without much success, to include migration in the UN's 2030 Sustainable Development Goals agenda. The fact that Sutherland had succeeded, along with his wider efforts in the field of migration, triggered a change in attitudes. By 2015, Sutherland had gained profound respect among civil society groups. Unfortunately, he was having a much harder time gaining the same recognition at state level.

After Sutherland was brought into the UN by Kofi Annan, the two men had developed a very close relationship. On 1 January 2007, Annan was succeeded by Ban Ki-moon, formerly South Korea's Minister for Foreign Affairs, for a 10 year term. The relationship between Sutherland and Moon was more transactional; Sutherland was never sure how much support he would receive from the new UN secretary general if he needed it. The answer came only in 2013, when, on the eve of the second High-Level Dialogue on Migration and Development, Sutherland attended a reception at the residence of the Mexican ambassador in New York. There he encountered John Ashe, the President of the UN General Assembly, and challenged him about his refusal to allow civil society to have a more prominent role at the dialogue. (Ashe, who was from Antigua and Barbuda, was subsequently arrested and charged for taking bribes from a Chinese billionaire. He died in 2016 while awaiting trial.) The exchange was acrimonious. Sutherland was furious; it was the third time that Maniatis saw him really shaken. Sutherland insisted that the two of them walk the thirty blocks back to his hotel. He told Maniatis that he would have no choice but to resign given the heat of the conversation that evening. When Maniatis told Jan Eliasson, Moon's deputy, how angry Sutherland was, Eliasson reported this to Moon. In response, Moon met Sutherland the next day and told him: 'As long as I'm here you are here.' At that moment Sutherland knew that he had Moon's full confidence.

Even though Sutherland had been successful in including migration as part of the 2030 agenda, he knew more immediate and co-ordinated action was needed. But there was very little appetite, either among governments or at an EU level, to take on the issue. It was still far too divisive. Meanwhile large numbers of refugees from Syria and economic migrants from Africa were compelled to make the journey across the Mediterranean with the aim of reaching Europe. In late 2014 and early 2015, Sutherland intensified his lobbying efforts, warning the UN once more about the scale of the looming crisis. There were up to five million refugees in Turkey, Lebanon and Jordan, and they were not going to stay there forever. He told Ban Ki-moon that the UN had to get involved, while he and Maniatis reached out to Alex Betts, an academic at Oxford University. Betts, who had studied the Vietnamese boat crisis and the international community's response, was possibly the world's leading expert on the looming migration crisis.

In the months before April 2015, Sutherland began urging Ban Ki-moon and Jan Eliasson to step up the UN's diplomacy on the Syrian refugee crisis. After April he escalated his campaign, proposing the creation of the UN Quartet – consisting of António Guterres, the UN High Commissioner for Refugees; Prince Said, the High Commissioner for Human Rights; Bill Swing, the director general of the IOM; and Sutherland himself – to lead the UN's response. He urged Moon to convene national and regional leaders to develop a plan of action.

'Peter was insistent that there had to be a comprehensive plan of action for the Syrian refugee crisis,' says Maniatis. 'We wanted something practical to happen. We wanted states to come together to feed these people, otherwise they were going to have to cross the Mediterranean. It is spectacular that this event was never systemically analysed. There was never a UN attempt to analyse what happened with the Syria crisis, and to try and figure out a plan of action. That is what really infuriated Peter. It led to the renationalisation of migration policy. It helped lead to the decay of the political centre in Europe.'

Sutherland's aim for the quartet was that the four offices would co-ordinate an international response to the migration crisis. The quartet went to Berlin in the summer of 2015 for a meeting with German Chancellor Angela Merkel, but there was no official response from the UN, no commitment to a plan of action. Sutherland wanted to arrange a meeting between Jean-Claude Juncker, the president of the European Commission, and Ban Ki-moon, but Moon did not want to get involved.

There are a number of theories as to why Sutherland was meeting so much resistance from the UN. According to certain well-placed sources, Moon briefed UN officials that he could not risk another high-profile failure. In 2009 the UN Climate Summit had taken place in Copenhagen, with about 45,000 delegates from around the world descending on the Danish capital. There was heightened expectation that the UN would broker a historic breakthrough on climate action. But the summit ended without agreement. It was Moon's first big challenge as secretary general, and it was a failure. He didn't want a repeat, which he thought would damage the UN, and in view of the fractured consensus on migration, the possibility of failure was considerable. There was also speculation at the time linking Moon with the presidency of South Korea. A high-profile setback of this scale would almost certainly dent his chances.

There is another explanation: the majority of UN member states were unaffected by the Syrian refugee crisis. Many of these countries felt that the problem was Europe's to solve. In theory the UNHCR sees its role as giving help to countries that cannot cope with refugees. The European Union is one of the richest blocs in the world; with a population of roughly 500 million people, it was faced with an influx of approximately one million refugees. Countries such as Pakistan and India took the view that the only reason this had been deemed a crisis was because it affected Europe; the EU should be able to manage it without the UN. But the scale of inaction would ensure that the crisis worsened, with yet more destabilising consequences.

The political stakes for the EU were increasing in proportion to the level of inaction. EU leaders lacked agreement in response to the crisis. The bloc was still recovering from the ravages of the financial meltdown; the single currency had come close to being sundered by member states, including Ireland, that faced solvency issues, while the austerity measures needed to restore fiscal rectitude had frayed the political consensus to breaking point. Insurgent populist parties were on the rise, particularly in the countries, such as Greece and Italy, that were most affected by the migration crisis. A number of emergency EU summits failed to agree a coherent and effective response to the migration crisis at its southern borders. Italy and Greece were demanding greater solidarity from northern member states, but a lurch to the right in some of those countries made finding a compromise almost impossible. Austria for example proposed a cap on the number of asylum seekers allowed entry to just eighty a day. In the autumn of 2015, it is estimated that 7,000 refugees were arriving in Greece from Turkey every day.

Sutherland gave up his role at Goldman Sachs altogether in 2015 to focus on the migration crisis. As a humanitarian he cared deeply about the plight of refugees, while as a passionate European he also believed in the inherent benefits of European integration. He made a decision around this time to mount a public campaign to raise awareness about migration. He opened a Twitter account, which became a magnet for every paranoid malcontent on social media. He also made countless appearances on TV and radio, and penned a number of newspaper articles on the subject.

Such pieces pulled no punches. The following was written for Project Syndicate, an international media organisation that publishes syndicated commentary, in 2015:

The EU is in disarray. Faced with waves of asylum seekers from conflict-ridden states, too many European countries have acted selfishly and unilaterally, undermining any chance of an effective collective response to the crisis.

Rather than calmly handling an eminently manageable situation, they have made Europe appear incompetent, near hysterical and without integrity.

This is not to deny credit where credit is due. Under the leadership of chancellor Angela Merkel, Germany has welcomed hundreds of thousands of people – not without controversy but in relative calm. Berlin also has been honest in declaring that the European asylum system is not working. 'If Europe fails on the question of refugees, if this close link with universal civil rights is broken,' Ms Merkel stated bluntly this week, 'then it won't be the Europe we wished for.'

Greece and Italy, which have rescued more refugees than any other member states – and Sweden, the EU state that has taken in most per capita – also have acted honourably. Countless thousands of private citizens and non-governmental organisations have done the same.

But Europe's failure to measure up to the human disaster has radically increased the human, financial and political costs of the crisis. One of the bedrocks of the EU, the Schengen free-movement zone, is now in jeopardy. It is not too late for the bloc to recover from a crisis largely of its own making. As hardline, anti-migrant parties surge in many countries, European governments must show they can work together to tame the chaos, uphold international law and show compassion to those in need.

Europe's leaders and media need to start calling the situation what it is: a refugee crisis, not a migration crisis. At least two-thirds of those crossing the Mediterranean come from Syria, Eritrea, Afghanistan and other states from which they are legitimately fleeing persecution. Refugees have inalienable rights under international law, and their plight is well understood by the European public. Only a minority of those taking to the seas are economic migrants.

The EU also needs to give far greater help – starting straight away – to Lebanon, Jordan and Turkey, which together host 4m Syrian refugees. Such aid will be far more effective than military missions or yet more dogs and barbed wire at border posts. Most refugees prefer to stay close to home. But, if there are no schools or jobs for them in front-line countries, they will move on. Four years into the Syrian conflict, this is what is happening.

Simultaneously, the EU must make every effort to establish safe and legal means for asylum seekers to seek protection in Europe without risking their lives. This could be done through massively expanded resettlement; by establishing private sponsorship programmes so that individuals, churches and NGOs can take responsibility for integrating refugees; by issuing humanitarian, labour, family reunification and student visas – or a combination of all these.

Finally, EU member states should agree to a permanent system of sharing responsibility for processing and hosting asylum seekers and refugees. The European Commission's plan to relocate 40,000 asylum seekers from Greece and Italy, rejected by member states, needs to be expanded and made mandatory. There are many details to work out, but such a programme is within reach.

This would be the first, necessary step towards a single European asylum system – not a hodge-podge of 28 systems that produce vastly different outcomes. So far this year, Hungary has granted asylum to just 278 out of 148,000 applicants – barely 0.2 per cent. By contrast, Germany has accepted 40 per cent of applications. This chasm makes a mockery of both the law and the notion of a common system.

An emergency meeting of EU interior ministers scheduled for September 14 needs to make inroads on this. But the rest of the world also needs to do far more. The world's 20m refugees, a historic high, are a shared responsibility – one that at present falls most heavily on the developing world, where 86 per cent of refugees live.

The global refugee system was originally created to help Europeans, and it has helped save and rebuild the lives of millions of them. Now, with the system strained, faltering and outdated, Europe should reciprocate. It is time for the EU to rescue its integrity and dignity before they, too, perish in the Mediterranean.[1]

During 2015, Sutherland had formed the view that the most effective way of addressing the Syrian crisis was through a UN summit. He pushed Moon and Eliasson to support a special conference to deal with the Syria crisis. He formed an alliance with the White House. When Sutherland took over the migration role, the US administration, under instructions from John Bolton, had tried to block every initiative he proposed. Under Barack Obama, that would change utterly. Throughout 2015, the US looked on in frustration at the growing inaction of both the UN and the EU, and in October of that year, Washington would back Sutherland in two crucial areas. Sutherland's lobbying since 2006 to get the IOM into the UN had been based on the rationale that because there was no single UN institution responsible for migration, it slipped between the cracks. These shortcomings had been cruelly exposed by the Mediterranean crisis. UN member states resisted his pleas on the basis that migration should remain a national competence. The most visceral opponent of integrating the IOM with the UN, when Sutherland initially proposed it in 2006, had been the US. In 2015, Sutherland had developed very good ties with US Secretary of State John Kerry, Tony Blinken, the Deputy Secretary of State, and Anne Richard, Assistant Secretary of State. A meeting in Istanbul in October 2015, shortly after the Alan Kurdi tragedy, was attended by Richards, António Guterres, Jan Eliasson and Bill Swing, as well as Sutherland himself.

For a brief period, this boy's death changed the tone of the debate about migration. In the Canadian general election campaign of October 2015, the death of Kurdi had featured prominently; the young boy had drowned on the first step of a journey where Canada was the final destination. Stephen Harper, the incumbent prime minister, equivocated in response to the tragedy. Justin Trudeau, his opponent, pledged to take in 40,000 Syrian refugees. Trudeau won a thumping majority. The Kurdi affair was not decisive, but it played a role in shaping public opinion.

October 2015 was also important for Sutherland for another reason. The US said it was prepared to lead on a special summit for Syria, with the specific aim of providing funding for the World Food Programme and assistance for Turkey, Jordan and Lebanon to prevent them being overwhelmed by the influx of migrants. Again the UN resisted the idea, and Sutherland found out through back channels the reason why. During a peacekeeping summit held by the UN that autumn, Jan Eliasson had felt that the US had strong-armed countries into taking roles as peacekeepers. He feared that the US would similarly bully countries into making commitments at a special summit for Syria. There began a diplomatic shoving match between the US and the UN.

Assistant secretary of state Tony Blinken focused his diplomatic efforts on the quartet. The UN finally announced on 20 November 2015 that a summit would be held in September 2016. But it would be a summit on refugees and migrants. Eliasson insisted that it couldn't only be about refugees and it couldn't only be about Syria. It fell far short of what Sutherland had hoped.

The life of young Alan Kurdi, however, was pivotal in one of the biggest institutional shifts in the approach to migration. Richard said she could persuade John Kerry to bring the IOM into the UN. And she did. The key moment came in June 2016 at a vote of the IOM council, when it agreed to become part of the UN. The official signing ceremony was scheduled to take place at the UN summit on 19–20 September 2016. But, as a result of the heart attack Sutherland had suffered a few days earlier, he would miss one of his most significant achievements as UN Special Representative for Migration. There was a round of applause from the floor in his honour.

In January 2016, Sutherland had missed Davos for the first time in nearly three decades. Instead he visited the beaches in Greece to monitor first hand the scale of the crisis. His frustrations with the UN occasionally spilled over, particularly in correspondence. Here is just one of countless emails sent by Sutherland to both Moon and Eliasson during this period:

Dear Jan

The UN, in my view, must demonstrate leadership at this vital moment – that is really what is being asked for by both the US and Germany. The Global Compact Conference will not, in itself, provide such a demonstration. It is probably a good thing but its time frame and general remit will not answer the obvious need for a Mediterranean initiative focused on Syria which I, at least, do not believe will be adequately covered by other proposed conferences (which are not, in any event, under UN aegis).

Another concern I have is that many of the persons that we should be protecting are not refugees at all and this is not merely a UNHCR matter. IOM have a big role to play for one so does Human Rights.

So I remain convinced that there is an urgent need for the Secretary General to call for an International Conference of two parts: firstly an immediate one relating to Syria and secondly to the Compact.

The UN must be seen to be a leader at this time.

Best regards,
Peter

The US was still determined to focus on refugees, and on Syria. Samantha Power, the Dublin-born US ambassador to the UN, pushed Eliasson on the matter. On 20 December 2015, the US, whose patience with the UN had by then run out, announced that it would hold its own summit – to be known as the Obama summit – in September 2016. Focused exclusively on Syria, it was looking for specific commitments from the countries involved.

Positive developments emerged from both summits, although they fell short of the outcomes that Sutherland had wanted. The UN summit led to the New York declaration on refugees and migrants, the 126 pages of which were mostly aspirational – but at least it clearly stated that it was the political will of member states to save lives, protect rights and share responsibility on a global scale. The summit itself achieved very little else. The countries that attended failed even to agree a plan to resettle 10 per cent of the world's refugee population. At the Obama summit, meanwhile, the US agreed to increase its intake from 85,000 to 110,000, while some countries that had never taken refugees pledged to do so.

*

The idea of a Sutherland Report on migration was originally conceived in 2012, but work started on it only in 2014. The aim was to put together a comprehensive plan and set of guidelines on how countries could work together to ensure orderly, safe migration. When, after two years, it was published, it turned out to be Sutherland's most important written legacy. The report was very mindful of the impact migration had on host countries, although it chimed with Sutherland's broad philosophy on migration: that it was a force for good but for it to work it had to be well managed.

In the opening of the report, Sutherland wrote:

Migration is generally good news, but its benefits can take time to materialize, while many of the associated costs arise upfront. And there are inevitably individuals – indeed some-times large social groups – for whom it is harmful. Their concerns can and must be addressed, not brushed aside. But that requires an effort, not only from governments but from society as a whole. Rather than playing on fears or exaggerating problems, we need to identify those problems systematically, and look for practical solutions. Above all, it is in everyone's interest for migration to happen safely and legally, in a regulated rather than a clandestine way. The latter not only exposes other workers to unfair competition, provoking resentment and lowering overall standards of welfare, safety and hygiene, but also puts migrants at the mercy of unscrupulous employers and traffickers, who may subject them to the worst abuses – sometimes described as 'modern slavery', which is abhorrent to all mankind.[2]

In the conclusion of the report, Sutherland reflected on the themes that had defined his decade-long tenure. He lamented that nothing could be achieved without trust – 'trust among governments, as well as between governments and their constituents'. Sutherland pushed the point that at no time in recent history had the bonds of trust been so frayed between governments, particularly on issues surrounding migration, 'about which the general public is fearful and badly informed'. Because of this, Sutherland knew that progress could only be made incrementally.

He continued:

That is why I suggest tackling problems at the lowest level where they can be solved. Sometimes that means the local or national level, but on some issues States need to work together, bilaterally, at the regional or even the global level – seizing on the initiatives of pioneers and champions, and working through what has been called 'mini-multilateralism', whereby small groups of interested states work together to develop and implement new ideas that can then be debated, and perhaps adopted, in more formal settings. Attending to the concerns of those who feel threatened by migration is necessary, if we are to avoid destructive reactions and achieve sustainable results. Confrontation will get us nowhere. Progress on international cooperation in this area must take the interests of all legitimate actors into account. As long as there are stakeholders for whom the system is not working, they will at best ignore it or worse, undermine it. Listening to each other, seeking tirelessly to identify shared goals and to agree on paths for reaching them, will – I am convinced – enable us to find solutions that hold out hope for us all.[3]

According to Maniatis, the UN was initially resistant. Normally this type of report would be requested by the UN system, but there was clearly no appetite at an institutional level for its putative aims. 'We wrote it but we didn't want to have to get UN support because we didn't want it to sound like a UN report. We needed a lot of leverage to get it published by the UN without having it reviewed by the UN. The main aim we had was to speak straight about the challenges facing migration, and to outline what could be the foundations for international co-operation. For example, if the IOM was placed within the UN, then what would it do? What should be the priorities that the UN should tackle? What should member states do? How do you go about that in a practical way?'

The Sutherland Report was finished at the end of 2016 and was the product of among the most systematic work ever conducted on migration. Sutherland had committed the funds needed to strengthen his New York team to work on the report. In drafting the report, Maniatis was joined by Doyle, Mortimer, Fouinat, and several other independent migration experts and other advisors – Colleen Thouez, Sarah Rosengaertner, Justin MacDermott, Katy Long, Kathleen Newland and Maggie Powers. Sutherland had read a final draft a few days before his heart attack. But because he had been unable to approve the final document, Maniatis and the team spent three months getting pushback from the UN.

'The UN view was, how can it be called the Sutherland Report when he hasn't signed off on the final draft? I ended up going personally to Guterres to get his support to publish it,' says Maniatis. Guterres ensured that the report was translated and published in February 2017, and it would help form the basis for the UN's Global Compact for Migration.

The Global Compact for Migration is not legally binding and allows countries to remain in charge of their own immigration policy, but commits signatories to improving co-operation on international migration. The pact was agreed by all 193 UN members, except the United States, in July 2018, and was to be formally ratified at a conference in Marrakesh in December 2018. That October, however, it became highly politicised. Sebastian Kurz, the coltish chancellor of Austria, who had flirted with the far right on his way to becoming the country's youngest ever leader, publicly expressed reservations about the pact. Viktor Orbán, the authoritarian prime minister of Hungary, came out against it. The Yellow Vest movement in France organised against it. The Belgian government collapsed because of the pact. Although the Global Compact for Migration was signed in Marrakesh on 16 December 2018, only 164 countries had formally adopted it at the ceremony on 10 December. Among those who refused to adopt the deal – in addition to the United States – were Hungary, Austria, Italy, Poland, Slovakia, Chile and Australia.

It was still a significant achievement. Maniatis has bittersweet memories of the ceremony. Sutherland had set out twelve years earlier to put migration on the agenda. There had been a number of victories along the way, but the signing of the global compact was by far the most important. Sutherland, however, would not live to see this outcome.

History very rarely repeats itself, but it often rhymes. Twenty-four years earlier, in the same city, Sutherland had presided over the ratification of the Uruguay Round of trade talks. That, some people would argue, had been the starting point of globalisation. The compact on migration directly addressed one inevitable outcome of that process.

*

Migration today is perhaps a less politically sensitive issue than it was in 2015 and 2016, but it is still divisive. It is still fuelling populism and the move to the far right, particularly in Europe. 'A lot of that is based on the misunderstanding of emigration,' observes Michael Doyle. 'There are lots of studies to show that well-regulated migration, not just opening your borders, is a net long-run positive on societies, but it has to be well managed so that the type of people who would be in competition with migrants have the resources invested in them that allow them to also prosper. That can be done. We see that in the UK migration was a big factor in the Brexit vote, but cities like London are dependent on migration.'

In 2015, at the height of the Mediterranean crisis, Angela Merkel, the German chancellor, took the very brave decision to announce an open border policy and accept an estimated one million asylum seekers. The move caused a backlash not only in her own country but also throughout Europe, and featured prominently in the Brexit campaign. When Sutherland met Merkel in the autumn of 2015, he whispered in her ear, 'You are my hero'; it is safe to assume that his reaction was quite different from most others she had encountered.

In retrospect, says Doyle, Merkel's policy had unfortunate consequences, because the image of open borders was played upon very heavily by the far right. But he wonders what she could have done differently in the circumstances. 'Tens of thousands of migrants were flowing through Austria and arriving at the German border. It is not clear they could have all been vetted adequately, which is what should have happened. The Austrians were threatening to close their border, which would have backed the problem into less humane circumstances in Hungary.

'The only migration that is good migration is when it is safe, orderly and regulated to ensure that there is proper vetting to keep out criminals, to ensure that refugees are legitimate and that labour migrants are needed in the recipient economy,' adds Doyle. 'Nobody would say Germany was a model of what should have happened, and I don't think Peter would have said so, but in the circumstances it was the only humane thing to do. It will probably take another ten years for the German investment to be recouped.'

Doyle was not surprised at Sutherland's passion for migration. Assessing his legacy on the matter, he believes, will take time. 'His main accomplishments are founding the GFMD and bringing everybody together to see what needed to be done.' The end result of his efforts, the New York Declaration of 2016, greatly improved understanding of refugees. Sutherland was on track, says Doyle, to create the kind of institutions that led to the WTO. 'We are not there and it was not achieved during his lifetime, but he was laying the intellectual foundations for a better regime for migration. I think he will be considered the pioneer who outlined a humane face for global migration.'

Mary Robinson commends Sutherland's practical approach to migration. 'I was very impressed about how articulate he was on the subject. He wasn't naive about migration.' She adds, 'He was very good at building alliances. He was very good at cajoling. When you have somebody who has a strong personality and has a passion, it's called leadership, although he could be a benevolent bully at times. I think Peter's main legacy is that he was hugely influential in making migration a central issue.'

According to Mortimer, Sutherland stayed in the UN migration role for longer than anybody expected. The Sutherland Report, he believes, would probably have had more of an impact if he had been able to personally present it at the UN. 'People took notice of him. As far as I could see he was not intimidated by the backlash on social media. He would have preferred to do it in a non-confrontational way.' Sutherland was, says Mortimer, 'a liberal with a small l'.

In October 2016, António Guterres was unveiled for his five-year term as secretary general of the United Nations, replacing Ban Ki-moon. Other candidates who had applied for the position included Helen Clark, the former New Zealand prime minister and head of the UN Development Programme; Irina Bokova, the Bulgarian chief of UNESCO, the cultural and educational agency; Danilo Turk, an ex-president of Slovenia and former UN assistant secretary general; Igor Lukšić, Montenegro's foreign minister; Natalia Gherman and Vesna Pusić, former foreign ministers of Moldova and Croatia respectively.

Although it was never publicly disclosed, Peter Sutherland had also thrown his hat in the ring. In the summer of 2015, he had held private discussions with several friends and associates about his intentions. As Gregory Maniatis explains, 'I don't think there was a time when he thought there was a decent chance it would happen. He spoke to people in Ireland and a few other countries. He was perfect for the role. He was visionary and he knew how to manage. He got enough positive feedback from countries to keep his campaign going for a year. We gamed out a lot of different scenarios. We could see a pathway for Peter. He had risen very much in prominence over 2015 and 2016. It wasn't such a strong field that you would think he didn't have a chance.'

There was one big problem, however. The UN Security Council had a veto – and Russia, as a member, could exercise that veto. Sutherland sensed that this presented a roadblock. When he was chairman of BP, he had taken on powerful Russian oligarchs close to Russian President Vladimir Putin, while the Russians were fundamentally opposed to his views on migration. 'He also had the sense that the French viewed him as too much of a free marketeer to be suitable for high office,' says Maniatis. Because of this, Sutherland quietly dropped his campaign in the spring of 2016.

19

A TURBULENT
RELATIONSHIP WITH IRELAND

T HE EARLY 1990S WAS A TIME OF PROFOUND change for the Irish and European economies, as member states began dismantling state monopolies in the telecoms, energy and aviation sectors. Ireland's economy had been highly protectionist from the inception of the state until the early 1990s. Like other countries, it faced challenges in ensuring that former monopolies were replaced with fair competition. As a result, it began opening up to outside investment. When Peter Sutherland returned to Ireland after his four-year stint as European commissioner to join AIB, he also took on presidential roles at the Institute of Bankers and Ibec, the employers' representative group.

Brian Cowen, Minister for Transport in the Fianna Fáil government at the time, observes of the privatisation era: 'It was a great opportunity for Ireland to get capital in. We had sectors that needed huge investment – aviation and telecoms in particular. The question was, how would you bring investment in while competition remained fair? It was important not to let companies cherry pick aspects that were profitable and leave the state with the rest. I got to know Sutherland during this period. He made himself available in terms of advice. He never crossed any lines. He made sure Ireland was au fait with the trends at the time. He made sure Ireland had the best policies that avoided the ravages of excessive capitalism.'

Sutherland has always been closely associated with Fine Gael, but when it came to matters of national importance, he was never afraid to cross the floor. The early 1990s was another difficult period for the Irish economy. While the structural reforms that would give birth to the rapid expansion of the economy from the mid-nineties onwards, known as the Celtic Tiger, had begun, Ireland's membership of the Exchange Rate Mechanism was fraught with risks. After the UK was famously forced to abandon the ERM on 16 September 1992, there was an immediate run on the Irish punt. It was the early days of the IIEA, and director Brendan Halligan decided something had to be done. When the staunch Labour Party man began putting together relevant information for the market, Sutherland was the only one who helped him. 'He rolled up his sleeves and spent days in the office. In the end we had to throw our hands in the air because the punt was devalued.' Sutherland went on *Morning Ireland* to argue that Ireland had to be at the core of Europe, and that meant joining the embryonic single currency.

When Sutherland joined GATT, Maruja and the family remained in Dublin while Sutherland made the weekly commute to Geneva. Sutherland kept a relatively low profile in Ireland for the next decade. There was the occasional interview or conference speech, but his business career was all-consuming. He briefly became embroiled in the tribunal into one of Ireland's biggest scandals.

In 1997, Michael Moriarty, who had devilled with Sutherland and who at that stage was a High Court judge, was appointed to oversee a tribunal of inquiry into alleged payments made to politicians. The long-running Moriarty Tribunal delivered the finding in March 2011 that Michael Lowry, the Minister for Communications, had secured the winning of the state's second mobile phone licence for the businessman Denis O'Brien's consortium, Esat Digifone, in 1995. O'Brien and Lowry have both denied any wrongdoing, and have rejected the findings. The tribunal was extensive and forensically looked under the bonnet of Irish public life over the previous few decades. Sutherland was dragged into its remit in January 2000 when the inquiry was looking at the activities of Guinness & Mahon, a bank that had an extensive network of offshore accounts, known as Ansbacher accounts, that had been a vital cog in a number of tax avoidance strategies. It emerged that when Sutherland had bought his house in Blackrock in 1976, the loan was secured by an account held in Guinness & Mahon's Guernsey branch. The beneficial owner of the account was Sutherland's Spanish father-in-law. Sutherland proved to the inquiry that he never had any improper offshore accounts. The tribunal never made any findings against him.

It was only at the time of the Lisbon Treaty referendum in 2008 that Sutherland again took a prominent role in his home country. A firm believer that Ireland's prosperity hinged on being a core member of the EU, he was horrified that the Irish electorate had voted down the first Nice Treaty in 2001, although the result had been overturned in a subsequent referendum in 2002.

Ireland's relationship with the EU changed in the 2000s. For most of the period from accession in 1973 onwards, the Irish people had been enthusiastic members of the bloc. Now, the Celtic Tiger imbued Ireland with a confidence that quickly morphed into arrogance. The Irish economic model of the mid-1990s onwards was based on a business-friendly environment with a corporate tax rate of 12.5 per cent. There was also a plentiful supply of well-educated young people, and Ireland was still a relatively low-cost location.

As a result the country became a magnet for US investment. The economy, which had been largely moribund since the foundation of the state, suddenly began to grow at double-digit rates. Unemployment, which had stood at 17 per cent in the early

1990s, was on its way to low single digits. No longer a country that exported people, Ireland was now a net recipient of inward migration. *The Economist* in the 1980s had described Ireland as the 'sick man of Europe'; it was considered the poorest of the rich countries. By the 2000s, the journal was feting the Celtic Tiger as an economic miracle and imploring other EU member states to follow Ireland's lead. The usual apologetic tone adopted by Irish ministers in Brussels was replaced by a swagger.

Mary Harney, the former Tánaiste and leader of the Progressive Democrats, summed it up with the pithy observation: 'Ireland has always spiritually been closer to Boston than Berlin.' It is safe to assume Sutherland would not have agreed with her assessment of Ireland's self-interest.

In an interview with the *Irish Times* in 2010, Sutherland said that Ireland had been a failed state in economic terms apart from a brief period between 1994 and 2002. 'This sent a signal to multinational investors that they didn't have to locate in France to sell in France. A low corporation tax rate of 12.5 per cent gave the country a dynamic boost. Then we reduced our competitive advantage by eating it up with waste and wage increases beyond what was possible for us to handle.' Ireland received 'incredible largesse' from the EU through the 1980s and 1990s, yet 'delivered virtually nothing in terms of improvement of the State. We never looked back and examined where the wastage happened.'[1]

Sutherland believed that a business-friendly taxation system delivered the economic dividends that governments could then use to improve a country's social infrastructure. He argued that this should be the pattern that should be adopted by the entire EU.

'He was intensely integrationist,' says Brian Cowen, who went on to be Minister for Foreign Affairs between 2000 and 2004. Cowen had a number of dealings with Sutherland over this period. 'He was very much of the [European] Commission view that there should be full-blown integration. He didn't believe in a European super state, but he was probably more integrationist than the Irish civil service would have been.' In an ongoing battle, the Irish government has remained opposed to ceding full autonomy in sensitive areas such as taxation. European integration has meanwhile become a political minefield for the governments of member states. The raison d'être of the EU is to raise the living standards of the citizens living within its borders, and the argument for integration is that by pooling sovereignty, the bloc is able to wield much more influence than the sum of its parts. But the trade-off between the pooling of sovereignty and the resultant economic dividends has become freighted with risks. Over the past decade the EU has been increasingly depicted as suffering from a democratic deficit that has become remote from the issues affecting member states; 'Taking back control' was the hugely emotive and effective campaign slogan of the leave side in the UK's Brexit referendum.

'Peter understood the national position,' says Brian Cowen, 'but his argument was that the benefits of integration would outweigh any downside. You could argue that point. There is no doubt that if you look at the banking collapse, the treaty kept states isolated. We didn't have banking union. It was a point in favour of integration. The nature of capital flows means you need cross-border oversight. Looking back now we were over-cautious on that one. We would have been better off being more integrationist.'

*

When the Lisbon Treaty referendum was called for June 2008, the mood had turned against the government. But it was the EU that would feel the brunt of simmering discontent at the ballot box. The country was coming to the end of a decade-long credit bubble and the backdrop had become increasingly uncertain. There was growing evidence that house prices were defying gravity.

Fianna Fáil had been in power for eleven years and there was a sense of voter fatigue. All the main political parties ran very bad campaigns, having seemingly taken the result for granted. After all, according to all Eurobarometer polls, Irish people were still overwhelmingly well disposed to the EU.

Declan Ganley, a businessman and founder of Libertas, spearheaded the opposition to the referendum alongside Sinn Féin. It was a very effective, if somewhat dishonest campaign. There were claims that if Ireland ratified the Lisbon Treaty, then the government would lose autonomy over crucial and sensitive issues such as taxation and neutrality. The spectre of a European army was raised with dizzying frequency. Even the pro-life movement weighed in, claiming that a vote for Lisbon would pave the way for the introduction of abortion.

Sutherland took to the campaign trail with his trademark intensity. His profile in Ireland had never been particularly high; it was twenty-five years since he had been attorney general and his main achievements over the intervening period had been on an international stage. As a result, the No side in the campaign declared open season on his background. Mary Lou McDonald, a Sinn Féin MEP who had failed the previous year to be elected as a TD in the general election, was looking to relaunch her national profile, and the treaty referendum was the perfect platform. At a referendum forum in Dublin Castle she referred in withering terms to Sutherland's background at Goldman Sachs and BP. Incoherent, unconvincing and toothless in the face of the No campaign's sophistry, the Yes side narrowly lost.

Lisbon went down because of the yawning chasm between the EU and ordinary people, says Cowen. 'In Lisbon there was a disconnect. It had been going on for a while. There was a big constitutional debate going on in Europe which was esoteric and irrelevant.' Jacques Delors had been able to emphasise the economic benefits of membership, such as the structural funds, reform of the common agricultural policy, and so on. 'It was seen as relevant to people's lives. If you asked people what was in the

Lisbon Treaty, nobody really knew or cared. By that stage, the UK right-wing press were having a field day on Europe and it was having an effect. What we found the second time is that we needed to do a lot more research.'

According to Cowen, a lot of the general political commentary in 2008 was 'lazy puerile analysis. They demonised Sutherland because he worked at Goldman Sachs. It is nothing more than name calling but it is effective.'

In October 2009, a second Lisbon Treaty referendum was called. This time 67 per cent of voters ticked the Yes box. But it was a campaign that Sutherland had to sit out. Earlier that year he had been diagnosed with throat cancer.

*

By the second time the Irish people went to the polls, the economic landscape had changed considerably. Ireland was on its way to experiencing one of the worst downturns any developed economy had ever experienced. House prices would collapse by just under 60 per cent from their 2007 peak to a trough in 2011. By 2008, the Irish banking system had become highly leveraged; by the time the global financial system became paralysed following the collapse of Lehman Brothers, the sector had become heavily reliant on wholesale money markets to fund its lending requirements. The problem was that Irish banks were borrowing in the short-term money markets while lending to the property sector, either in the form of mortgages or development loans, which are by nature long-term transactions. Any disruption to the wholesale money markets and Irish banks would be dangerously exposed.

The first portents of the looming banking crisis happened in March 2008. At the start of that month US investment bank Bear Stearns collapsed because of its exposure to the US sub-prime market. Over most of the 2000s, US banks had bundled together US mortgages and sold them as collateralised debt obligations (CDOs). Investors snapped them up, which increased the demand for these complex and opaque products. CDOs were cited as an example of how financial innovation was reducing risk for investors. The problem was that these CDOs had been stitched together with mortgages with different credit ratings, ranged from A grade high quality down to sub-investment grade. When the US sub-prime market hit the buffers at the end of 2007, investors didn't know which CDOs were carrying toxic assets. Irish businessman Ulick McEvaddy summed it up rather colourfully on RTÉ radio at the time as 'like going to a swingers' party. Everybody puts their car keys into a bowl and then you find out two people have Aids. You don't know which two. That's it, the party is over for everybody.' In the space of a few months, CDOs went from being an essential part of an investment portfolio to kryptonite.

Investment banks were carrying billions of dollars' worth of these products on their balance sheets, and Bear Stearns was merely the first to buckle under the strain. On what is now infamously known as the St Patrick's Day massacre, Irish banking stocks plummeted as investors looked suspiciously at the make-up of their balance sheets. Between March and September, the pressure on the banking system increased. The Irish government blamed hedge funds for adding to the instability by shorting banking stocks – in other words, their investors were taking a bet that stocks were set to fall in value. With the collapse of Lehman Brothers on 14 September, international money markets went into a tailspin. Irish banks lost access to the funding needed to cover day-to-day operations. The government took the highly controversial decision on 29 September to introduce a blanket guarantee of the domestic banks.

The decision to give the banks a backstop put the government on the hook for €64 billion of liabilities. That would have been a manageable strain on the national coffers if done in isolation, but the fiscal position was simultaneously deteriorating. The government had ramped up spending during the 2000s based on surging receipts from the property market, particularly via stamp duty. When the market crashed, an important source of revenue dried up. Brian Lenihan, who became Minister for Finance in June 2008 – or, in his own memorable words, 'It was just my luck to take over when the economy came to a shuddering halt'[2] – had to preside over one of the most savage periods of austerity in the history of the state. In 2009 the budget deficit ballooned to 14.3 per cent of GDP, the highest in the EU. By 2011, following the rescue of the banking system, it had climbed to over 30 per cent.

Sutherland developed a close relationship with Lenihan over this period. Both men had similar backgrounds: they were Jesuit-educated and had both trained as barristers. 'Peter was very supportive from 2008 onwards when we had to make massive cutbacks. We took the view that the sort of decisions we have to make are going to make us unre-electable, but it had to be done. It was a very adversarial time,' says Brian Cowen.

Sutherland's advice to Lenihan, continues Cowen, was to stick with the strategy they had embarked upon. 'There was no other choice. Then he was quite laudatory when we did do it. In that sort of a way he was very straightforward and patriotic and mindful of the country's future. He was of the view it had to be done right. If there was a delay or prevarication, then the country would end up like Greece. He made some public pronouncements, but mostly in private. Bankers were not exactly flavour of the month.'

From the end of 2008, and over the next two years, there was a steady flow of bankers and financiers into government buildings offering their services. Some of these were legitimate, others were snake-oil salesmen. Lenihan leaned heavily on Sutherland during this period. With his extensive network of contacts in the financial markets, Sutherland carried out background checks on several people and reported back to Lenihan as to who was worth talking to and who was a mere opportunist.

For much of this period Sutherland was recuperating from his treatment for throat cancer. 'I knew by looking at him he clearly wasn't well. But we never discussed his illness. Peter was an intensely private man,' says Cowen.

Lenihan was himself diagnosed with pancreatic cancer in December 2010. According to the *Irish Times*, he phoned Sutherland two days before Christmas to tell him about his diagnosis. 'Do the best you can to maintain your lifestyle,' Sutherland told Lenihan. 'If he is told to cut back,' he said, 'then that is what he should do – what he has to do is get better. There is a long way to go but I think there is a sort of national understanding that was reflected in the attitude to the appalling news about Brian Lenihan. We have limited talent in this country and we have to apply it.'[3]

During the same interview Sutherland lauded the approach Lenihan had taken to restoring fiscal rectitude. He described it as 'a crucial moment in Irish history' as the country fought to bridge the substantial gap between high public expenditure and low tax revenues. He pointed out that the country had only had the first of four austere budgets that this very difficult correction would require. 'We are very different, but if the Greek problem were to spiral out of control – and I hope it doesn't – the question is, have we done enough to dig a moat around the Irish problem in a way that distinguishes us quite clearly? There will be moments over the next twelve months when we will have to stand up domestically and be counted.'

Throughout 2010 the Irish government was effectively swimming against the tide. A debt crisis was sweeping through the periphery of the Eurozone. Greece was the first member state to lose its economic sovereignty, and it was a matter of time before Ireland would have to apply for an EU–IMF bailout package. When that happened, at the end of November 2010, it was a national humiliation unparalleled in the history of the state. The taxpayer-funded rescue of the banking system pushed the budget deficit to 32 per cent of GDP in 2011. Never in peacetime has a developed country had to contend with finances that were in such a parlous state. A senior Fine Gael source says that around this time, some senior members of the party became resentful of the relationship between Sutherland and Lenihan. 'There was a feeling he should get off the pitch and let Fine Gael have a clear run at Fianna Fáil,' according to one person familiar with the situation.

'To be critical of him was not to realise he was in a different sphere of influence,' Cowen says. 'He had a very strong international reputation. He had a reputation as a straight shooter, he was very influential and had a great contact list. He had contacts with people in the financial world that the government did not have access to. He was a man of the highest integrity. He was never a partisan politician. He was never really the same stock as the rest of us. He would be the first to say if he had a conflict of interest. He was a very ethical guy. He had a huge commitment to public service. A lot of these guys never get credit for it, they are of a different mentality. He could have put his own career first, but he didn't. He wanted to make a contribution.'

The political backlash was unforgiving and immediate. When the Fianna Fáil government collapsed shortly after Christmas 2010, Cowen became the focus of the backlash. 'From 2008 onwards, the atmosphere was toxic. People were being fed a very pessimistic picture. At the time, there was an easy narrative to blame a few people – Ahern, Cowen, throw Sutherland into the mix.' What would have happened, asks Cowen, if they had ducked the decision to guarantee the banks? What if a company went to pay its employees' wages and its bank had run out of money? 'There was no easy way out. We brought our debt way down. If we didn't have that cushion we would have been shagged. I was criticised for going to the IMF, but if I hadn't done that where would I have got the money?'

When Michael Noonan took over as Minister for Finance in March 2011, Ireland had just started a three-year bailout programme, and the prospects of the country exiting the bailout at the scheduled date looked bleak. Noonan had been very close to Sutherland when they were justice minister and attorney general respectively. Now the circumstances were different, but the two men took up where they had left off thirty years previously.

'I found him very helpful. He had access to parts of the decision-making world which no other Irish person had – not even the civil service.' Sutherland organised dinners and other meetings on Noonan's behalf. 'I was fortunate,' says Noonan. 'Tim Geithner was one of the people who stopped Brian Lenihan burning bondholders. I had him on the phone. Larry Summers was another. He became a friend and contact. I would have Peter in that group. I would get different views from different people. The civil service had low morale. There was a lot of blame going around. It was important for them and important for me that I could have these people. The difference was that Larry Summers would give me advice but Peter would put me in touch with serious people.'

There have been a number of official reports on the cause of Ireland's economic downfall. The broad conclusions are that the banking system grew too quickly, lending standards were too lax, and eventually the size of the sector came to pose an existential threat to the overall economy. Since the crisis a number of reforms have taken place in the direction favoured by Sutherland. The most important of these is EU banking union. The Single Supervisory Mechanism (SSM) based in Frankfurt is now responsible for the supervision of the Irish banking system. The pro-cyclical policy operated by the government during the period leading up to the crash in 2008 stoked inflationary pressures to unsustainable levels. There is a lot of wisdom in hindsight, says Cowen, who admits that much of the advice he was getting at the time did not raise any red flags. He also points to the opposition parties and media commentators who spent most of the 2000s calling on him to ramp up spending. The reality is that there was a system-wide failure.

Sutherland was responsible for bringing the Trilateral Commission's annual meeting to Dublin in May 2010. The Commission was founded in 1973 by David Rockefeller, scion of the Rockefeller dynasty, to promote dialogue between the US, Japan and Europe. Its membership included some of the most prominent industrialists, financiers and politicians from these countries. Sutherland was the European Chairman of the Trilateral Commission for over a decade. Henry Kissinger, the controversial US statesman, was among the attendees at the Dublin meeting. Sutherland was also a member of the Bilderberg Group, which was founded in 1954 to foster closer economic ties between the US and Europe. It is understood Sutherland started attending the Bilderberg meetings from the later 1980s onwards. Much like the Trilateral Commission, the annual Bilderberg gathering includes some of the most powerful people from the worlds of business, finance and politics. According to one Irish attendee, even in these rarefied surroundings, Sutherland was one of the most sought-after participants. The semi-secretive nature of both organisations has energised generations of conspiracy theorists. Bilderberg in particular is often depicted as a private cabal influencing world events without any accountability.

Alongside Noonan, Sutherland also developed close ties to Simon Coveney, currently Tánaiste and Minister for Foreign Affairs but in 2011 the Minister for Agriculture. Indeed, there is a video on social media – shared extensively by conspiracy theorists – of Sutherland and Coveney going for a walk during a Bilderberg meeting in Copenhagen in 2014. Sutherland's relationship with Taoiseach Enda Kenny was less close; he confided to a number of associates his disappointment that Kenny had not taken up his offer of help.

Sutherland did have one foray into domestic politics in 2011. Suzanne Kelly, the daughter of Captain James Kelly, met Sutherland at a theatre in London in 2014, they chatted about events over forty years previously. Sutherland told her that the Public Accounts Committee's 'lies and treachery' had motivated him in 2011 to campaign against a referendum to amend the constitution to give the Oireachtas special powers of investigation. His argument was that widening the remit of Oireachtas committees had the potential to limit civil liberties. Sutherland persuaded seven other former attorneys general – Patrick Connolly, John Rogers, Dermot Gleeson, Harry Whelehan, David Byrne, Michael McDowell and Paul Gallagher – to sign a letter calling for a no vote. The motion was unexpectedly defeated and the Oireachtas committees did not receive any extra powers.

In the years before 2008, Sutherland had not featured prominently in the Irish media, but when he did it was generally favourable. That changed around the time of the financial crisis. His ties with Goldman Sachs made him an obvious target, and there were a number of unflattering profiles; the most excoriating, penned by Fintan O'Toole in May 2010, was titled 'Sutherland could have led by example'. The piece focused on Sutherland's chairmanship of AIB and how his alleged failure of leadership in the DIRT scandal had helped foment a rotten culture that eventually led to the entire sector's demise.

'It hurt him deeply,' Brendan Halligan says. 'It wasn't just the O'Toole attack. There were a number of them around that time. He took it very badly. He said he psychologically and physically withdrew from Ireland as a consequence. He felt he had become an impediment to the pro-European cause. I tried to tell him that he was loved dearly. He was very hurt by what happened. His friends tried to tell him it wasn't as bad as he thought, but he wouldn't believe them. If, as I have, you have been on the receiving end of a nasty campaign, then you do develop a siege mentality.' Sutherland made only fleeting appearances in Ireland after the crisis.

He nevertheless convened a Sunday morning breakfast briefing every time he was in Dublin. At these gatherings a group of self-styled 'grumpy old men' met in Donnybrook Fair to discuss the challenges facing the country. Its members included Garrett Sheehan, Dáithí Ó Ceallaigh, Patrick Masterson, the former president of UCD, Dermot Gleeson, the former attorney general and chairman of AIB, businessmen Declan McCourt, and Lochlann Quinn, accountant John Blake Dillon, former attorney general

Paul Gallagher, Eoin McConagle, a senior counsel, and in the early years Derry Hussey. The meeting still takes place once a month in Sutherland's honour.

Among Sutherland's sparing appearances in Ireland in the aftermath of the crisis was to give the Barrett Family Lecture at the Nanovic Institute for European Studies in Dublin in March 2015. Choosing a subject that would generate few favourable headlines, he took aim at Ireland's position on neutrality. He believed, he said, that Ireland needed to take part in the defence of Europe, even though the Irish political consensus was very much moving in the opposite direction:

> It is hard to see the situation changing here because there is little evidence that anyone wishes to discuss it politically. Our situation on this subject stands as something of a contradiction [to] our ostensible belief in an integrated European Union. Ireland, which has made a disproportionately significant contribution to UN peacekeeping operations, has demonstrated a capacity that will enable it to play an openly active role in developing the European defence policy and should not be afraid to be seen to do so. Then, our ministers and Taoiseach made it clear that Irish neutrality would not inhibit us, in due course, from participating in the development of European defence policy when the time came.[4]

Article 42.7 of the Treaty of Lisbon, he said, provided that "'if a member state is the victim of armed aggression on its territory, the other member states shall have towards it an obligation of aid and assistance within Article 51 of the United Nations Charter. This shall not prejudice the specific character of the security and defence policy of certain states." Other neutral states within the Union have not been slow to consider their positions following this treaty. They have made domestic declarations of solidarity to other member states in clear and unambiguous terms. They were not bound to do so but they have seen it as their duty to express their responsibilities to other member states as they see them.'

Neutrality remains a divisive and emotive issue in Ireland, but overall sentiment towards the EU is moving in a direction that Sutherland would have approved. Britain's vote to leave the bloc has pushed Ireland's enthusiasm for EU membership to record levels.

20

BREXIT: A NIGHTMARE UNFOLDS

O N SATURDAY 10 SEPTEMBER 2016, THE DAY before Sutherland suffered his heart attack, he was at a British-Irish Association seminar in Oxford on Brexit. Also on the panel was Theresa Villiers, the former Northern Ireland Secretary and arch-Brexiteer. During the proceedings, Sutherland vented his views on Brexit with a robustness that shocked some members in the audience. It was almost three months after Britain had voted to leave the EU and much of the sloganeering that underpinned the Leave campaign had begun to unravel. There had moreover been very recent history between Sutherland and Villiers.

Speaking on the BBC's *Sunday Politics* Northern Ireland programme on 12 June, two weeks before the referendum, Sutherland had said a UK exit from the EU would cause a 'grave, serious and prolonged period of great uncertainty'. The agriculture industry and cross-border trade with the Republic of Ireland would suffer the consequences of a Leave vote, and foreign investors would overlook Northern Ireland and take their business to countries inside the EU, Sutherland told the programme.

'Those who invest in Ireland, north or south, are doing so because it provides them with the manufacturing base to sell to the European Union. The uncertainty, the borders created by

270

Britain leaving and the inevitable period of prolonged negotiation will lead to a drying up of investment.' Of the Democratic Unionist Party's campaigning for Brexit, Sutherland described it as 'incredible' that any political force in Northern Ireland could conceivably consider the UK's departure from the EU to be good for the province. He also said the UK's exit from the EU would 'create a border control requirement that we had thought banished to history. If in some perverted way there is an ideological desire to recreate that border, it's an act that would be incredibly foolish and very damaging.'

During the BBC programme, Villiers dismissed Sutherland's views and those of 'other so-called experts', saying a withdrawal from the EU would be 'great for Northern Ireland. It enables us to take back control of our own trade policies so that we can make deals not just with the European Union, but also with countries around the world where they have huge markets. Those could create jobs and opportunities for young people. There's no reason why we can't press ahead pretty rapidly with trade deals with the rest of the world. It is the EU that's failing economically, not us.'

That exchange was a perfect distillation of the broader campaign. The Leave camp had very effectively, and cynically, tapped into an anti-establishment undercurrent that would eventually sweep it to victory. Sutherland, the man who had set up the World Trade Organisation, knew the rules better than anybody. If the UK left the single market and customs union, then one result would be a hard border on the island of Ireland. But then again, Ireland and the implications for the border hardly featured in the referendum campaign. This deeply irked Sutherland. According to people around him at the time, he thought the Leave campaign dishonest and opportunist.

As one close friend notes, Sutherland was particularly aggrieved at the role played by Boris Johnson, the journalist and Conservative MP. When Sutherland chaired a debate at the London School of Economics on the future of London and the UK on 10 December 2013, Johnson – who was then Mayor of London – treated the audience to his trademark bloviated rhetoric. Having taken a few gratuitous swipes at the EU during the course of the evening, Johnson told Sutherland at a private dinner afterwards, according to one of Sutherland's close associates, that his Euroscepticism was a 'bit of fun' and he was really 'a bit of a Europhile'. It was an interaction that would prey on Sutherland's mind over the next few years, and one he recounted to a number of people. He found it hard to believe that a campaign of crucial importance for both the UK and the EU would be conducted in such a glib manner by some of the leading figures in the Leave camp.

Johnson in particular was guilty of making highly inflammatory comments. In one piece written for the *Sunday Telegraph*[1] before the referendum, he compared the EU to the Nazis. Interviewed by Newstalk radio, Sutherland described the comments as 'bizarre and utterly uncalled for. I don't understand what his real position is, nor do I know whether he knows what will happen to Britain if there is a Brexit. Making any comparison to the EU in the same breath as Hitler is so ludicrous as to be beyond parody.'[2]

Britain has had an uneasy relationship with the EU since it first joined the bloc in 1973. But the campaign to leave began in earnest following Margaret Thatcher's Bruges speech on 20 September 1988. In her address to the College of Europe in the Belgian city, she postulated her thoughts on Britain and the EU. Far from the fire-and-brimstone sermon that is often depicted, the speech is colourful and erudite, with none of the flinty prose that is often imagined. Thatcher spoke about Britain's shared history with Europe and how it had been mutually beneficial. She firmly ruled out any moves towards federalism, but she was willing to embrace integration where it made sense – in areas such as trade and security. The fact that the speech was wide ranging and nuanced has been lost over the years. Instead a few lines in the middle energised a new generation of Eurosceptics:

Indeed, it is ironic that just when those countries such as the Soviet Union, which have tried to run everything from the centre, are learning that success depends on dispersing power and decisions away from the centre, there are some in the Community who seem to want to move in the opposite direction. We have not successfully rolled back the frontiers of the state in Britain, only to see them re-imposed at a European level with a European super-state exercising a new dominance from Brussels. Certainly we want to see Europe more united and with a greater sense of common purpose. But it must be in a way which preserves the different traditions, parliamentary powers and sense of national pride in one's own country; for these have been the source of Europe's vitality through the centuries.[3]

These words have assumed a bewitching quality for Eurosceptics. They would form the opening salvo in the Brexit campaign, although it is highly unlikely that was Thatcher's intention at the time.

*

From the early 1990s, and indeed for most of that decade, Europe caused internecine warfare in the Conservative Party. It was partly why the Tories were annihilated at the 1997 general election. In the same year that Sutherland moved full time to the UK, Tony Blair swept New Labour to victory with the biggest majority in UK election history. Even though Labour had traditionally been the Eurosceptic party, it had evolved under the leadership of Neil Kinnock to take a more outward-looking, progressive approach. Blair was possibly the most pro-EU leader Britain has ever had, and possibly will ever have. He set about putting the UK at the heart of the EU. He wanted to join the single currency, until he was blocked by Gordon Brown, his Chancellor of the Exchequer. Sutherland developed a good relationship with both Blair and Brown, and indeed with John Major.

Sutherland loved living in London. He had an enormous respect for Britain's history, culture and society. He was very proud to have been appointed chairman of the LSE in 2006. He was also the master of St Dominic's College in Oxford. And he was awarded an honorary knighthood in May 2004 for services to philanthropy, although he could have accepted a full knighthood as he was born in 1946, three years before Ireland became a republic.

Sutherland spoke to a number of people about his decision, including David O'Sullivan, then the secretary general of the European Commission. O'Sullivan remembered that moment: 'He rang me and said he was going to be given this. And he said, "I do have the possibility because I was born before 1949." But he said he didn't think he should take it.' He asked O'Sullivan, 'What do you think?' O'Sullivan agreed, adding, 'I think that would kill you in Irish terms ever if you wanted to represent the country.'

'I'm not very comfortable with it myself, I won't do that.'

'I don't think he ever got the credit for being patriotic or for being Irish,' says O'Sullivan. 'But he was absolutely Irish. He could only have ever been Irish.'

*

Not long after he had stood down as a European commissioner, in the early 1990s, Sutherland attended a party at Conrad Black's house. The Canadian, who owned the *Telegraph* newspapers, was famous for throwing lavish soirees with the cream of the business and political worlds in attendance. Sutherland bumped into Margaret Thatcher at the party. Perhaps still sore from her bruising encounters with the former competition commissioner, she decided to launch a verbal attack on Ireland as a means of retaliation, taking aim in particular at the country's war record. Sutherland took exception and politely but firmly informed her that on a pro rata basis, more Irish soldiers had been killed in the Great War than any other nationality. It was something of a conversation stopper, and the Iron Lady was quickly on her way. Sutherland subsequently admitted that he had no idea if his peroration had any factual basis, but that he was relieved to find that Thatcher had no idea either.

Sutherland lived under the reign of New Labour for his first thirteen years in London. He never publicly expressed a preference for either Labour or the Tories, but for such a committed Europhile, life under Labour must have been easier, at least from that perspective. As soon as Conservative David Cameron became prime minister in 2010, Sutherland saw the ominous portents for the UK's relationship with the EU.

Sutherland gave the annual Cardinal Newman Lecture in St John's College Oxford on 19 May 2010, a fortnight after the general election and a week after the Tories had formed a coalition with the Liberal Democrats. It was a most prescient speech. The following is an edited version (a more complete version can be found in Appendix 3):

> The more that I have reflected on this lecture, the more I have been struck by how alien and even destructive it may sound in Britain. Religion and values have not formed part of the narrative here of the troubled relationship between Britain and the process of European integration. But if the EU is no more than a Common Market, as many here believe, why should they be part of the story? In fact these subjects may be seen rather as added complications to a debate by those who seek a more constructive dialogue on European issues. The result of this is they are not much spoken of, particularly within and by the Churches. While this lecture is not intended to be exclusively focused on Britain in the European Union (which is not in any sense 'Europe'), I will initially look at this issue.

> Perhaps there is an unspoken suspicion that the whole business of European integration is a little too Catholic for British tastes. Even though the religious influence of the Reformed Churches, particularly in Germany, was profound in its creation and development, this would not be at all

275

visible here, whereas the Founding Fathers, as they are perhaps annoyingly described by Europhiles like me, were to a man Catholic. Monnet, Schuman, de Gasperi and Adenauer were all Christian Democrats too, and only Paul Henri Spaak in the early European pantheon was a socialist. But others from the reformed tradition, such as the Danes, Swedes and Finns, however reluctant initially, have begun to put suspicions of this kind behind them. Increasingly they demonstrate a real belief in the integration process. This is particularly true of Finland.

It is indisputable that the United Kingdom has a fundamental problem with European integration. The evidence of polls suggests that the negativism here is qualitatively different from all other cases not merely in its consistency but in its depth. Thus it remains at the lowest position in Eurobarometer polls in its positivism towards the European Union. Indeed it is far from clear what the result of a referendum on membership would be today.

This ambivalence has been evident from the earliest days. In the lead-up to the Treaty of Paris that created the Coal and Steel Community and started the whole process, Dean Acheson counselled the French not to inform London because he foresaw its potential for destructive opposition.

The reasons for this antipathy are many, varied and in part understandable. It is apparent that history plays a substantial part in this, not merely through the memory of terrible continental wars but also in the sense of distinctiveness born out of the inviolability of Britain itself, an island that has not been invaded for a thousand years. Britain had pragmatic economic grounds, too, for its initial opposition to European integration. Its loyalty to and connection with an empire, already disintegrating but still connected in the 40s and 50s, and 'the English speaking peoples', was an essential element in such limited profound political debate as took place during the 1950s on the whole subject of Europe.[4]

Sutherland's fears were well founded. In January 2013, Cameron sought to lance the euro boil that had plagued his party for decades. He pledged a referendum on the UK's membership of the EU if the Conservatives won an overall majority in the 2015 general election. In May 2015, after the Tories upset the odds and won such a majority, Cameron found himself under pressure to follow through on his commitment. On 20 February 2016, the British Prime Minister called a referendum for 23 June.

At the EU Council meeting in March, Cameron was given a cool reception by the heads of other member states when he entered the chamber. He made an immediate beeline for Enda Kenny, the Taoiseach, and assured the Fine Gael leader that the referendum would confirm Britain's membership. The Irish delegation was not so sure. Ireland has had a chequered history with referendums. The old maxim – you get an answer you didn't want to a question you didn't ask – immediately sprang to mind.

The backdrop could not have been less favourable. From 2010 onwards, there were legitimate questions about the feasibility of the euro and the future of the EU. The 2008 financial crisis had exposed the flawed architecture of monetary union. From the early 2000s onwards, capital had been flowing from core countries to those on the periphery. When the resulting Irish property bubble collapsed in 2008 and the debts of the country's banks were no longer sustainable, there was no mechanism for burden sharing; the financial backstop put in place by the government raised question marks over the solvency of the Irish state. Italy, Spain, Greece, Portugal and Cyprus faced similar problems. The commission's response was a programme of chastening austerity. The inevitable societal backlash seemed at one stage as if it would sunder the euro and unravel European integration.

As if financial disintegration wasn't enough to test the cohesion of the EU28, there was a migration crisis on its southern border. Brexiteers had a field day. Sutherland had opened a Twitter account on 22 September 2015, using the handle @PDSutherlandUN, primarily as a forum to express his views on migration, but in

2016 he also used it to talk about Brexit. The responses to his posts are illuminating. Overwhelmingly negative, they mostly depict Sutherland as a Jewish banker intent on undermining British sovereignty.

British Euroscepticism is an amorphous force, which made it more challenging to put together an effective argument to remain in the EU. The bedrock of British anti-EU sentiment is the alleged irreconcilability of two different cultures. According to this narrative, there can be no dilution of British sovereignty and the values that flow from it. These include an unconditional commitment to democracy, freedom and the rule of law. For this worldview to hold water, the EU is portrayed in equal and opposite terms.

Catherine Day believes the UK has always had a problem with the European Commission. 'They have made a bogeyman about it, but a lot of it just wasn't true.' She says the commission had the power of ideas and persuasion, and that what the British hated was that, once a commission proposal was on the table, it generally had a lot of support from other member states and that made it harder for the British to derail it.

But esoteric arguments about the alleged democratic deficit of the EU, while effective, would not be enough to swing a vote in favour of Leave. Instead, the campaign coalesced around the slogan 'Take back control', with its numinous undertones. Migration became the lodestone of the movement. Louise Mensch, a former Conservative MP and prominent Brexiteer, told one of Sutherland's associates that the Leave camp was delighted he had joined the fray on the Remain side. His close association with migration meant that he would himself be a useful bogeyman for a campaign that was about taking back control.

Sutherland became quite active in the Remain campaign. He appeared on the BBC's *Newsnight* on two occasions, as well as on *Channel 4 News* and a raft of other programmes, and penned a number of opinion pieces. It can be said with some certainty that his contributions hardened the resolve of Leave voters. It wasn't just his association with migration: even worse, he was dismissed as an expert. The Leave side carried the day on 23 June 2016, winning by a narrow margin with just under 52 per cent of the vote.

Basil Geoghegan discussed Brexit with Sutherland on a number of occasions. 'If Peter was around now I think the real question would be how would he react to Brexit and how would he have reacted to the reform that is probably needed in the EU. For a committed Europhile, that is the real question. He was never going to be shy and retiring about putting his views forward. He spent a lot of time in the world of politics but he was never a politician. He spoke his mind. He never worried about winning approval.'

On 19 May 2016, Sutherland had given a speech on Brexit at the IIEA in Dublin. According to Brendan Halligan it was the sort of speech that had been missing from the debate in the UK – passionate, but most importantly well informed.

Sutherland opened with a warning that Brexit had unleashed uncomfortable echoes of the country's past. 'Anybody who is unfortunate enough to read British tabloids will see this virulent strain of nationalism and xenophobia.' He said he didn't know which way the referendum would go. 'The bookies say one thing. The taxi drivers will tell you another.' He took aim at Boris Johnson: 'How anybody could be persuaded by these meanderings I do not know.' Ireland and the EU, he said, would be faced with a very long period of negotiation.

Then he reached the substantive part of the speech, which concerned what would happen if Britain voted to leave. 'We move into a period of uncertainty that will be profound. The Council will agree guidelines for the Commission to negotiate with Britain. That will be for a period of two years. This puts the UK in an extreme position of vulnerability. There will be highly complicated talks about how the relationship will exist after Brexit.' To go by previous experience, the process might take five years or more, and the prospects for the UK economy and for inward investment would change.

He cited warnings by the IMF, the OECD and Mark Carney, governor of the Bank of England:

> They all say this will be a disastrous position. On the other side you have Boris Johnson, Norman Lamont and Lord Lawson saying it won't. I know which way I would vote.
>
> It will have very serious implications for Ireland. There will be concern about access to British markets at the end of all of this. A drawbridge won't be erected but the conditions will be very different. The UK will be scrambling to negotiate sixty free trade agreements. This is a formidable challenge. Even though the British civil service has a very good reputation, there will be very grave concerns about its capacity to deal with the challenge it presents.

Before the referendum many Brexiteers had cited the Norwegian model as the template to follow in the event of a no vote. Sutherland warned that the Norwegian model would require Britain to accept free movement, budget contributions and be a rule taker.

> If that deal is brought back to Westminster, the political reaction might be, what was this all about. What will Parliament do? There is a majority in Parliament who don't want Brexit. One can foresee chaos and severe trauma in the British political system.
>
> The argument that Britain is a net importer and therefore Germany will have an overwhelming interest in retaining an open free market is also flawed. Undoubtedly every country wants an open and free market. But the other side of that is never referred to in these comments, and that is that Britain exports substantially greater services than it takes from others. It is a services-based economy. These will be excluded on the models we are talking about. The WTO does not work to cover services, and services will be key in

this negotiation. What will happen to commerce and investment? It will be positive for Ireland in terms of greater flows
of FDI (foreign direct investment).

Sutherland insisted it would be impossible for Britain to retain
the benefits of the single market, which is what many prominent
Brexiteers had pledged, while at the same time ditching the free
movement of people and EU legislation:

There will be a great deal of support to find a new relationship that works for everybody, including from Ireland. But
to do so destroys the essence of membership and creates a
Europe à la carte and one in which the EU is disintegrating
– that is inconceivable. That won't happen. The fear factor
of a country leaving the union at a time of such turbulence
may well ensure negotiations are not going to be easy. Nobody
will wave goodbye at no price. I don't believe negotiations
will be so terrible that a border will be erected. It could
happen, but I think a way will be found. The consequences
for Ireland north and south will be very destabilising. Indeed
I am taken aback that there is one party in Northern Ireland
so imbued with exceptionalism that it is in favour of Brexit.

Huge uncertainty and damage will be caused. The outlook
is deeply worrying. We [Ireland] have a huge interest in
Great Britain staying. They have a very similar outlook in
terms of free trade. They were the most supportive government when I was at the WTO. They are responsible for us
not being in Schengen. I don't agree with that but it was
because of the common travel area. The evidence is overwhelmingly in favour of staying in the union. The case has
not been explored or articulated in any way in the UK. I
know trade policy can be opaque but how could anybody
say it will be fine? Britain will have to recreate negotiating
positions with the rest of the world. Foreign direct investment
into the UK is on the basis of access to the EU.[5]

Sutherland pointed to the slump in sterling when Boris Johnson announced he was running on the Leave side; the impact if the UK left would be unimaginable:

> I have nothing remotely constructive to say about Brexit. I can't believe that if they do leave then anybody would think it would be a good idea for Ireland to leave. We should do the opposite and bind ourselves to Europe. The days of being dependent on one country are over. We need Britain in. We have to stand firm and not be afraid to say it. We need to stand firm on European principles and not be afraid to say it in front of our friends. We cannot let Brexit in any way affect our relationship with the EU. If it does we have to stand firm.[6]

Clearly, Sutherland was more or less right, in almost every warning he issued. Yet at the time he was dismissed as being a mere expert. The following September Sutherland became ill, although it wasn't publicly disclosed, while at the same time Bertie Ahern proposed that he should have been made a representative for Ireland in Brexit talks. 'He would have been brilliant. He would have been a huge asset for the country. When I proposed him I had no idea he was ill. It was very unfortunate for everybody.'

21

FAITH AND PHILANTHROPY

I T IS A SIGN OF HOW MUCH IRELAND HAS CHANGED
over recent decades that a declaration that someone had a
deep faith can have such an uncomfortable subtext. Since the
1990s, the Catholic Church in Ireland has been rocked by a series
of scandals. Whereas the church was once the bedrock of Irish life,
it is now floundering at the margins. In 1980, 96 per cent of all
weddings were Catholic; in 2018, it was 47 per cent. Of course,
that reflects a changing, more multicultural society, but Ireland is
now a very different country from the one in which Peter Sutherland
grew up. His faith, nevertheless, was very important to him.

Gonzaga and Fr Joe Veale were important factors in shaping
Sutherland's value system, but there were others. According to
Diarmuid Martin, the archbishop of Dublin, Sutherland and his
contemporaries would have been heavily influenced by changes
in the church itself in the early 1960s: 'At the time of the Second
Vatican Council there was a reflection of the church's role in the
world. And this was a reflection of a change in the geography of
the world. It was the 1960s and a time of decolonisation. There
was a belief that we needed to assist these countries to develop.
Peter's vision of migration comes from the same thing. Movement
is a natural corollary to globalisation. Migration means enrichment
of societies.'

Martin and Sutherland encountered one another for the first time in the small village of Cernobbio, on Lake Como in Italy, in the early 1990s, where Archbishop Martin was representing the Vatican at an international financial conference. The two afterwards met a number of times at Davos, and over the years they got to know each other. Martin returned to Ireland in 2004 as archbishop of Dublin, and he recalls of Sutherland: 'He came to my residence on a number of occasions to talk about the church and the financial aspects of the church and migration. He was very generous to church organisations. He didn't just dole money out. He came to me to talk about particular projects and I would tell him if I couldn't recommend that he do it.' If so, that was usually the end of it.

Archbishop Martin tells of an acquaintance who was a high-ranking IMF official. 'He was Chilean and he was educated at a Jesuit university. He studied a subject called Catholic sociology. There is no such thing as Catholic sociology. They were basically sent out to poorer parts of the city to help people. That also shaped Peter. I think Peter got from the Jesuits the ability to understand inter-relations. You could see that from the WTO, the ability to introduce a rules-based system and how that would be a positive development for the developing world.'

Sutherland's faith was expressed in many ways, but particularly through his generosity. Although Hywel Jones still regrets that Sutherland did not set up a foundation with his windfall from Goldman Sachs' flotation, close associates of Sutherland say that he was very generous with his money; but his donations were made privately. How much he gave to charitable causes is unknown, but it is likely to run into tens of millions.

In 2007, Dáithí Ó Ceallaigh was the Irish ambassador to Britain when Irish President Mary McAleese gave a lecture at Westminster Abbey. He organised a dinner for McAleese at the Irish embassy after the event, for which she requested that an invitation be extended to Annie Maguire, the victim of one of the gravest miscarriages of justice in British judicial history. In 1975 the

Maguire family had been arrested as part of the investigation into a 1974 bombing in the Surrey town of Guildford. Paul Hill, Gerry Conlon, Paddy Armstrong and Carole Richardson were wrongly convicted of being IRA members who planted the bombs, while the Maguires were convicted in 1976 of handling explosives. The convictions were eventually quashed in 1991 following an appeal which found that the case against them had been manufactured.

There were roughly 100 people at the dinner, and Ó Ceallaigh put Maguire at the same table as McAleese and Sutherland. When Sutherland and Maguire fell into a lengthy conversation, she told him that her youngest son Patrick, who was fourteen at the time of his incarceration, had developed mental health issues and would need treatment for the rest of his life. 'Peter made arrangements to cover the bill,' says Ó Ceallaigh.

Ó Ceallaigh had spent three years on a mission station in Zambia before he entered the diplomatic corps. Andrew Turnbull, the former UK Cabinet Secretary, who had himself spent a number of years in Zambia, set up a small charity to educate orphans in the country when he retired in 2005, and asked Ó Ceallaigh if he would launch it. The launch took place in the embassy, and Ó Ceallaigh invited Sutherland to attend. 'I then discovered that he was already financially supporting a hospital in Zambia. He couldn't come but he sent Garrett Sheehan instead. He was helping people all over the place but he never talked about it.'

One act of Sutherland's generosity was revealed by the *Sunday Times* in 2012 through the workings of the National Asset Management Agency (NAMA). Seán MacRéamoinn, a well-known Irish-language journalist and broadcaster, had fallen ill in 2006 and was struggling financially. At the time two businessmen had stepped in to help by buying his family home, putting in place a confidential agreement that MacRéamoinn be allowed to live there until his death. The men had learnt of MacRéamoinn's financial difficulties from contacts in Fine Gael and paid the market value for the former broadcaster's home in Eden Park Drive in Goatstown, south Dublin, taking out a mortgage with the Anglo Irish Bank. The names of the two businessmen were never known to MacRéamoinn; but one was Pat Doherty, who created the Titanic Quarter in Belfast. The other was Peter Sutherland.

Four years later, when NAMA moved in on Doherty's Harcourt Developments, the loan for MacRéamoinn's former home was also swept into the agency. When, according to the *Sunday Times* report, Sutherland became aware that a loan partly in his name was under NAMA's control, he agreed to buy out Doherty's share, and NAMA then released its hold on the mortgage. Sutherland then rented out the property. Neither Sutherland nor Doherty were close to MacRéamoinn; they were simply approached because they were in a position to help.

Sutherland was immensely proud of University College Dublin, which he supported continuously over the years. Education was one of his great interests. He believed that Ireland needed a world-class education system if it was going to compete in the global economy, But his interest in education didn't stem entirely from economic considerations. He believed that a well-resourced and accessible education system was one of the best ways of tackling inequality.

Sutherland had studied law at UCD when the campus was located in Earlsfort Terrace. The college moved to its current Belfield site in Dublin 4 in the 1970s, and the law faculty was housed in the Roebuck Building, which by the early 2000s was no longer suitable. Hugh Brady, UCD's president, put together a committee made up of prominent barristers and major law firms in Dublin, and chaired by Declan McCourt, to consider the future of the school. The cost of a new school was estimated at €27 million. Mary Hanafin, education minister at the time, agreed in 2007 to put up one-third of the final cost, with the agreement that the rest would have to come from donations.

'I asked Peter would he be lead donor. In principle he said he would. He was also asked would he fund a chair in European law.' Imelda Maher was identified as a suitable candidate, and she came back from the London School of Economics to take the position. Sutherland, says McCourt, was very reluctant to have his name associated with the project at the beginning, and only agreed when he was sure that it was what everybody wanted. 'He put together a multi-million euro package for the building and the chair. The Sutherland School of Law is one of the most modern law buildings in the world,' concludes McCourt.

*

In 2001, Sutherland had become chairman of the Ireland Funds in the UK. Basil Geoghegan, who was on the board at the time, says that Sutherland wanted the fund to have a clear identity and practical focus like the Ireland Funds in the US, which had become a prominent player in the peace process in Northern Ireland. Sutherland came up with the idea of the Forgotten Irish after visiting a shelter in Camden Town in north London, largely occupied by Irishmen who had emigrated in the 1950s and 1960s. They could no longer work, but had no homes and nowhere to go, and many had mental health issues or problems with alcohol. That, says Geoghegan, would not have prevented Sutherland from offering help: 'He was in no way judgemental.'

In 2007 the Ireland Fund commissioned research from Middlesex University in order to identify, locate and quantify the numbers of vulnerable and elderly Irish in the UK. The 'Forgotten Irish' Report was the first such study to be conducted on a UK-wide basis, focusing on the fifty-plus age bracket, although it included a caveat: due to its very nature the statistics were likely to under-represent the size of the 'Forgotten Irish' community in England, as such figures could not include Irish people who were homeless or who did not access state provisions or services.

The report found that most of the 'Forgotten Irish' had come to Britain in the second half of the twentieth century. The majority came to find work and sent billions of pounds home to their families, while thousands of others came to escape the hardship, the marginalisation and, all too often, the abuse of institutional life. They paved the way for more recent generations of Irish immigrants to Britain. At the end of their working lives, many lacked the means to go home, however; often they were living in isolation, poverty and deprivation, without the support of friends or family.

The key findings of the report were that the largest concentrations of older Irish migrants were in areas such as Yorkshire and Humberside and the West Midlands. Census figures showed that a high proportion of Irish lived in the UK's most deprived boroughs and local government areas. Some regions, such as south-west England and East Anglia, had low Irish populations, but among those were a high proportion of elderly Irish. There were few if any Irish community groups or centres in these areas. Almost 20 per cent of Irish pensioners in the UK lived alone. More than 10 per cent of the Irish population in the UK – some 67,000 people – were not working because of permanent sickness or disability, while Irish men were 15 per cent more likely than their British counterparts to be single, divorced, separated or widowed from the age of fifty onwards. Deaths from cancer among Irish people in Britain was 20 per cent higher than the national average.

Sutherland headed the campaign, and tried, according to Dáithí Ó Ceallaigh, to involve the big Irish property developers in the UK with the Ireland Fund and the campaign. 'He had some success with them, but not as much as he would have liked.'

It is understood that Sutherland contributed generously to the campaign from his own resources. But Hugo MacNeill says it wasn't just about money, and that Sutherland was also very generous with his time. He recalls a night in London when he went for a drink with Sutherland and another colleague after an Ireland Funds board meeting. 'He left for quite some time. I thought something must have happened. It turned out he had to deal with three people who had got into terrible difficulty in their personal lives. I'll never forget that. This was about eleven at night. He was very apologetic about leaving us for so long. This wasn't about finance. It was a very difficult position that one person in particular had found himself in. Nobody would have known about this. It was never about grand gestures with Peter. He did it all behind the scenes. There was nothing for him apart from his own satisfaction.'

The death of Brian Murphy, an eighteen-year-old student, outside the Anabel nightclub in Dublin in August 2000 gripped the country for much of the decade. Four students from Blackrock College – Dermot Laide, Sean Mackay, Desmond Ryan and Andrew Frame – were charged with manslaughter and violent disorder. All charges against Frame were dropped, but Mackay and Ryan were convicted of violent disorder, although Ryan's conviction was overturned on appeal. Laide was convicted of manslaughter and violent disorder and sent to prison; his conviction for manslaughter was overturned in 2005 following an appeal. Sutherland did not know Laide, nor did they have any mutual acquaintances. Nevertheless, Sutherland made contact with him. 'He thought Laide had been hard done by. The other three boys came from establishment families in Dublin, whereas Laide was from Monaghan. He was having a very hard time of it when he got out of prison and Suds believed he deserved a second chance,' says a close friend of Sutherland's. Sutherland introduced Laide to a number of people to help him build a life. He is now an undertaker in the Blackrock district of Dublin.

Sutherland had played a few times against Gordon Wood when the former Irish international was coming to the end of his rugby career. After Wood died tragically young at the age of fifty-one in 1982, his son Keith became one of the best hookers in the history of the game, playing with the same intensity and determination as his father. When Keith Wood retired after the 2003 Rugby World Cup, Sutherland – knowing that the transition back to normal civilian life is difficult for many players – rang him, although they had never met, and offered him advice and support. The two men subsequently became good friends.

*

Even though faith was an important part of Sutherland's life, his first formal role with the Catholic Church came about only in 2011, when he became an adviser to the Vatican's Administration of the Patrimony of the Holy See. 'There were a number of good financial people on the board. It was Cardinal Cormac Murphy O'Connor with whom he was very close.' It was the former archbishop of Westminster, says Archbishop Martin, who proposed Sutherland to the Vatican.

However, adds Martin, Sutherland was unhappy that the system was not transparent. The Vatican has been embroiled in financial scandals over much of its existence, and in the early 1980s it had played a cameo role in one of the most notorious murders in Italy. Roberto Calvi, who among other roles had been the Vatican's banker, was found hanging from Blackfriars Bridge in London in June 1982 in an apparent suicide. It took until the mid-1990s to prove that he had been murdered by the mafia as a result of certain murky dealings. By the start of the noughties the Vatican Bank had been engulfed in accusations of money laundering and fraud.

Sutherland was a member of a panel of consultors, who met once or twice a year and were available to be contacted individually for advice. But they were advisers rather than a policy board, and like any group of advisers their advice might or might not be taken. Sutherland told colleagues at Goldman Sachs that, one year when he was attending the annual meeting of his board, he reviewed the financial advice he had given the previous year to find that the markets had gone in the opposite direction. An envelope slipped under the door of his room at the Vatican hotel contained the minutes of the previous year's meeting, changed to make it look as if his advice had been correct. 'They must have been trying to spare my feelings,' he told colleagues.

Sutherland's panel reported to the board of clerics. 'This board was comprised of cardinals but their knowledge of financial markets and investments was patchy,' says Archbishop Martin, who adds that Sutherland found this frustrating. 'He didn't feel as if it was being run effectively or efficiently. When Pope Francis was appointed in 2013 he set about a radical reform of the Vatican's finances. The board of advisers that Peter was a member of was sidelined.'

When Pope Francis summoned Sutherland to the Vatican in 2013, asking for advice on the reforms necessary to safeguard the reputation of the Vatican Bank in future, Sutherland emphasised the need for transparency. So Pope Francis created the new role of Prefect of the Secretariat for the Economy to oversee the required reforms. There was speculation at the time that Sutherland was interested in the position, although Archbishop Martin says he does not know whether there was any truth in the rumour. In any case, in 2014, Pope Francis appointed Cardinal George Pell to the post. (In 2019, Pell was convicted on charges of child sex offences committed in Australia in the 1990s, and sentenced to six years in prison.)

Archbishop Martin had extensive discussions with Sutherland about the church. 'He was liberal in his faith and he was unashamed of that. He felt the Irish church had become fossilised a little bit. He was known for his generosity to Catholic institutions and he would have been courted by them. I never asked him for anything.'

Criticisms were often made that there was an inconsistency between Sutherland's faith and his business career. 'I've no idea how he made so much money,' says Archbishop Martin, who notes that many of Sutherland's colleagues went from Goldman Sachs back into government. Oil, he observes, is a controversial business. 'If I was going to canonise Peter I would look into the files of what practices his businesses got up to. For example, take a country like Angola. Oil hinders its development. I don't know about his personal role in it. You would have to get out your diary and match the times. He could have been one of the few who understood the mitigating circumstances. I don't know enough about his roles. I don't know enough about his private work and whether BP and Goldman Sachs lived up to the ideals of inter-relations at a global level.'

Fr Barber would address these contradictions at Sutherland's funeral mass:

> One never finds greatness in gaining credit of a great name
> on earth, but in conforming one's life to that of Christ. If
> one achieves that then one is great, no matter how the life
> is otherwise. This was something of which Peter Sutherland
> was quietly convinced and that he accepted in faith. This
> may seem strange to say of one who had Peter's ambition,
> wealth, prestige and power in high places. Yet it was his faith
> and the practice of his faith that gave him his moral compass.[1]

Fr Barber paid tribute to Sutherland's philanthropy – 'to his countless acts of generosity that were and remain hidden . . . Then
there was his passionate devotion to the cause of refugees that
the Vatican and the UN called on and that passion came from a
deep religious consciousness. He promoted globalisation because
he saw it was a means of lifting billions out of grim poverty and
of countering a narrow nationalism, which avoids global responsibility.' While pointing out that Sutherland's enthusiasm for the
benefits of globalisation perhaps blurred his view of its downside,
he praised the contribution Sutherland had thereby made to
benefiting the poorer countries of the world, and concluded:

> He was a committed Catholic whose Catholicism was open,
> tolerant and gracious and the absence of these characteris-
> tics raised his temperature. I recall the appointment of a
> man to high ecclesiastical office producing language from
> Peter quite unsuitable to repeat in church. His convinced
> faith enabled him to accept without self-pity his illness,
> which eventually led to the enfeebled body, the weakening
> mind, and a total dependency on others. These are the brute
> facts, but we are not here to celebrate brute facts but to
> celebrate Peter's life in the light of Christ's death and resur-
> rection. We look on the cross above this altar and we see

that when Christ was at his weakest, frailest, when he was helpless and humiliated, then was he at the point of his entry into glory. So with Peter, he has moved from his frail and broken state into that place of peace and happiness that was prepared for him from before the foundation of the world.[2]

22

FAMILY

SUTHERLAND WAS AT THE HOP AT BELVEDERE Rugby Club one Saturday night in 1969 when a young woman caught his eye. Her name was Maruja Cabria Valcarcel, and she came from a farming background just outside Santander in northern Spain. She had come to Dublin to work as an au pair and to improve her English. Even though connections to the UK at the time would have been much better, many Spanish parents wanted their daughters to go to Ireland – like Spain, a devoutly Catholic country.

Sutherland was smitten with the young Spanish woman. They courted briefly, but the romance was cut short when she had to return home. Undeterred by the distance of half a continent, a daunting prospect in the days before Ryanair and cheap travel, Sutherland put together his backpack and hit the road. Maruja's father was naturally suspicious of this young Irishman trying to prise his daughter away, but Sutherland's efforts paid off, and the couple were married in Santander in September 1971. Paddy Kevans, who was courting a Spanish girl at the time, was one of Sutherland's few friends to make the ceremony.

For some men of power, influence and peripatetic lifestyle, affairs are part of the package. Not so Sutherland. Friends, former colleagues, everybody who knew him, said that if there was one constant in his life, it was his unstinting devotion to Maruja. Theirs was an extremely close marriage. 'There was never ever any question of him breaking the sixth commandment,' says Nicholas Kearns, while Niall FitzGerald emphasises the importance of their relationship. 'The real secret of Peter being successful was Maruja.'

Their first child, Shane, was born in June 1972. Ian followed a couple of years later and Natalia towards the end of the decade, Shane and Ian being named after the two boys Maruja had looked after as an au pair. Shane later studied history at UCD and subsequently law at Buckingham University in the UK, and has since spent most of his career at the European Commission. He has most recently worked in the cabinet of Phil Hogan, when Hogan was European Commissioner for Agriculture, and is at the time of writing a programme manager at the Centre for Advanced Studies at the European Commission. Ian studied law at Trinity and did a master's at Georgetown University in the US. He qualified as a solicitor and is a senior partner at private equity firm Colt. Natalia studied Spanish and economics at UCD and completed an MBA in Madrid. All three are married, and they have ten children between them.

When the children were young, Sutherland already had a formidable work ethic. During the 1970s, when he was in the process of building up a thriving practice at the Bar, he would rise at 6 a.m. on a Sunday morning to clear his paperwork for the week. He also became involved with Fine Gael, and there was rugby at weekends. Shane says that from his earliest recollections, home life was hectic 'to say the least. There are memories of important people visiting our house in Sydney Avenue in Blackrock. There were ministers dropping by in the evening on the way home. It was the days before mobile phones so people visited a lot more. Garret [FitzGerald] was a regular visitor.'

Sutherland's hard-line approach to paramilitaries as attorney general during the Troubles in Northern Ireland would have consequences for family life. During his time in office there was a constant Garda presence outside the family home, and he had a Garda driver.

Shane remembers a phone that hung from the wall and was used for official business. 'Certainly at the weekends there were a lot of calls with a lot of colourful language. My mother would always be telling him to tone it down. Even though my father was very busy, he was also very hands-on. He brought the kids swimming every Saturday morning. He would never get in, he would read the newspapers. But for a man with such weighty issues on his mind he would insist on making sure that our hair was dry. I don't know whether that was out of a genuine worry we would get pneumonia or because he was afraid of what my mother would do to him.' Sutherland very rarely spent his free time unaccompanied by his children. 'Whether it was rugby, or the horse show or a boxing match, he always wanted his kids around him.'

When Shane and his siblings were growing up, Sutherland's parents sold their home in Monkstown and moved to Foxrock, another middle-class suburb in south Dublin. The entire family would go to the grandparents for Sunday lunch, which invariably ended up in a forceful discussion between Sutherland and his father Billy, and sometimes his brother-in-law David Brennan. 'They were good-natured discussions but they would become very heated.'

Shane says his father lived for family moments. 'When you arrived home, it was like the prodigal son had returned. Towards the end he was keeping a physical or mental log of whether the in-laws were getting more time than him. He was making sure he wasn't being short-changed on holiday time with his children and grandchildren. If he felt he was missing out he would let you know. He would organise boutique hotels that he would take over for family holidays in France, Italy or Spain.'

Sutherland took his two sons to the Hong Kong Sevens rugby tournament, and to the Rugby World Cup in Australia. He never returned home from work trips without a gift, although that presented its own danger. 'He came through Dublin airport once with toy guns that looked very real. They were snaffled, but he managed to get them released because he was attorney general at the time.

'He was very hands on when he was here,' says Shane. 'He would read us stories before bed. He was always encouraging us to take up new sports, whether that was tennis or rowing or whatever. When he was present you always felt like numero uno. You could go to him with any problem. He had very simple rules. He never wanted us to lie. It is something that stuck with me through the years.'

Decades later, Sutherland rang Fr Barber in panicked tones to say that Paul McEnroe, his son-in-law, and his daughter Natalia, were veering towards sending their son Patrick to St Mary's College in Rathmines. He enlisted Fr Barber's help to successfully change their minds. Patrick started at Gonzaga in September 2018.

It didn't matter where his father was in the world, says Shane, there would always be a phone call. 'They were invariably at the wrong time for us, but he always got through. He would get quite annoyed if he couldn't.' Even though, Shane adds, such calls would usually end with 'My flight has been called, you've served your purpose,' or 'My car has arrived, buzz off.'

Later acquaintances also remember Sutherland's phone habit. Rory Godson, who now runs the strategic communications company Powerscourt, was a close friend of Sutherland from the 1990s onwards. He recalls that he would often have six missed calls from Sutherland over a space of twenty minutes. The messages usually started with a simple request to call him back, but Sutherland would grow increasingly exasperated with each missed call, and his last message was usually a mixture of anger and despair. Godson would ring in a panic thinking that something awful must have happened, only to find Sutherland nonplussed by his sense of urgency. 'I only rang you because I was bored,' usually came the reply.

Sunday mornings, says Shane, were spent going to mass with his father. 'We would always go to mass with him in Booterstown. My mother would always be busy doing the roast. It wasn't forced down our throat.' It was a source of regret for Sutherland that Shane's children were not baptised while Peter was alive. 'He would lament this when the issue arose. But we agreed not to discuss it. We went through the motions at school. It was not rammed down our throats. But it fundamentally guided him in everything he did, whether it was popular or not.'

*

Sutherland battled with his weight for most of his life. Before he went to parties when he was a child his mother, Barbara, would stuff him with rice pudding to ensure his appetite was sufficiently sated that he would leave enough food for other kids. When he got older, Barbara would be forced to hide the Sunday roast that she had prepared on a Saturday night in case Sutherland returned from the rugby and the subsequent hop and decided to devour the whole thing.

Sutherland was well aware of the problem. When he once met with the chairman of the China National Petroleum Company (CNPC) on a visit to the country, the two men had a conversation that extended well beyond business interests. They found that they shared a passion for reading, and the chairman told Sutherland he found some books so interesting that he would forget to eat. Sutherland asked him to pass on the names of these books, 'as my wife would be very interested'.

In later years, travelling and receptions would take a toll on Sutherland's health. He was always a moderate drinker, but he smoked cigars. His physical appearance in later years was moreover often used against him. Unfortunately for him, he became the public epitome of a 'fat cat' banker. Over his last decade any media profile of him usually contained a sly reference to his girth. 'We worried every day about his health. You'd implore him to eat less and exercise more. This was a constant refrain. At times the situation improved. We would ask him to eat less and look after his diet. But he would tuck in anyway. Every time he was away on a business trip we would ask him to bring a pair of trainers or swimming togs, but it never happened. Every day at the back of my heart I had a feeling something was going to happen. My grandfathers lived to a very old age. I think he thought he would live forever. He had warnings. His lifestyle was aeroplane food and receptions. He ate everything put in front of him,' says Shane.

Even though Sutherland was a very wealthy man, he enjoyed a relatively modest lifestyle. There was no private jet, fleet of luxury cars or trophy villas. That is not to say that he embraced ascetic values. There was a family home on Eglinton Road, Dublin; a house in London; a house in Goleen in west Cork, and another house in Spain. But they were all used. One of the highlights of his year was the trip to west Cork every August. His forebears were from Cork and, according to Shane, 'he claimed to be related to half the county'.

*

Friendships meant a great deal to him. Garrett Sheehan, John Arrigo and Paddy Kevans were lifelong friends going back to Gonzaga and Monkstown while Nicholas Kearns was another close friend from the time they met at UCD. He stayed close to people.

Sheehan and Sutherland spoke most days. 'There was a private, very generous side to Peter that he didn't want to publicise. He wasn't that thick-skinned. He was actually quite sensitive.' But, as Sheehan notes, Sutherland had an extraordinary capacity to move on. 'He didn't dwell on things. He was never depressed. How he managed to keep up so many friendships I do not know.'

Loyal, generous, kind, humorous, empathetic and passionate

are the words most often used by friends, former colleagues and associates to describe Sutherland. They joke that he was an outrageous name-dropper. He could also be very direct. He could sometimes deliver a very blunt assessment if he thought somebody had made a wrong decision, either in a professional or a personal capacity.

He was also very sensitive. He needed constant validation. It was not uncommon, in the aftermath of a speech or a TV appearance, for him to ring close associates to get their feedback. He might ring the same person a number of times in one evening.

John O'Hagan was friendly with Sutherland at UCD, but they saw little of each other for the next thirty-five years. It was only in the mid-2000s that they picked up where they left off. 'He didn't like to be criticised. He could be very insecure. When in public he was very confident but in private he could be insecure. I never got the impression he was at ease despite his amazing success. That's the hallmark of a lot of great people. He was always striving.'

'The thing about Peter is who else has done what he has done,' says Gregory Maniatis, who is now a director of the Open Society Migration Initiative, funded by the philanthropist George Soros. 'I only fell out with him three times in eleven years and that was always momentarily. He always knew instantly if he was in the wrong. He was very aware of the power he exerted when he walked through a room. In that world he was peerless. He even made prime ministers fade into the background. Everybody stood up and took notice of him. He was a businessman. He was a lawyer. He negotiated GATT. He became the UN special representative on the key issue of the past decade. So he had this aura. But he was totally down to earth about his place in the world. He was not bombastic, he was not hubristic. He had that ability to connect with people. He was profoundly respectful of institutions. He respected the rules and procedures. He recognised the importance of individuals but it had to be about the institution – the person cannot be bigger than the institution as it would weaken the institution. That applied to the EU, the UN or whatever.'

Richard Gnodde, from Goldman Sachs, says his abiding memory of Sutherland is being 'extremely compassionate'.

'The migration story will support that. But he was also extremely competitive and driven. If he wanted something he would bash down doors to get it. He had a fantastic sense of humour and was a great raconteur. He always stayed very well connected. He made an enormous contribution to everything he touched: to Ireland, Europe, the world, through WTO and migration, to us, to BP, and the Vatican. In that sense he was extremely self-deprecating. He was always happy to laugh at himself. If someone was in trouble, financially or in any way, he helped a lot of people out. That was the thing about Peter, he was a globalist, a European and most importantly an Irishman. I look around me today and I wonder why people have to make a choice.'

*

In 2009, on a family holiday, Maruja noticed a lump at the side of her husband's neck. He had it checked out immediately, and the family's worst fears were confirmed. It was throat cancer.

Sutherland underwent immediate surgery, followed by aggressive chemotherapy and radiotherapy. But he never fully recovered from the treatment. He suffered afterwards from throat ulcers, which meant that he couldn't eat certain types of food or drink wine. Yet he didn't let up on his punishing regime of travel and work commitments. His passion about migration, in particular, ensured that he pushed himself beyond his physical capabilities. On the bright Sunday morning of 11 September 2016 he left his house in London to go to mass. He would never return home. He spent the first year in a private hospital in London. The family hoped against the odds that he would make a recovery, but the heart attack he had suffered inflicted too much damage.

Friends visited, but because Sutherland had been larger than life it was hard to see him in a reduced state. He was eventually transferred to a private nursing home in Rathgar, where he became prone to infections. He finally succumbed to a chest infection in St James's Hospital on 8 January 2018, aged seventy-one.

23

LEGACY

A S A COUNTRY IRELAND HAS ALWAYS PUNCHED above its weight. Irish people have at various times been world leaders in the fields of arts, sports, literature, international affairs and academia. Freddie Boland, Sean McBride, John Hume, Mary Robinson, John Bruton, Bertie Ahern, Bono, Catherine Day, David O'Sullivan, Conor Cruise O'Brien, Tony O'Reilly, Michael Smurfit and Denis O'Brien are just some of the Irish men and women who have made an impact on the international stage.

But Sutherland is unique in terms of his spheres of influence. A roll call of his achievements speaks for itself. He received sixteen honorary doctorates and was a member of the Royal Irish Academy. He was made a Chevalier of the French Légion d'Honneur and a Papal Knight of St Gregory, while his other awards include an honorary knighthood, the Gold Medal of the European Parliament (1988), the first European Law Prize (Paris 1988), the David Rockefeller International Leadership Award in 1998 and the Robert Schuman Medal for his work on European integration.

He became attorney general at the age of thirty-five; he was one of the most successful European commissioners ever; he is widely regarded as the best president the European Commission never had; he brokered the first global multilateral trade agreement;

he shaped the global migration debate, possibly more than any other individual; he was chairman of the third largest company in the world, and chairman of the international arm of one of the most successful investment banks in the world. He had access to world leaders like no other Irish person. He was one of the head-line acts at Bilderberg. He was the European chairman of the Trilateral Commission between 2001 and 2010. In fact, he is among the most influential international powerbrokers of the last thirty years or so.

Indeed, the tributes paid to Sutherland in death were wide-spread and generous. Irish and international civic and business groups issued statements. Fianna Fáil and Labour joined Fine Gael in extending sympathies on his passing, and in acknowledging his achievements. European and world leaders as well as the pope acknowledged his many accomplishments.

Yet he spent the latter years of his life the subject of unrelenting attacks. With the exception of George Soros, there is probably no other individual who was such an effective lightning rod for disaffection from the hard left and the hard right. He was a very late adapter to social media and it was not a forum to which he paid too much attention. It is probably just as well. He wasn't spared even in death.

The attention he received from the traditional media was much harder for him to ignore. Over the latter years of his life, he was the subject of a series of ad hominem attacks. Strangely, for somebody who championed free trade and open markets, he became something of a *bête noire* for the British right-wing press. The *Daily Mail* stuck the boot in on a number of occasions. In Ireland too there were a number of bruising encounters. Fintan O'Toole wrote two critical pieces about Sutherland, one in 2010 at the height of the financial crisis and one in the immediate aftermath of his death.

There were common themes to the attacks on Sutherland. In no particular order or ranking they were: That there were double stand-ards between his highly lucrative business career and his public service, particularly in the area of migration. That he worked for Goldman Sachs. That he worked for BP. That he had been on the board of Royal Bank of Scotland when it had to be rescued. That he was partly responsible for Brexit and the presidency of Donald Trump, because the type of globalisation he advocated fuelled rampant inequality in the developed world. That his zest for deregulation and support for the financial sector had contributed to the global financial crisis in 2008. That his failure to show leadership when he was chairman of AIB spawned a banking culture that seriously harmed the country. That the migration agenda he pushed had politically destabilising consequences for many countries.

Sutherland first entered the public eye during the Arms Trial in 1970. For the next forty-eight years until his death, he was never far from the public eye. His career was multifaceted. There were a number of high-powered positions across the public and private sectors. It would have been inconceivable for him not to have encountered controversies along the way. In some cases, criticism is merited; in others, not so. Very often there is a yawning chasm between the facts and supposition.

What is crucial to understanding Sutherland's legacy is the changed landscape over the past decade. The tectonic plates have shifted. Before 2008, globalisation had its discontents, but Sutherland's worldview broadly chimed with the prevailing economic orthodoxy in the West. The globalisation of trade in the 1990s presaged a period of unprecedented global prosperity. Traditionally left-wing and right-wing parties moved to the centre. Leaders eschewed ideology and instead focused on managing the economy and spreading the fiscal gains, although with more regard to the ballot box than to shaping society.

The collapse of the western economy in 2008 exposed the growth chimera of the previous decade. Wealth had very often been based on the accumulation of debt. During the recession, governments were forced to consolidate; the consequent painful belt-tightening caused a real drop in living standards for most countries, and for Irish people in particular.

Grievance with growing inequality – real or otherwise – has only heightened the level of disaffection. Globalisation has pitted communities that have lost out to lower-cost locations against alleged elites.

Since the economic downturn, there has been a backlash against globalisation, migration, Europe and big business – the financial sector in particular. Sutherland was associated with all of these. It was inevitable that he would become a bogeyman. But many of the charges laid against him need to be put in context.

For example, what about the claim that if he had intervened in the DIRT scandal it might have changed the course of Irish banking and steered it on a more virtuous path? The scandal was indeed a shameful episode in Irish banking. But AIB was rumbled. It was hauled over the coals in a very high-profile Public Accounts Committee investigation. Findings were made against individuals. The bank had to pay over €90 million in restitution, and public opprobrium was heaped upon it. Politicians lined up to give it a kicking.

The Irish Central Bank pledged that nothing like this would happen again – except it did, with far more devastating consequences. The banking sector brought the country to the brink of national bankruptcy. There was a change of personnel at executive level across all the banks, and public acts of contrition. And yet over the past few years there has been the tracker mortgage scandal. Roughly 40,000 customers have been either wrongly taken off or denied a tracker mortgage, which could cost the banks up to €1 billion in restitution and fines. In other words, only an appropriate regulatory framework and a sufficiently robust regulator will keep banks on the straight and narrow.

The light-touch approach to regulation, which Ireland heartily embraced in the early 2000s along with a raft of other countries, was a central component in the subsequent economic crash. It was a political choice made by a Fianna Fáil government which won three successive elections based largely on its management of the economy. Sutherland, moreover, was chairman of AIB, not an elected public official. His job was to do what was in the best interests of the bank. He was given information that the DIRT issue had been resolved through an agreement with Revenue. It is highly unlikely that any chairman in existence would have insisted that the bank instead pay a €100 million liability and make a public act of contrition when no arm of the state, and certainly not Revenue, was looking for such a move.

That is not to say Sutherland is without blame. Not only was he chairman of AIB when the DIRT scandal was in full flow, he was a board member of RBS when the bank had to be bailed out by the British taxpayer, and chairman of Goldman Sachs when the bank was charged in 2010 with securities fraud by the US Securities and Exchange Commission (SEC) in relation to the subprime crisis. There was never any evidence of Sutherland's culpability or impropriety, but as an executive he shares responsibility.

However, there is little evidence that Sutherland favoured the sort of casino capitalism that wreaked so much damage. The EU has introduced a series of reforms over the past few years in the area of banking and has achieved much closer fiscal union. If these reforms had been introduced in Ireland and elsewhere a decade earlier, then the worst ravages of the financial crisis could have been avoided. Sutherland was always an enthusiastic supporter of this sort of integration.

He certainly believed in competition and open markets, but he believed too in fair trade. More than any other European commissioner he dismantled barriers to competition across the EU which helped develop the single market. The vision for the EU is closely aligned with the centre-right European People's Party, the largest bloc in the European Parliament. To take aim at that is a political charge.

Take, for example, the claim that as an Irishman he failed to show leadership when it mattered, with grave consequences for the governance of the country. It is important to note that apart from the role of attorney general, Sutherland never held public office in Ireland. From January 1985 onwards, he contributed to public life solely on a voluntary basis. People were free either to take heed of his public pronouncements or to ignore them.

Sutherland was a fiercely proud Irishman, whose success never diminished his Irishness. He was motivated by the best of intentions. He cared passionately about Ireland. He wanted the best for his country. He believed the only way Ireland could emerge from the economic crisis was if it recognised the importance of fiscal consolidation. However, in an era of austerity, anybody who had risen as high in the corporate world as Sutherland was going to be a target. He recognised that belatedly.

For the last decade of his life he showed immense leadership with respect to one of the most crucial issues of these times. It was Sutherland, possibly more than any other individual, who improved the lives of migrants and fought tirelessly to alleviate their plight. He cajoled governments into action. He committed his own money to the cause. He didn't do this because he had a successful business career. He did so because it was consistent with his personal values. He believed in the free movement of goods and people in a regulated environment.

The type of globalisation that he helped shape lifted 500 million people out of poverty. It is true that in the last years of his life, there was a backlash against Europe and globalisation. Perhaps he was naive about the impact of globalisation. But again, it would be fanciful to pin the pitfalls of globalisation on the shoulders of one man. Globalisation created wealth. It was up to governments to use the proceeds to ensure that developed countries could adjust and compete in the new world. They didn't. That is why Donald Trump became the forty-sixth President of the US.

*

Assessing Sutherland's legacy will take time. The things about which he felt most passionately are still a work in progress. What can be said with certainty is that it is unlikely that any Irish person will match his achievements again.

A memorial day for Sutherland was held at the Sutherland Law School in UCD on 29 March 2018. Former colleagues and friends gathered to pay tribute to him. Bill Swing, the head of the IOM, flew in from New York for the day. 'In the field of migration, Peter Sutherland will be remembered as a giant. And I shall remember him as a faithful friend and a companion in arms in a noble fight for the rights of migrants. If migrants' lives, rights and prospects are better in future years than they are today, if fewer migrants die in the sands of the Sahara or in the depths of the Mediterranean, this will be due largely to Peter Sutherland and his great humanity, compelling advocacy and strategic thinking.'

Others have spoken about Sutherland's legacy – not just the one he leaves to the world, but also on a more personal level. For Roddy Kennedy, he still has a great deal of respect and affection for Sutherland. 'I admired him for his kindness and his sense of humour, which came into play even at the trickiest of moments. He was deeply regarded by everyone who worked with him. All of the secretaries and personal assistants he had at BP and Goldman Sachs flew to Dublin at their own expense for his funeral.'

Adrian Jones has said that Sutherland had a hugely positive impact on his life. 'For him to take such a personal interest in me was incredible. We would have dinner every couple of weeks. We had a very nice, easy relationship. He was a fundamentally decent human being. He was highly moral and extraordinarily loyal. I spent time with men his age who had gone to school with him who were up the creek. He was helping sort their finances. He had a loyalty to his faith. The migration role was a gift to him. It allowed him to use his talents in an area that he felt passionately about. I think he felt hurt and frustrated in the negativity he faced. I think he felt his voice was stymied by the fact that he was now a very wealthy man. He was frustrated by that. Just as he was by the tribalism and the peevishness of the Irish press. He would work through it and move on. It is how you deal with people. There was a moral compass at his core and he never compromised that.'

Dáithí Ó Ceallaigh had a working and personal relationship with Sutherland for over thirty-five years: 'My personal view is that Peter was one of the most morally upright people I have ever met. There was a deep, deep morality to the man and a deep concern for humanity.'

In an interview with the UCD magazine in 2010, Sutherland said the most important thing in life to him was that he was a good husband and father. According to his son Shane, Sutherland achieved this – and then some. 'When he was around we always felt safe. There was nothing he wouldn't do for us. He meant the world to us.'

ACKNOWLEDGEMENTS

I first interviewed Peter Sutherland in 2005 for *Business & Finance Magazine*. I had intermittent contact with him over the next few years. I had a very brief conversation with him in 2009 about writing his biography: it was just before he was diagnosed with cancer, so nothing came of it. I only met Peter once again – briefly, at a conference in 2014.

I contacted Ian Sutherland in March 2018, seeking permission from the Sutherland family to do what I had originally proposed nine years previously. I am very grateful for all the assistance provided by Maruja, Shane, Ian and Natalia. I would also like to thank Rory Godson and Richard O'Toole for all the help they provided, as well as Gregory Maniatis for all his help and advice. Indeed, there are too many to name individually, but I would like to thank everybody who agreed to be interviewed for this book. A full list is provided in the pages that follow. There is obviously a huge gender imbalance in the list of interviewees. Unfortunately, that is a reflection of the times.

I would like to thank Eoin McHugh, my editor at HarperCollins, and the wider team for agreeing to publish this book. I would also like to thank Dr Brian Jackson and Stephen Collins for their help and advice. Finally, I would like to thank my wife, Mary Minihan, and our two sons, Hugh and Dominic, for being so patient over the past twelve months.

LIST OF ILLUSTRATIONS

February 1960 Gonzaga Junior Cup team. Sutherland can be seen at the front, kneeling, second from left. (© The Gonzaga College Archive)

The 1969-70 rugby season, Landsdowne Football Club. Sutherland can be seen on the back row, third from the right. (© Lansdowne Football Club)

Called to the Bar, 1968. Sutherland can be seen on the back row, second from the right. Notable other members of the class of 1968 include Professor William Binchy, The Hon. Declan Budd, Conor Doyle, John Hurley, The Hon. Justice Nicholas Kearns, Declan McCourt and The Hon. Esmond Smyth. (© Declan McCourt)

The attorney general in his office, 1982 (© *The Irish Times*)

Meeting of the first Delors Commission, 1985. Sutherland is seated at the front of the picture. (© European Union, 2019/ Christian Lambiotte)

The EU Commissioner cabinet. From left to right, David O'Sullivan, Eugene Regan, Richard O'Toole, Peter Sutherland, Colm Larkin, Catherine Day and Michel Richonnier. (© Catherine Day)

The EP President awards a medal to Commissioner Peter Sutherland in December, 1988. (© Communautes Europeennes 1988 - Source : PE)

Sutherland, then chairman of AIB, with the bank's then chief executive, Gerry Scanlan, 1991. (© *The Irish Times*)

A press conference after BP and US oil giant Amoco announced plans for their merger. From left to right, Sir John Brown, Laurance Fuller and Peter Sutherland. (© JOHNNY EGGITT/ AFP/Getty Images)

Sutherland as head of GATT at the Uruguay round of global trade talks. Richard O'Toole is to the left of Sutherland. (© World Trade Organization)

Peter Sutherland as General Director of the GATT shows one of numerous documents on the final act of the Uruguay Round, 15 April 1994. (© ABDELHAK SENNA/AFP/Getty Images)

Secretary-General Kofi Annan meets with Peter Sutherland, Special Representative of the Secretary-General for Migration, in Davos, Switzerland. (© UN Photo/Eskinder Debebe)

A joint press conference at the conclusion of the Global Forum on Migration and Development. From left to right, Esteban Conejos, Undersecretary for Foreign Affairs of the Philippines, Secretary-General Ban Ki-moon and Peter Sutherland. (© UN Photo/Mark Garten)

Sutherland addresses the Security Council meeting on cooperation between the United Nations and regional and sub regional organizations in maintaining international peace and security. Gregory Maniatis is seated directly behind Sutherland. Federica Mogherini, the High Representative of the European Union on Foreign Affairs is to Sutherland's right. (© UN Photo/Loey Felipe)

Sutherland visiting a refugee camp in Athens, 12 May 2016. (© Gregory A. Maniatis)

Sutherland with Angela Merkel and Martin Schulz at the Valletta Summit on migration, 2015. (© Darrin Zammit Lupi)

Sutherland with Pope Francis at the Vatican, 26 June 2015. (© Servizio Fotografico - Vatican Media)

Peter Sutherland and his family at the 2007 Business & Finance Awards in Dublin. From left to right: Paul McEnroe, Natalia Sutherland McEnroe, Peter Sutherland, Maruja Sutherland, Shane Sutherland and Ian Sutherland. (© Ian Hyland/Business & Finance)

APPENDICES

Appendix 1

UCD vs Trinity team sheet, 17th Annual Colours Match, 4 December 1968

	UCD	TCD	
15	A. HICKIE (St. Mary's)	G. MURPHIE (Midleton College)	15
14	T. GRACE (Newbridge)	H.R. HERRON (Belfast Royal Academy)	14
13	G. O'HAGAN (St. Mary's)	D.P. DONOVAN (Belmont Abbey)	13
12	B. BRESNIHAN (Gonzaga)	R.C. HUTCHINSON (Hurstpierpoint)	12
11	H. BLAKE (Glenstal)	K.G. KELLY (St. Patrick's Armagh)	11
10	H. MURPHY (St. Mary's)	W. McCOMBE (Campbell College)	10
9	R. COOKE (Mungret)	A.M. CARROLL (King's Hospital)	9

1	P. SUTHERLAND (Gonzaga)	P.R. EVANS (Portora Royal)	1
2	J. O'HAGAN (Capt) (St. Mary's)	A.H. McKINLEY	2
3	T. FEIGHERY (Clongowers)	J.W. GOODE (St. Andrews)	3
4	G. SHEENAN (Gonzaga)	R. DAVIES (Cowbridge C.S)	4
5	C. FEIGHERY (Castleknock)	M.G. ROBERTS (Magee College)	5
6	G. GILL (Blackrock)	R.E. DOHERTY (Campbell College)	v
8	S. DEERING (St. Mary's)	C.J. HAWKESWORTH (Campbell College)	8
7	P.J. SMYTH (C.B.C. Monkstown)	K. SHERIDAN (Downside)	7

Appendix 2

Sutherland's full advice, as attorney general, on the Eighth Amendment to the Fine Gael–Labour government, 1983

The use of the word 'unborn' in the proposed amendment is significant because it has not to my knowledge been used before in a similar context, that is as a noun standing on its own. The word is usually taken in association with 'child', 'person' or 'human being'. The word, used as a noun, is not in fact defined in any of the standard English dictionaries. The reason why it is used in the proposal, without any supporting noun, deserves detailed consideration, as this is the word which defines the class to be afforded protection.

The Irish text of the proposed amendment, which must prevail in cases of conflict and which corresponds to 'the unborn' in the English, can be translated as 'the unborn living' or 'the living unborn'.

In the event that the Supreme Court is called upon to construe the proposal, it could come to a number of different conclusions as to the definition of the class which is afforded protection. Undoubtedly a view which might commend itself to the court is that all human beings fall within the ambit of the amendment, and that a human being comes into existence when the process of fertilisation is complete.

It is, I believe, the position of many in the community that the inalienable right to life attaches to the newly fertilised ovum prior to implantation. The consequences of such a definition of the commencement of human life are matters on which medical opinion would be required.

If, as would appear to be the case, it is correct to state that certain contraceptives can operate after fertilisation, then these would be abortifacient if human life commences on conception. Thus the importation, dissemination and use of such contraceptives would be prohibited, and as an example, the use of the 'morning-after' pill in the treatment of rape victims will not be permissible, nor will the use of such contraceptives in certain conditions of the health of a woman – e.g. valvular heart disease, diabetes.

As I stated earlier there are, however, other conclusions that the Supreme Court might reach in defining what is meant by 'unborn'. It might simply conclude that the question cannot be answered definitively. (In considering the rights, if any, attaching to life before birth in the United States the Supreme Court there determined that to attempt to reach a conclusion on the issue would be to speculate because 'those trained in the respective disciplines of medicine, philosophy and theology are unable to arrive at any consensus'.) Other conclusions might be that human life commences at the moment of implantation of fertilised ovum or when brain activity commences.

However, the point of time for which the most compelling legal argument could be made, other than the time of fertilisation, as being the moment of commencement of protection, could be said to be the time when the foetus becomes independently viable. I understand that this is probably at some time between 25 and 28 weeks of pregnancy.

Such a construction could be supported by an argument that 'unborn' could be regarded as being applicable only to something capable of being born. The word 'unborn' used as a noun must, as a matter of language, mean 'unborn person', 'unborn child' or 'unborn human being'. It could be argued that neither a fertilised ovum, a fertilised and implanted ovum, an embryo or even a foetus prior to the time when it is independently viable, would come within this definition.

The consequences of such a finding could be that there would be no constitutional prohibition on abortion prior to this stage of pregnancy.

The next issue that is raised by the proposed amendment is the meaning and effect of the words 'with due regard to the equal right to life of the mother'.

The meaning of 'with due regard to' is entirely unclear. These words are generally perceived to allow for, at least, termination of the life of the foetus in the case of ectopic pregnancy or cancer of the uterus. The words 'with due regard to' have been understood by many to suggest that the right to life enjoyed by the unborn was to be confined in some way. That interpretation is in my opinion incorrect. (The word 'comh cheart' in the Irish text is literally 'the same right'.)

The right to life of both the unborn and the mother is stated in the proposed text to be equal, and in these circumstances I cannot see how it could be possible knowingly to terminate the existence of the unborn even if such termination were the secondary effect of an operation for another purpose.

The issue of intention does not arise in the proposed amendment, and thus, it seems to me, that even if the termination of the pregnancy is an incidental consequence of an operation to save the life of the mother, it could be prohibited. The correct logical consequence is that the right to life provided for the unborn is absolute.

If a doctor were to be faced with the choice as to saving the life of one, and thereby terminating the life of the other, then I believe that the only lawful conclusion to this dilemma would be that he could do nothing, absolutely nothing, which is infringed on either right. It is only where there is no possibility of the foetus surviving, even without the doctor's intervention, that no difficulty will arise.

Whatever about such a clear-cut factual situation, the difficulties of applying the provision to other circumstances will be considerable. There may be cases where a doctor will have to consider whether he can treat a prospective mother for an illness which might otherwise shorten her life expectancy if this treatment will threaten the life of the foetus.

The proposed amendment will in my view tend to confuse a doctor as to his responsibilities, rather than assist him, and the consequences may well be to inhibit him in making decisions as to whether treatment should be given in a particular case.

The consideration of the points which I have raised is of particular importance having regard to the difference in principle between an ordinary legislative provision and a statement in the Constitution.

While a view may be formed as to the likely interpretation of a given constitutional provision at a particular time, such an interpretation is open to review in the future. One is considering in this instance a provision which is intended to stand the test of time. This type of constitutional provision, by its nature, is a statement of broad general principle. The fact that the interpretation of such provisions is often a complicated and difficult task is evident from the very many reported judgments on the Constitution which have been delivered by the Supreme Court. I draw attention to the ambiguities in the proposed draft because to do otherwise might suggest that the words are susceptible to only one interpretation.

It is further to be borne in mind that this constitutional provision, whilst a statement of general principle, will be susceptible to enforcement in various ways through the civil and criminal law. Uncertainty as to its meaning and effect could have the most serious consequences. These ambiguities and uncertainties are inherent in any statement of a general right, since the scope and extent of such a right must be settled by the Supreme Court, and often this will become definitive only after perhaps a number of references to the court.

Appendix 3

Part of Sutherland's speech at the annual Cardinal Newman Lecture in St John's College Oxford on 19 May 2010, a fortnight after the general election and a week after the Tories had formed a coalition with the Liberal Democrats

The more that I have reflected on this lecture, the more I have been struck by how alien and even destructive it may sound in Britain. Religion and values have not formed part of the narrative here of the troubled relationship between Britain and the process of European integration. But if the EU is no more than a Common Market, as many here believe, why should they be part of the story? In fact these subjects may be seen rather as added complications to a debate by those who seek a more constructive dialogue on European issues. The result of this is they are not much spoken of, particularly within and by the Churches. While this lecture is not intended to be exclusively focused on Britain in the European Union (which is not in any sense 'Europe'), I will initially look at this issue.

Perhaps there is an unspoken suspicion that the whole business of European integration is a little too Catholic for British tastes.

Even though the religious influence of the Reformed Churches, particularly in Germany, was profound in its creation and development, this would not be at all visible here, whereas the Founding Fathers, as they are perhaps annoyingly described by Europhiles like me, were to a man Catholic. Monnet, Schuman, de Gasperi and Adenauer were all Christian Democrats too, and only Paul Henri Spaak in the early European pantheon was a socialist. But others from the reformed tradition, such as the Danes, Swedes and Finns, however reluctant initially, have begun to put suspicions of this kind behind them. Increasingly they demonstrate a real belief in the integration process. This is particularly true of Finland.

It is indisputable that the United Kingdom has a fundamental problem with European integration. The evidence of polls suggests that the negativism here is qualitatively different from all other cases not merely in its consistency but in its depth. Thus it remains at the lowest position in Eurobarometer polls in its positivism towards the European Union. Indeed it is far from clear what the result of a referendum on membership would be today.

This ambivalence has been evident from the earliest days. In the lead-up to the Treaty of Paris that created the Coal and Steel Community and started the whole process, Dean Acheson counselled the French not to inform London because he foresaw its potential for destructive opposition.

The reasons for this antipathy are many, varied and in part understandable. It is apparent that history plays a substantial part in this, not merely through the memory of terrible continental wars but also in the sense of distinctiveness born out of the inviolability of Britain itself, an island that has not been invaded for a thousand years. Britain had pragmatic economic grounds, too, for its initial opposition to European integration. Its loyalty to and connection with an empire, already disintegrating but still connected in the 40s and 50s, and 'the English speaking peoples', was an essential element in such limited profound political debate as took place during the 1950s on the whole subject of Europe.

Winston Churchill of course, in his famous speech in the University of Zurich on 16 September 1946, though extolling the common inheritance of Christian faith and ethics and the prospect of a united Europe, saw Britain standing apart. So the Commonwealth and the United States form part of the backdrop to this, but so does simple nationalism. It is not hard to recall George Canning's remark in 1826, following the collapse of the Congress of Vienna system, that 'things are getting back to a wholesome state, every nation for itself, and God for us all'. It still has a resonance here even in this era of interdependence.

At the end of the day it is difficult to avoid the conclusion that Britain essentially dislikes, in principle, the sharing of sovereignty and, indeed, any interference with the constitutional principle of the supremacy of Parliament. So even the supremacy of European law, established beyond doubt in Britain by the Factortame case in 1989, has been erroneously characterised by many establishment figures as an unwarranted and unjustified intrusion of their basic understanding of what they joined in 1973.

In Britain there has never been sympathy for, or even a comprehension of, the political and indeed moral purpose of the project to pursue 'an ever greater Union' of the peoples of Europe. It has had few true advocates in the political world or even academia, and the Conservative party in the current government is the most Eurosceptic in the last twenty years. At every revision of the Treaties since accession, Britain has been the most reluctant member state to move forward and has always pressed for 'co-operation by sovereign states' rather than integration. In other words it has pressed for intergovernmentalism rather than supranationalism. This has been a tragedy for many of us who had hoped for constructive leadership in another direction from Britain. It seems tragic because Britain has so much to give to the process, its tolerance, longstanding democracy and commitment to the rule of law being particularly noteworthy and generally respected.

The real tragedy, however, may be that a debate on the substance of the issues has never truly taken place. In particular the overwhelmingly Christian intellectual foundations for European integration have not been explored in any substantive manner in political circles, and academia has not been much better.

The question may be asked whether the issue is relevant following the delayed conclusion of the agonising debate on the Lisbon Treaty and the general agreement on its adoption that further constitutional change was not on the agenda. Many contributions in recent times have pointed to the fact that there is no appetite for further constitutional change in Europe generally and this is clearly true for the majority for the moment. However, the debate is only in temporary abeyance. For one thing it is increasingly obvious that the dynamics of globalisation will demand a more united Europe if we are to play a real role in determining our own destiny. Furthermore the issues surrounding the survival of the Euro following the debt crisis will, in the view of many observers, probably result in a new drive for economic governance at European level. Mrs Merkel has already trenchantly said this and last week linked this issue to the survival of the Union itself. This argument about the future will undoubtedly be essentially about federalism and Britain, though not in the Eurozone will have to be part of it.

The word federal has taken on such pejorative connotations here that it can scarcely be mentioned in public company, and this notwithstanding the fact that for many continentals it is at the heart of the process and is inextricably linked to maintaining the admirable vision of its founders.

REFERENCES

List of interviewees

Abbott, Roderick; number two in the EU negotiating team during Uruguay Round of trade talks. Phone interview on 26 July 2018.

Ahern, Bertie; former Taoiseach and leader of Fianna Fáil. Interview took place in Dublin on 19 March 2019.

Barber, Fr Noel; former teacher at Gonzaga. Interview took place in Dublin on 21 July 2018.

Barrington, Colm; friend and former Gonzaga classmate. Interview took place in Dublin on 11 October 2018.

Byrne, David; former Attorney General and European Commissioner. Interview took place in Dublin on 12 September 2018.

Cowen, Brian; former Taoiseach and leader of Fianna Fáil. Interview took place in Tullamore on 2 March 2018.

Day, Catherine; former Secretary General of the European Commission. Interview took place in Dublin on 24 July 2018.

De Buitléir, Donal; economist and former AIB deputy head of taxation. Interview took place in Dublin on 25 September 2018.

Doyle, Michael; former assistant to Kofi Annan and professor of International Relations at Columbia University. Phone interview on 30 January 2019.

Dukes, Alan; former leader of Fine Gael and Minister for Finance. Interview took place in Dublin on 21 July 2018.

Ehlermann, Claus-Dieter; former Director General of the legal service of the European Commission. Phone interview, 28 August 2018.

Fennelly, Nial; former Supreme Court Judge. Interview took place in Dublin on 3 October 2018.

FitzGerald, Mark; son of Garret FitzGerald. Phone interview on 7 August 2018.

FitzGerald, Niall; former Chairman and Chief Executive of Unilever. Interview took place in London on 17 September 2018.

Geoghegan, Basil; former Managing Director of Goldman Sachs and patron of the Ireland Funds of Great Britain. Phone interview, 30 July 2018.

Gnodde, Richard; Chief Executive of Goldman Sachs International. Phone interview on 9 January 2019.

Griffiths, Katherine; Banking Editor at *The Times*. Phone interview on 18 January 2019.

Halligan, Brendan; former Labour Party MEP and founder of the Institute of International and European Affairs (IIEA). Interview took place in Dublin on 28 January 2019.

Hussey, Gemma; former Fine Gael Minister for Education. Interview in Dublin took place on 15 August 2018.

Jacobs, Francis; former European Parliament senior official. Interview took place in Dublin on 3 October 2018.

Jones, Adrian; Managing Director of Goldman Sachs. Phone interview, 3 October 2018.

Jones, Hywel; former Director for Education and Training at the European Commission. Interview took place in Dublin on 9 October 2018.

Kantor, Mickey; former US Trade Representative and Secretary for Commerce in the Clinton administration. Phone interview, 5 September 2018.

Kearns, Nicholas; former Supreme Court Judge. Interview took place in Dublin on 25 September 2018.

Kennedy, Roddy; former Global head of Communications at BP. Interview took place in Cambridge on 6 February 2019.

Lamy, Pascal; former head of the WTO and European Commissioner. Phone interview on 14 August 2018.

Lillis, Michael; lead negotiator for Irish Government in Anglo-Irish Agreement. Interview took place in Dublin on 5 February 2019.

MacNeill, Hugo; head of Goldman Sachs' investment banking business in Ireland. Interview took place in Dublin on 4 December 2018.

Maniatis, Gregory; assistant to Peter Sutherland when he was UN Special Representative on Migration. Interview took place in Dublin on 8 February 2019.

Martin, Diarmuid; Archbishop of Dublin. Interview took place in Dublin on 22 March 2019.

McCourt, Declan; friend and former UCD classmate. Interview took place in Dublin on 15 April 2019.

McKillop, Sir Tom; former Chairman of Royal Bank of Scotland and BP board member. Phone interview on 8 January 2019.

Mortimer, Ed; former journalist with the *Financial Times* and speechwriter for Kofi Annan. Phone interview on 15 January 2019.

Noonan, Michael; former Fine Gael Minister for Justice and Minister for Finance. Interview took place in Dublin on 10 October 2018.

O'Callaghan, Con; AIB's company secretary 1988 – 94. Interview took place in Dublin on 16 August 2018.

Ó Ceallaigh, Dáithí; former Irish Ambassador to the UK. Interview took place in Dublin on 30 January 2019.

O'Sullivan, David; former EU Ambassador to US and former Secretary General of the European Commission. Phone interview, 26 August 2018.

O'Toole, Richard; Chef de Cabinet for Sutherland at European Commission and WTO. Interview took place in Dublin on 26 August 2018.

Paulson, Henry 'Hank'; former chief executive of Goldman Sachs and former US Treasury Secretary. Phone interview on 2 October 2018.

Pavcnik, Nina; Professor of Economics at Dartmouth University. Phone interview on 7 January 2019.

Regan, Eugene; Judge at the European Court of Justice and former member of Sutherland's cabinet at the European Commission. Phone interview on 15 August 2015.

Robinson, Mary; former President of Ireland and UN High Commissioner for Human Rights. Interview took place in Dublin on 7 November 2018.

Schwab, Klaus; head of the World Economic Forum. Phone interview on 14 February 2019.

Sheehan, Garrett; Gonzaga classmate, lifelong friend and former High Court Judge. Interview took place in Dublin on 24 July 2018.

(Lord) Simon, David; former Chairman and Chief Executive of BP. Phone interview on 2 March 2019.

Spollen, Tony; former Gonzaga classmate and friend. Former head of AIB internal Audit. Interview took place in Dublin on 27 July 2018.

Spring, Dick; former Tánaiste and leader of the Labour Party. Phone interview on 3 April 2019.

Sutherland, Shane; son of Peter Sutherland. Interview took place in Dublin on 28 March 2019.

Yerxa, Rufus; number two in the US negotiating team during Uruguay Round of trade talks. Phone interview on 15 August 2018.

ENDNOTES

1 *Gonzaga and childhood in Monkstown*

1. *Doctrine and Life*, September 2000 edition, Dominican Publications.
2. Fr Joseph Veale appreciation, *Irish Times*, 4 November 2002.
3. 'Fr Joe Veale, An Obituary', *Sunday Independent*, 3 November 2002.

3 *The Arms Trial*

1. 'Ex Master of the High Court and Champion Cricketer', *Irish Times*, 22 July 2006.
2. Sutherland's private papers, provided by the Sutherland family.
3. Sutherland's private papers, provided by the Sutherland family, based on research carried out by Dr Brian Jackson, Head of Postgraduate Studies at the Carlow Institute of Technology.

4 *Fine Gael*

1. Sutherland's private papers, provided by the Sutherland family.

5 *The Eighth Amendment time bomb*

1. Sutherland's private papers, provided by the Sutherland family.

6 *The Troubles: negotiating the Anglo-Irish Agreement*

1. Sutherland's private papers, provided by the Sutherland family.

2. Released by the Irish government from the national archives in December 2016.
3. Released by the Irish government from the national archives in December 2015.

7 Getting Competition: becoming a European Commissioner

1. 'Leadership at a time of transition and turbulence', speech delivered by Peter Sutherland to Gresham College London, 8 March 2011.

8 Shaping EU competition policy

1. 'Michael O'Leary: Flying high in the battle for Europe's skies', *Irish Times*, 24 July 2017.
2. Sutherland, 'Leadership at a time of transition and turbulence'.
3. Ibid.

9 President of the European Commission?

1. Case law 294/83 Gravier (1985) ECR 593.
2. 'Britain tolls division bell: The Dehaene fiasco at the Corfu Summit has repercussions for the shape of Europe to come', *Independent*, 26 June 1994.
3. 'Peter Sutherland: A profile', *Sunday Tribune*, 22 December 1993.

10 Brokering the Uruguay Round and setting up the WTO

1. 'Arthur Dunkel, Diplomat and pioneer of the World Trade Organisation',*Guardian*, 16 June 2005.
2. Interview with Keith Rockwell, WTO spokesman, 14 February 2011, WTO in-house channel.
3. Ibid.

11 Globalisation and its discontents

1. Interview with Hillary Clinton, *Financial Times*, 3 December 2007.
2. Interview with Peter Sutherland, *Financial Times*, 12 December 2007.
3. Interview with Keith Rockwell.

12 Allied Irish Bank: the DIRT scandal

1. 'Lunch with the FT: Peter Sutherland', *Financial Times*, 3 January 2009.

14 *Goldman Sachs*

1. 'The Great American Bubble Machine', *Rolling Stone*, 5 April 2010.

15 *Clipping Goodwin's wings at RBS*

1. Ian Fraser, *Shredded: Inside RBS: The bank that broke Britain* (Birlinn, 2014).
2. RBS sheds Goodwin's $32 million jet', *Guardian*, 8 May 2009.

16 *The longest serving chairman*

1. 'Sun King of the oil industry', *Financial Times*, 13 July 2002.
2. This account was relayed first hand by two separate, confidential sources.

17 *Migration: UN Special Representative*

1. Memorandum outlining the objectives of the Global Forum on Migration and Development sent by Sutherland to Kofi Annan in June 2006, supplied by Gregory Maniatis.
2. 'Peter Sutherland: The Globe's Grandee', *Daily Mail*, 27 June 2012.
3. Peter Sutherland, evidence to House of Lords EU home affairs sub-committee on 21 June 2007.

18 *The biggest crisis of our time*

1. Peter Sutherland, op-ed for Project Syndicate, *Financial Times*, 2 September 2015.
2. Report of the SRSG on Migration (A/71/728), UN Publications, February 2017.
3. Ibid.

19 *A turbulent relationship with Ireland*

1. 'The Ultimate Social Networker', *Irish Times*, 30 January 2010.
2. Brian Lenihan, Seanad Éireann debate, 9 July 2008.
3. 'The Ultimate Social Networker'.
4. Peter Sutherland, Barrett Family Lecture, 17 March 2015.

20 *Brexit: a nightmare unfolds*

1. Boris Johnson, *Sunday Telegraph*, 15 May 2016. 'The EU wants a superstate: just as Hitler did.'

2. Newstalk, 'Lunchtime' programme, 24 May 2016. Interview with Peter Sutherland.
3. Margaret Thatcher, speech to the College of Europe, 20 September 1998.
4. Peter Sutherland, Cardinal Newman Lecture, St John's College Oxford, 19 May 2010.
5. IIEA speech on Brexit Sutherland gave on 19 May 2016.
6. Ibid.

21 *Faith and philanthropy*

1. Fr Barber, Sutherland's funeral homily, Donnybrook Church, Dublin on the 11 January 2018.
2. Ibid.

INDEX